Financial Reporting:
An Accounting Revolution
Third Edition

William H. Beaver
Stanford University

D0780746

Prentice Hall, Upper Saddle River, New Jersey 07458

Editor-in-Chief: P. J. Boardman
Editorial Assistant: Jane Avery
Editorial Director: James Boyd
Executive Marketing Manager: Deborah Hoffman Emry
Production Editor: Marc Oliver
Production Coordinator: Cindy Spreder
Managing Editor: Katherine Evancie
Senior Manufacturing Supervisor: Paul Smolenski
Manufacturing Manager: Vincent Scelta
Interior Design: Donna Wickes
Cover Design: Kiwi Design
Composition: Pine Tree Composition, Inc.

Library of Congress Cataloging-in-Publication Data
Beaver, William H.
    Financial reporting : an accounting revolution / William H. Beaver.—3rd ed.
      p. cm.—(Prentice-Hall contemporary topics in accounting series)
    Includes bibliographical references and index.
    ISBN 0-13-737149-7 (alk. paper)
    1. Accounting—United States. 2. Financial statements–United States. I. Title. II. Series: Contemporary topics in accounting series.
HF5616.U5B36   1998
657′.3′0973—dc21   97-25886
                CIP

Prentice-Hall International (UK) Limited, *London*
Prentice-Hall of Australia Pty. Limited, *Sydney*
Prentice-Hall Canada, Inc., *Toronto*
Prentice-Hall Hispanoamericana, S.A., *Mexico*
Prentice-Hall of India Private Limited, *New Delhi*
Prentice-Hall of Japan, Inc., *Tokyo*
Simon & Schuster Asia Pte. Ltd., *Singapore*
Editora Prentice-Hall do Brasil, Ltda., *Rio de Janeiro*

Printed in the United States of America

10 9 8 7 6 5 4 3 2

To Sue, Marie, Sarah, and David.

Contents

Preface ix

1 **THE REVOLUTION** 1

2 **INFORMATION** 18

3 **CERTAINTY** 38

4 **UNCERTAINTY** 59

5 **THE EVIDENCE** 89

6 **MARKET EFFICIENCY** 125

7 **REGULATION** 159

INDEX 175

Preface

As I indicated in the previous editions, I am indebted to the late Sid Cottle, who coauthored *Security Analysis* with Benjamin Graham and David Dodd, for first suggesting that the changes in perspective regarding financial statements were revolutionary. The revolution began in the mid-1960s and a question arises whether it is still appropriate to refer to an accounting revolution. Although the transition is by no means complete, the conceptual shifts in recent years have been milder.

In discussing this issue with others, some suggested that the series of political events in France that began in 1789 is still called the French Revolution, even though the transition to democratic forms of government is largely complete. It refers to a historical period that is dominated by changes in perspective of governance. At the risk of mystifying the younger readers, who have known only the postrevolutionary period, I have decided to still refer to these changes in perspective as an accounting revolution.

Of course, the revolution is not complete, particularly in the regulatory processes for financial reporting. In retrospect, the revolution was much more of an academic revolution and reflected a major shift to an informational perspective accompanied by a substantial explosion of empirical research that adopted an informational perspective. Much of the regulatory rhetoric is still the language of measurement, and recently we have seen an expansion of research that embraces a measurement perspective.

The major changes in this edition are in the last half of Chapter 4 and all of Chapters 5 and 6. Chapter 4 now includes the Feltham–Ohlson framework and discusses key features of financial reporting such as clean surplus, delayed recognition, conservatism, and discretionary accruals. In retrospect, it is striking how much early research and, as a result, the first and second editions were focused on an earnings-only valuation approach from an informational perspective. The third edition attempts to acknowledge the broader perspective of recent research that incorporates balance sheet as well as earnings variables. Chapter 5 has been updated to reflect recent empirical research that adopts a balance sheet perspective and to discuss the dual book value and earnings valuation studies. Many of these studies adopt a measurement rather than an informational perspective. Chapter 6 has undergone major revisions, largely because of empirical research documenting systematic patterns in security returns, such as the postearnings announcement drift and the forecasting of future returns as a function of the book-to-market ratio.

A major issue in the revision is what recognition to give, if any, to the new millennium. After all, they don't come around very often. I had originally included a lengthy section in Chapter 7 with speculation on financial reporting in the twenty-first century. I am reminded of reading issues of *Popular Science* in the 1950s, which contained ambitious forecasts of what future technology could bestow on us. One issue and the attendant cover I particularly remember contained the prediction that within 20 years (in other words, the 1970s) every suburban home would have its own personal helicopter. Indeed, some prosperous homes would have more. During the morning rush hour, thousands of helicopters would leave their launch pads in the driveways and fill the skies. Traffic jams in the skies would be a major problem. Well, I guess they are around major airports today, but the prediction of a personal helicopter (or two) in every driveway has hardly come to pass.

In retrospect, I do not want the third edition to suffer the same fate as an issue of *Popular Science* from the 1950s. Therefore, I have decided to keep forecasts for financial reporting for the next millennium to a minimum. The concepts underlying the first and second edition are the main focus of the third edition.

I am indebted to many people who have made this and previous editions possible. Their numbers increase, and there are too many to list them all. A special debt is owed to Chuck Horngren and Joel Demski, my colleagues and friends with whom I have shared the Chicago and Stanford experiences. Chuck is now emeritus and Joel has departed for the frontiers of Connecticut and then Florida. However, my debt to them is undiminished. I am also indebted to my colleagues, my coauthors, and my doctoral students, especially Mary Barth, Wayne Landsman, and Stephen Ryan, who have significantly affected my thinking. I also wish to thank P. J. Boardman of Prentice Hall and Katherine Schipper for their encouragement and support in undertaking a third edition. I would also like to acknowledge the helpful reviews of Teresa P. Gordon, University of Idaho; Steven R. Jackson, University of Southern Maine; Frank J. Kopczynski, Plymouth State College; Wayne Landsman, University of North Carolina; and James M. Wahlen, University of North Carolina. My assistant, Bryan Brown, was very helpful in preparing many of the new tables, figures, and revised bibliographies.

Most of all, I am indebted, as ever, to my wife, Sue, and to my children, Marie, Sarah, and David, for their love and support.

William H. Beaver

Financial Reporting

1

The Revolution

On the eve of a new millennium, financial reporting is a subtle mixture of the old and the new. Double entry accounting is 500 years old and still forms the backbone of the structure of financial statements. Early in the twentieth century, accounting theory evolved into a stewardship theory of how best to measure assets, liabilities, equity, and earnings and compared the accounting measures with economic concepts.

The past 35 years have experienced a rapid growth in the quantity and complexity of financial reporting requirements mandated by the Financial Accounting Standards Board (FASB) and the Securities and Exchange Commission (SEC).[1] Both the American Institute of Certified Public Accountants (AICPA 1994) and the Association for Investment Management and Research (AIMR 1993) have evaluated whether the current system is adequate for the challenges of financial reporting in the twenty-first century and have called for significant changes in that system.[2] Many of these proposals, which call for disclosures of nonfinancial data, forward-

[1]The SEC is an independent agency of the federal government created by the Securities Acts of 1933 and 1934. It is empowered to ensure "full and fair" disclosure by corporations. The nature of its activities is described in an excellent text by Skousen (1983). The FASB is a private-sector organization that determines the financial accounting standards to be used in preparing annual reports to shareholders. Throughout, the Statement of Financial Accounting Standards of the FASB are referred to as FAS followed by the number of the standard. The generic term *financial reporting* is used to include financial statements and financial disclosures.

[2]The American Institute of Certified Public Accountants (AICPA) is the professional organization primarily composed of members of the public accounting profession, and the Association for Investment Management and Research (AIMR) is the professional organization primarily consisting of financial analysts.

looking data, and fair market value data, can be viewed as natural extensions and implications of adopting an informational approach to financial reporting. As its implications are pursued, an informational approach can have dramatic effects on the way financial reporting is viewed, evaluated, and regulated. This change in perspective is called a *financial reporting revolution* and is the main subject of this book.

This introductory chapter provides a brief historical perspective on the purposes of financial reporting, with a special emphasis on the objectives of financial statements. The informational approach is then introduced, and the role of accrual accounting from an informational perspective is discussed. The major constituencies and the economic consequences of the financial reporting environment are also described. In presenting this framework, several trends in financial reporting are identified. Key features of the environment are its complexity, diversity, and impact on the preferences of the constituencies for financial reporting.

The selection among financial reporting systems by management or by the financial reporting regulators is a substantive choice, which involves making tradeoffs with respect to the effects on the different constituencies. A particular financial reporting requirement is the outcome of a political (or social choice) process.

This chapter provides the basis for understanding the financial reporting revolution and provides a perspective for the remaining chapters, which are briefly summarized at the close of this chapter.

1-1 HISTORICAL PERSPECTIVE

The stewardship function of management was dominant in early views of the purpose of financial statements. Under this view, management is the steward to whom capital suppliers (in other words, shareholders and creditors) entrust control over a portion of their financial resources. In this context, financial statements provide a report to capital suppliers that facilitates their evaluation of management's stewardship. A variety of reporting systems could conceivably fulfill this purpose. However, in financial accounting it has long been presumed that merely reporting cash flows is inadequate and that some form of accrual accounting is appropriate.

This basic faith in the superiority of accrual accounting is epitomized in Paton and Littleton's (1940) monograph, which focuses on the *matching concept*. This monograph has been called one of the most important contributions to financial accounting of the twentieth century.[3] The matching concept states that revenues and expenses should be recorded such that efforts and accomplishments are properly aligned. Reporting cash receipts and cash disbursements will not properly match, and some form of accrual accounting is called for. Accrual accounting is essential to proper financial reporting. However, the accrual process is ambiguous and not well-

---

[3]American Accounting Association Committee on Concepts and Standards for External Financial Reports (1977).

defined. For example, for virtually every major event that could affect the financial statements of a firm, there exists a variety of alternative methods for matching costs and revenues. LIFO versus FIFO methods of inventory valuation and straight-line versus accelerated methods of depreciation are two prominent examples within the framework of historical cost accounting. Departures from historical cost accounting, such as various forms of current cost and market value accounting, further increase the alternatives available. The question then arises as to which accrual method is "best." This question has been viewed as essentially a normative one.

One approach to evaluating alternative accrual methods is to attempt to infer criteria from general definitions, such as *net income*. Net income can be defined as the difference between revenues and expenses (plus or minus gains and losses). This is tautologically correct, but it is not particularly insightful. Attempts to dig deeper by exploring various definitions of *revenues* and *expenses* suffer from the same problem. An expense is typically defined as an *expired cost,* but the definition is silent on the basis for determining expiration. For example, consider the definition of *depreciation,* which has been described as the allocation of the original cost over the estimated useful life. Again this is tautologically correct, but it provides no insight into what criteria to use in selecting an allocation method from among a large number of possibilities.

Another approach is to ask, "What properties should the 'ideal' net income have?" Accounting alternatives would then be evaluated in terms of these "desirable" criteria. When a "desirable" properties approach is pursued, financial accounting theorists have usually adopted an *economic income* approach. Under this approach, accounting alternatives are evaluated in terms of their perceived proximity to this "ideal." It is assumed that economic income is a well-defined concept, and in most cases certainty is assumed or uncertainty is treated in a casual manner. In a multiperiod setting the discounted present value of future cash flows is usually adopted as the valuation model for the firm and its securities. _Economic income_ is defined as the change in the present value of the future cash flows, after proper adjustments for deposits (for example, additional common stock issues) or withdrawals (for example, dividends). _

As will be shown in Chapter 3, this concept is virtually unassailable under conditions of perfect and complete markets. For example, it not only reflects the effects of management's actions on current year's operations (for example, current cash flows), but also incorporates the future effects into this year's measure of net income. Hence, from a stewardship perspective, economic net income has appealing qualities.

This perspective can be traced to the early classics of Paton (1922), Canning (1929), and Alexander (1950). It has been applied to the comparison of specific accounting alternatives, such as depreciation methods, lease accounting, and the treatment of long-term receivables and payables. This approach also motivates proposals for market value or current cost approaches to financial reporting, which appear in Edwards and Bell (1961), Chambers (1966), and Sterling (1970).

1-2   INFORMATIONAL PERSPECTIVE

In the late 1960s the perspective shifted from economic income measurement to an "informational" approach. This is reflected in financial accounting research in information economics, security prices, and behavioral science. The emphasis is reflected in the FASB's *Statement of Financial Accounting Concepts No. 1 (1978),* which states:

> Financial reporting should provide information that is useful to present and potential investors and creditors and other users in assessing the amounts, timing, and uncertainty of prospective cash receipts. . . . Since investors' and creditors' cash flows are related to enterprise cash flows, financial reporting should provide information to help investors, creditors, and others assess the amounts, timing, and uncertainty of prospective net cash inflows to the related enterprise. (p. viii)

The notion that financial statement data ought to provide useful information on the assessment of future cash flows appears to be relatively innocuous. However, if taken seriously, the informational perspective has several dramatic implications for financial statement preparation and interpretation.[4] Chapter 2 will explore the informational approach and its implications.

There are at least two reasons for this shift in emphasis. (1) The concept of economic income is not well-defined when there are imperfect or incomplete markets for the assets and claims related to the firm. For example, in the simple case of certainty, the value of the firm is described in terms of the present value of the future cash flows. The present value model effectively collapses the multiperiod cash flows into a single number called the *present value.* Perfect and complete markets are sufficient to permit the vector of cash flows to be adequately described by a single number. Without perfect and complete markets, the properties of such a collapsing operation are not clear. Given that many of the assets and claims reported on the financial statements are represented by imperfect or incomplete markets, the concept of economic income is not well-defined. Hence, the "ideal" that financial statement data are attempting to represent is not clear conceptually. (2) Moreover, even in situations in which the relevant markets for claims exist (for example, marketable equity securities) there seems to be an inability to reach a consensus of the "best" method of reporting. More is at stake in the setting of financial accounting standards than is evident when adopting an economic income approach. Various groups or constituencies, such as shareholders, creditors, financial analysts, regulators (for example, the FASB and the SEC), management, and auditors, are affected by the choice of the financial reporting requirements. Hence, they have interests in which requirement is chosen. These interests are not incorporated within the framework of an economic income approach. In any event, the economic income perspective does not lead to a consensus on what financial standards should be, and the reasons for the lack of consensus are obscured by this perspective.

---

[4]Armstrong (1977) reported substantial opposition to adopting an informational perspective. Stewardship was cited most often as the preferred alternative. However, according to the FASB (1976b), stewardship is subsumed under the informational perspective.

Financial reporting data play two distinct, but related, informational roles. One role is to facilitate decision makers, such as investors, in selecting the best action among the available alternatives, such as alternative investment portfolios. A second role is to facilitate contracting between parties, such as management and investors, by having the payment under the contract defined in part in terms of financial reporting data. Management incentive contracts defined in part in terms of the firm's accounting net income would be an example. Both roles aid in the understanding of why management and financial reporting regulators perceive the choice of accounting method to be a substantive issue. This perspective also helps us understand why the standard-setting is the result of a political process. Chapter 2 describes both roles in greater detail.

1-3 ACCRUAL ACCOUNTING IN AN INFORMATIONAL SETTING

Although the informational perspective potentially represents a dramatic shift in the purpose of financial statements, the FASB concluded that accrual accounting with its attendant net income number is still superior to cash flow accounting with respect to the "new" purpose—information about future cash flows. According to the FASB (1978),

> Information about enterprise earnings based on accrual accounting generally provides a better indication of enterprise's present and continuing ability to generate cash flows than information limited to the financial aspects of cash receipts and payments. (p. ix)
>
> *The primary focus of financial reporting is information about earnings and its components.* (p. ix; emphasis added)

Notwithstanding the assurances of the FASB, there has been some questioning of the efficacy of the accrual system. One trend in security analysis is away from earnings-oriented valuation approaches to discounted cash flow approaches. Deficiencies in current financial reporting rules are given as a primary reason. Ijiri (1978) has expressed concern over the importance of accruals. He suggested that financial statements be based on a cash flow orientation, and he offered several reasons for this recommendation: (1) There is a direct logical link between past cash flows and future cash flows (in other words, they are of a similar nature or character). (2) Cash flows offer a more primitive system. By the principle of Occam's razor (a principle approximately 700 years old), the simpler method should be used until the more complex one has proven that it adds something. (3) Cash flow is less misleading in the sense that it does not have the same connotations that earnings do, which are often viewed as an indicator of economic income.

To challenge the accrual process strikes at the heart of financial accounting and financial statements as they are currently structured. It is not surprising that the FASB chose to reaffirm the importance of accrual accounting. Accrual accounting represents one way of transforming or aggregating cash flows, as illustrated in the

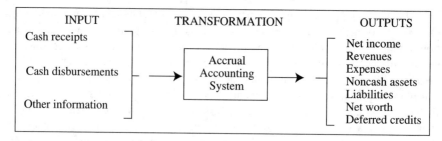

FIGURE 1-1   The Accrual Process

Figure 1-1. Accrual accounting reflects information in addition to cash receipts and disbursements. For example, information on the aging of receivables may be reflected in the allowance for estimated uncollectible accounts. Inventory, under a lower of cost or market rule, may reflect information on salability of inventory. More generally, the accruals reflect management's expectations about future cash flows and are based on an information system potentially more comprehensive than past and current cash flows. Accruals can be said to involve some implicit or explicit prediction of the future, and accrual accounting can convey information not contained in cash receipts and disbursements. As suggested by the FASB, accrual accounting may transform cash flows to provide a better indicator of future cash flows and dividend-paying ability than current cash flows do.

However, the efficacy of accrual accounting is an open issue. Why not merely place the underlying source data in the public domain? One issue is the comparative costs of processing the data. To the extent that data items would be processed (for example, aggregated) by investors in a relatively uniform manner, it may be cost-effective to have the corporation perform the process once instead of having the process performed several times over by analysts and investors. Of course, there may be no consensus on the method of aggregation, and generally there is a loss of information when aggregating. Hence, when presented with aggregated data, users may incur costs in an attempt to restore the lost information. So the cost of processing may not be related to the level of aggregation in any simple fashion. Moreover, in addition to the cost issues, there are other consequences of nondisclosure due to aggregated data. Hence, the appropriate level of aggregation is not a trivial issue, and income determination can be viewed as one special case. In this context, accrual accounting can be viewed as one potentially cost-effective compromise between merely reporting cash flows and a more ambitious system of fuller disclosure. These issues are discussed more fully in later chapters.

1-4   THE FINANCIAL REPORTING ENVIRONMENT

The shift toward an informational perspective can be better understood in light of the current financial reporting environment. This environment consists of various groups or constituencies who are affected by and have a stake in the financial reporting requirements of the FASB and the SEC. These groups include investors, information intermediaries, regulators, management, and auditors, among others.[5]

The investment process, a central feature of the financial reporting environment, involves the giving up of current consumption for securities, which are claims to future, uncertain cash flows. The claims to uncertain future cash flows are of value because they represent command over future consumption. Hence, investment is the giving up of current consumption for future, uncertain consumption. The investor must decide how to allocate wealth between current consumption and investment and how to allocate funds set aside for investment among the various securities available. The investor naturally has a demand for information that will aid in assessing the future cash flows associated with the securities and the firms that offer those securities.

However, the investor is not acting in isolation but within a larger investment environment. This environment consists of several characteristics: (1) Investors, some perhaps with limited financial and accounting training, have the opportunity to avail themselves of the services of financial intermediaries, such as investment companies, to whom they can defer a portion of the investment process. (2) Investors, some perhaps with limited access to and ability to interpret financial information, have the opportunity to avail themselves of the services of information intermediaries, such as analysts, to whom they can defer a portion or all of the information gathering and processing function. (3) Investors have the opportunity to invest in a number of securities and to diversify out of some of the risks associated with a single security. (4) Information intermediaries compete with one another in gathering and interpreting financial information. (5) Managements, competing with one another for the investors' funds, have incentives to provide financial information to the investment community. (6) Investors and intermediaries have information available that is more comprehensive and perhaps more timely than the annual report to shareholders or the SEC filings. (7) Security price research suggests that security prices reflect a rich, comprehensive information system. (8) The flow of financial information to the investment community is regulated by a dual regulatory structure that consists of the private-sector FASB and the public-sector SEC.

---

[5]Unless otherwise indicated, the term *investors* will refer to common shareholders. This usage is consistent with that of the FASB quotation cited earlier. The primary user orientation of both the FASB and the SEC is the common stock investor. This orientation is natural given the intent of the Securities Acts of 1933 and 1934. Other groups include creditors and employees. Neither will be given explicit treatment here. Creditors are a form of investor (supplier of capital). Although their interests may not be the same as those of the stockholders, many of the general statements made with respect to investors also apply or could be easily extended to creditors. As a result, creditors will not be treated here as a separate constituency. The reason is parsimony of exposition and does not imply that creditors are unimportant. In the United States employees have played a relatively minor role in the financial reporting environment. However, in many countries of Western Europe employees play a more active role, and they may eventually do so in the United States as well.

Investors

Investors are a heterogeneous group in many ways. For example, they may differ with respect to tastes or preferences, wealth, beliefs, access to financial information, and skill in interpreting financial information. These factors can affect their demand for financial information. In general, the demand for information will be a function of the investor's wealth, tastes (for example, attitudes toward risk), and beliefs about the future. Because these attributes differ across investors, their demand for financial information can also naturally differ. In addition, investors may also differ in their access and ability to interpret financial information. As a result, the information demands of professional users, such as the financial and information intermediaries, may differ from that of the nonprofessional users, such as individual or noninstitutional investors.

Nonprofessional investors can also differ in many respects. Such investors may not operate in an unaided fashion and have a variety of investment strategies available. These options illustrate some reasons for heterogeneity among investors with respect to demand for financial information: (1) direct management of portfolio versus deferral of investment function to an intermediary, (2) use versus nonuse of information intermediaries, (3) diversified versus undiversified portfolio policies, and (4) active versus passive portfolio management.

If an individual investor defers a portion of the investment process to a financial intermediary, that individual may have a reduced direct demand for financial information.[6] To the extent that the individual relies on the analysis and recommendations of an information intermediary, the direct demand for financial information may also be reduced.[7] The individual, perhaps because of limited access and ability to interpret financial information, may choose to defer such functions to an intermediary. The individual is substituting the analysis and recommendations (in other words, the information) of the intermediary for the financial information. In this sense, they constitute competing sources of information. In both cases (deferral to a financial intermediary and deferral to an information intermediary), there may be an indirect demand for financial information by the individual investors.

Apart from options involving the extent to which the individual investor can defer to intermediaries, investors may also differ with respect to portfolio strategies. One dimension of this investment choice is the extent to which the investor chooses to be diversified. For example, mean-variance portfolio theory (Sharpe 1995) indicates that individual securities are relevant to the investor only in so far as they af-

---

[6]The term *financial intermediary* as used here includes those involved in investing the funds of others. Specifically, it includes mutual funds, closed end investment companies, investment trusts, and pension funds, among others.

[7]The term *information intermediary* as used here includes those involved in the gathering, processing, analyzing, and interpreting of financial information. It includes financial analysts, bond rating agencies, stock rating agencies, investment advisory services, and brokerage firms, among others.

fect the risk (variance of return) and expected return associated with the portfolios. Under this view, the objects of interest to the investor are the risk and expected return of the entire portfolio. Individual securities are means by which different portfolios can be constructed. From this perspective, interactions or correlations among the returns of securities are of interest, as well as the expected return and variability of return of the individual security. In fact, for well-diversified portfolios, some aspects of individual security return behavior may be relatively unimportant because they can be diversified away, such as the so-called unsystematic risk. Portfolio theory stresses the importance of diversification, which can reduce much of the uncertainty or risk associated with holding a single security. For example, a single security may have considerable uncertainty as to the return, yet through diversification much of this risk (unsystematic or diversifiable risk) can be eliminated at the portfolio level.

As a result, the demand for financial information may be a function of the extent to which the investor chooses to diversify. The investor is concerned with financial information only in so far as it is useful in assessing the attributes of the portfolio return. For the well-diversified investor, factors such as unsystematic risk may be relatively unimportant, and financial information that helps assess such risk may not be of value. However, for the less diversified investor, such information may be perceived to be extremely valuable.

In a similar vein, the demand for financial information can be influenced by the extent to which the investor adopts an "active" versus a "passive" trading strategy. Under a passive trading strategy, the investor essentially buys and holds a security and anticipates little trading until liquidation for consumption purposes. In the limit, the investor would simply purchase a well-diversified cross section of securities (for example, an "index" fund) and the direct demand for firm-specific financial information would be essentially nonexistent. By contrast, an "active" trader has a speculative demand for information. In other words, an active policy involves continually seeking information that will permit the detection of mispriced securities and continually trading on such information. By definition, the turnover of the active portfolio will be greater than that implied by a passive policy. In many cases, an active trading policy is attempting to take advantage of perceived short-term aberrations in security prices and expects to open and close the speculative position in a relatively short time period. Here, information that helps predict short-run movements in security prices is of interest to the active trader, but it would not be of interest to the investor who follows a passive policy and tends to adopt a longer-term perspective.

These classifications by no means exhaust the possibilities and they are not mutually exclusive. They do, however, illustrate a fundamental point. Investors are heterogeneous, and their demand for financial information can be heterogeneous. Moreover, they operate in an environment in which they can rely on financial and information intermediaries and in which they can adopt portfolio strategies that can substantially alter their direct demand for financial information.

Information Intermediaries

The information intermediaries can be viewed as an industry whose factors of production include financial information and other types of data and whose product is analysis and interpretation. The output of the information intermediaries is also a form of information. The intermediaries take primitive information and transform it into another type of information, which reflects their ability to understand, synthesize, and interpret the raw data. As indicated earlier, the nonprofessional user may have less direct demand for financial information if that user relies on the information provided by an intermediary.

More specifically, information intermediaries can be viewed as performing three information-related activities: (1) the search for information that is not publicly available (hereafter called *private information search*), (2) the analysis, processing, and interpretation of information for prediction (hereafter called *prospective analysis*), and (3) the interpretation of events after the fact (hereafter called *retrospective analysis*).

As a result, the relationship between financial reporting and the information intermediary is not simple. At one level, public financial reporting provides one source of input factors for the intermediaries. However, if part of the function of the intermediary is to obtain more comprehensive and more timely information, financial reporting can be a competing source of information to that provided by the information intermediary. Moreover, information intermediaries compete with one another in the gathering and interpretation of financial information.

Information intermediaries engage in private information search. This private-sector information system is large and active.[8] The competition among analysts for disclosures and for the interpretation of disclosures may result in security prices that reflect a broad information system. Statements of legislative intent at the time of the enactment of the Securities Acts indicate that at least some were relying on the competition within the professional investment community to interpret the SEC filings and to effect an "efficiently" determined market price.[9] Chapter 6 will discuss further the relationship between security prices and financial information.

The role of the information and financial intermediaries in the financial reporting environment has been receiving increasing recognition by the financial reporting regulators. The recognition of the professional user as a prime target for the financial reporting system is reflected in the following ways:

1. Information intermediaries, such as analysts, are viewed as major representatives of investor demand for additional financial reporting. As a result, the FASB and the SEC look to this community as a source of ideas for further disclosures. As long as the financial reporting policy makers rely on information intermediaries,

---

[8]The role of analysts as information intermediaries is discussed in Schipper (1991).
[9]Consider the following statement by Justice William O. Douglas (1933), who at the time was teaching at Yale: "Even though an investor has neither the time, money, or intelligence to assimilate the mass of information in the registration statement, there will be those who can and who will do so, whenever there is a broad market. The judgment of those experts will be reflected in the market price."

their preferences will be an important barometer of future financial disclosure requirements. Analysts' interest in segment or divisionalized reporting and in management forecasts are prominent examples.[10]

2. The financial reporting requirements assume that the user has a greater sophistication and technical skill to interpret the data reported than has previously been assumed. The FASB's standards on foreign currency translation, pensions, other post-employment benefits, and stock options as compensation are prominent examples of financial reporting requirements that require a considerable amount of expertise in interpretation.

3. There is greater emphasis on the reporting of so-called soft data, such as future-oriented disclosures and current cost data.

4. There is greater emphasis on disclosure and less emphasis on a single earnings number. Disclosures are used to report financial aspects of certain events without an attempt to prescribe exactly how those disclosures are to be used to arrive at "the" net income or earnings for the firm. This shift away from a single "best" measure of earnings affords users a greater opportunity to structure the analysis of financial disclosures in a manner they perceive is appropriate. This is particularly important to the extent that users are heterogeneous in their demand for and analysis of financial information.

Financial Reporting Regulators

A prominent feature of the financial reporting environment is the regulation of the flow of financial information to investors. The primary regulators are the FASB and the SEC, although Congress and the independent regulatory agencies can also influence financial reporting requirements.

The SEC and the FASB share a concern over the effect of the financial reporting on investors (FASB 1976b, Chapter 2, and SEC 1977, Introduction). The investor orientation is natural given the intent of the Securities Acts of 1933 and 1934. This orientation appears to be partially motivated by a concern over the welfare of investors, the "fairness" of the markets in which they buy and sell securities, and the prevention of perceived adversities and inequities that may befall investors due to informational deficiencies, such as a failure to disclose material financial information. However, the policy makers also appear to be concerned with the effects of financial reporting on resource allocation and capital formation.

A distinctive feature of the regulatory system is its dual structure. The relationship between the FASB and SEC has not been clearly defined, although a similar perspective on the purposes of financial reporting has been suggested for both. The SEC Advisory Committee on Corporate Disclosure (SEC 1977) suggested a purpose of corporate disclosure similar to the FASB's statement of purpose cited earlier. The Advisory Committee states that the SEC's objective in corporate disclosure is

---

[10]The financial analyst community has made several suggestions for increased financing reporting (see AIMR 1993).

to assure the public availability in an efficient and reasonable manner on a timely basis of reliable, firm-oriented information, material to informed investment, and corporate suffrage decision making. (p. D-8)

This similarity of objectives further blurs the historically fuzzy distinction between the two aspects of financial reporting: disclosure and financial accounting. This distinction has been previously invoked to define the jurisdictional lines between the FASB and the SEC. In principle, the jurisdiction of the FASB was said to be the setting of financial accounting standards, whereas the jurisdiction of the SEC was said to be disclosure. Yet the distinction has never been well-defined, and, as a practical matter, the distinction is not operational. The standards of the FASB typically also include disclosure requirements. In fact, some standards, such as the standard on segment reporting, are viewed by many as primarily disclosure standards. Similarly, the SEC influences financial accounting standards, as has been well documented by Horngren (1972, 1973) and Armstrong (1977). Chapter 7 explores these issues further and provides a framework for viewing the FASB–SEC relationship.

Management

Managements, competing with one another for investors' funds, have incentives to provide financial information to the investment community (Healy and Palepu 1993). Moreover, management can be viewed as an agent to whom investors have entrusted control over a portion of their resources. This stewardship view implies that management has a responsibility to act in the interests of the investors. Management plays many roles including productive agent, risk bearer, and supplier of information. A prime responsibility of management is financial reporting, which can help to evaluate the stewardship of management. This financial reporting responsibility is reinforced by the legal liability of management under the Securities Acts of 1933 and 1934. Legal liability for financial reporting and the major determinants of litigation risk are discussed in Francis, Philbrick, and Schipper (1994). Financial reporting by management can influence the terms on which management can obtain additional financing and can affect the competitive position of the firm, among other effects. Hence, management clearly has a stake in the financial reporting environment and plays an important role as the preparer of the financial statements and a supplier of financial information.

Auditors

The incentives of management with respect to financial reporting are an open issue, and their reports are subject to "monitoring" or certification by an auditor. The concept of the "independence" of the auditor from management is a part of the auditor's professional ethics and underscores the responsibility of the auditor to users (for example, investors) of the financial statements. As with management, this responsibility is reinforced through the legal liability of the auditor under the Securi-

TABLE 1-1 Constituencies in the Financial
Reporting Environment

I. Investors
  A. Diversified vs. Undiversified
  B. Active vs. Passive
  C. Professional vs. Nonprofessional
II. Information Intermediaries
  A. Financial Analysts
  B. Bond Rating Agencies
  C. Stock Rating Agencies
  D. Investment Advisory Services
  E. Brokerage Firms
III. Regulators
  A. FASB
  B. SEC
  C. Congress
IV. Management
  A. Large vs. Small Firms
  B. Publicly vs. Closely Held Firms
V. Auditors
  A. National vs. Local Firms
  B. SEC Practice vs. Non-SEC Practice

ties Acts. Auditors, in addition to also being risk bearers, are major suppliers of information and have an obvious stake in the financial reporting environment.

Summary of Environment

The financial reporting environment consists of the five major constituencies discussed above, although other groups may be involved to some extent. The role and the interests of each of these constituencies differ. Moreover, each group is not homogeneous. The constituencies and possible subgroups are summarized in Table 1-1. As a result of the diversity and complexity of the environment, financial reporting can induce a variety of economic consequences and the various constituencies may not be affected by these consequences in a similar way.

1-5 ECONOMIC CONSEQUENCES AND SOCIAL CHOICE

Financial reporting has a number of potential economic consequences, including the effects on the following: (1) the distribution of wealth among individuals, (2) the aggregate level of risk and allocation of risk among individuals, (3) the aggregate consumption and production (for example, effects on the rate of capital formation), (4) the allocation of resources among firms, (5) the use of resources devoted to the production, certification, dissemination, processing, analysis, and interpretation of

TABLE 1-2 Economic Consequences
of Financial Reporting

Wealth Distribution
Aggregate Risk Incurred and Risk Allocation
Aggregate Consumption and Aggregate Production
Resource Allocation
Resources Devoted to Publicly Available Information
Resources Devoted to Regulation
Resources Devoted to Private Search for Information

financial information, (6) the use of resources in the development, compliance, enforcement, and litigation of regulations, and (7) the use of resources in the private-sector search for information. These are summarized in Table 1-2 and are discussed more fully in Chapter 2.

Because these consequences may affect the various constituencies differently, the selection of a financial reporting system is a social choice. There may be no consensus among the constituencies on what financial reporting system is "best." The selection among financial reporting systems by the FASB and the SEC involves making trade-offs among consequences *and among constituencies.* Moreover, it involves trade-offs within constituencies. For example, well-diversified investors may not have the same preferences for a financial reporting system as less diversified investors would. Similarly, investors with passive portfolio strategies may not have the same preferences for financial reporting systems as would investors with active portfolio strategies. The section on investors hinted at the reasons these diversities might induce heterogeneous preferences for financial reporting systems.

Debates over the "best" financial accounting standard not only emphasize traditional "technical" issues, such as which method produces the "best" matching of cost and revenues, but also focus on the economic consequences.

Considerable controversy exists over which economic consequences and constituencies should be considered by the financial reporting policy makers (Armstrong 1977, Rappaport 1977, and Zeff 1978). To address such issues requires a framework that recognizes the role of information in a multiperson setting (Chapter 2) and the rationale for regulation as an institutional solution to resolving social choice questions (Chapter 7).

1-6 CURRENT TRENDS IN AND KEY FEATURES OF FINANCIAL REPORTING

This chapter identifies several trends in financial reporting, which are summarized in Table 1-3. The chapter also provides a historical perspective within which to view these trends, and it provides a description of the financial reporting environ-

---

TABLE 1-3 Current Trends in Financial Reporting

I. General
   A. Shift in financial accounting from an economic income to an informational perspective
   B. Increased emphasis on the complex nature of the financial reporting environment and the professional user of financial information
   C. Recognition of social choice nature of selection among financial reporting systems

II. Specific
   A. Rapid growth in reporting requirements
   B. Less emphasis on earnings and more emphasis on disclosure
   C. Emphasis on disclosures that require a greater expertise to interpret
   D. Emphasis on "soft" data
   E. Debate over economic consequences

---

ment within which the trends are occurring. A key feature of the environment is its complexity and its diversity. This feature can affect preferences for financial information across and within the major constituencies (inventors, information intermediaries, regulators, managements, and auditors). A variety of consequences can result from a financial reporting policy and can affect the constituencies in diverse ways. As a result, there may be a lack of consensus on the "best" reporting system. The selection among financial reporting systems can be viewed essentially as an issue of social choice involving trade-offs among constituencies. Under this view, standard-setting is the outcome of a political process.

Table 1-4 lists ten key features of financial statements. These features capture the major characteristics of financial statements as they are currently prepared and will be discussed in the subsequent chapters.

TABLE 1-4 Key Features of Financial Reporting

1. Reporting at discrete intervals, quarterly for many items and annually for others
2. Accrual accounting
3. General purpose financial statements that include both balance sheets and income statements
4. Discretion and judgment exercised in accruals and elsewhere
5. Footnote disclosures as part of the financial statements
6. Clean surplus relation for most transactions
7. Delayed recognition arising from historical cost accounting
8. Conservatism
9. Audited financial statements, mandated for publicly held firms
10. A dual regulatory system that includes both SEC and FASB

1-7 SUMMARY OF REMAINING CHAPTERS

Chapter 2 explores in some detail and depth the nature of information in a single-person and multiperson setting. The chapter discusses the potentially dramatic implications of adopting an informational perspective and examines the potential economic consequences of financial reporting.

Even though the FASB has adopted an informational perspective, it has indicated that the prime focus of financial reporting is still information about earnings and its components. As a result, Chapters 3 and 4 explore in detail the concept of earnings under conditions of certainty and uncertainty. The chapters discuss the relationship of earnings to the valuation of securities and indicate why earnings information is of potential value to investors in conducting security analysis. The chapters also examine how the nature of earnings differs under an economic income perspective as opposed to an informational perspective. Chapter 5 reviews the empirical evidence regarding the relationship between earnings and security prices. The evidence indicates that security prices behave as if earnings are an important source of information but only one such source.

Security prices play an important role in the financial reporting environment, and security price research has been a major area of financial reporting research. Chapter 6 explores in detail the relationship between prices and information and its implications for the various constituencies in the financial reporting environment.

A prominent feature of the financial reporting environment is that the flow of financial information to the investment community is regulated by a dual regulatory apparatus. Chapter 7 explores the potential economic rationale for the regulation of financial information. It also discusses the relationship between the financial reporting policy makers under the dual regulatory apparatus.

BIBLIOGRAPHY

AICPA. "Improving Business Reporting—A Customer Focus." *Report of the Special Committee on Financial Reporting.* New York: AICPA, 1994.

AIMR. "Financial Reporting in the 1990s and Beyond." Position paper prepared by P. Knutson. Charlottesville, VA: AIMR, 1993.

Alexander, S. *Five Monographs on Business Income.* New York: Study Group on Business Income, AI(CP)A, 1950.

American Accounting Association Committee on Concepts and Standards for External Financial Reports. *Statement on Accounting Theory and Theory Acceptance.* Sarasota, Fla: AAA, 1977.

———. "The Politics of Establishing Accounting Standards." *Journal of Accountancy* (February 1977), 76–79.

Canning, J. *The Economics of Accountancy.* New York: Ronald Press, 1929.

Chambers, R. *Accounting, Evaluation and Economic Behavior.* Englewood Cliffs, N.J.: Prentice-Hall, 1966.

Douglas, W. "Protecting the Investor." *Yale Review* (1933), 523–524.

Edwards, E., and P. Bell. *The Theory and Measurement of Business Income.* Berkeley: University of California Press, 1961.

Financial Accounting Standards Board. *Scope and Implications of the Conceptual Framework Project.* Stamford, Conn.: FASB, December 2, 1976b.

————. *Statement of Financial Accounting Concepts No. 1* Stamford, Conn.: FASB, November 1978.

Francis, J., D. Philbrick, and K. Schipper. "Shareholder Litigation and Corporate Disclosures." *Journal of Accounting Research* (Autumn 1994), 137–164.

Healy, P., and K. Palepu. "The Effects of Firms' Financial Disclosure Strategies on Stock Prices." *Accounting Horizons* (March 1993), 1–11.

Horngren, C. "Accounting Principles: Private or Public Sector." *Journal of Accountancy* (May 1972), 37–41.

————. "The Marketing of Accounting Standards." *Journal of Accountancy* (October 1973), 61–66.

Ijiri, Y. "Cash Flow Accounting and Its Structure." *Journal of Accounting, Auditing and Finance* (Summer 1978), 331–348.

Paton, W. *Accounting Theory.* Chicago: Accounting Studies Press, Ltd., 1962 (originally published in 1922).

———— and A. Littleton. *An Introduction to Corporate Accounting Standards,* Columbus, Ohio: American Accounting Association, 1940.

Rappaport, A. "Economic Impact of Accounting Standards—Implications for the FASB." *Journal of Accountancy* (May 1977), 89–98.

Schipper, K. "Analysts' Forecasts." *Accounting Horizons* (December 1991), 105–121.

Securities and Exchange Commission. *Report of the SEC Advisory Committee on Corporate Disclosure.* Washington, D.C.: U.S. Government Printing Office, November 1977.

Sharpe, W. *Investments,* 5th ed. Englewood Cliffs, N.J.: Prentice-Hall, 1995.

Skousen, K. F. *An Introduction to the SEC,* 3d ed. Cincinnati, Ohio: South-Western Publishing Company, 1983.

Sterling, R. *Theory of the Measurement of Enterprise Income.* Lawrence: University of Kansas Press, 1970.

Zeff, S. "The Rise of Economic Consequences." *Journal of Accountancy* (December 1978), 56–63.

2

Information

This chapter explores the implications that financial statement data is to provide information useful to investors, creditors, and others. The discussion begins with the context of an individual user of financial statement data, and the analysis is then extended to a multiperson setting. Each setting will be general, characterizing the role of any type of information, of which financial reporting is one example. For illustrative purposes, the user context chosen here will be that of the common stock investor (hereafter, simply investor).[1]

The chapter consists of two major parts: (1) information in a single-person setting in which the investor is used to illustrate the role of information, and (2) information in a multiperson setting in which other investors and other constituencies are also considered.

The single-person setting is a natural prelude to the multiperson setting. Many of the intuitive notions about the value of financial information are based on a single-person setting (for example, if additional disclosure is costless, more is at least as good as less). It provides a benchmark for showing how the role of information changes or expands when a multiperson context is adopted.

The chapter begins by illustrating the role of information for a single investor. A simple illustration is provided, and implications are discussed. A key feature is

---

[1]The investor's decision is a primary orientation of the FASB (FASB 1978) and the Securities Acts of 1933 and 1934 (SEC 1977). Other users include creditors, bondholders, potential acquiring firms (for example, takeovers), employees and governmental organizations, consumers, and "public interest" groups, among others.

that the value of information is personal and subjective and can vary across investors as their personal characteristics differ.

A multiperson setting introduces several additional aspects or effects of information. In a multiperson setting, a key feature is that the economic consequences of a financial information system may affect the constituencies in different ways. The chapter closes with viewing the selection among financial reporting systems as a social choice, involving trade-offs among the various constituencies.

2-1 INFORMATION IN A SINGLE-PERSON SETTING

Before the role of information can be understood, the decision context in which the information is to be used must be described. Decision making under uncertainty is typically characterized as choosing the act that maximizes the expected utility of the decision maker. The decision-making process involves the following components: (1) acts, (2) states, (3) consequences, (4) a preferences function for consequences, (5) a probability distribution across states, and (6) an objective function.

Acts

Acts refer to the various alternative choices available to the decision maker. In an investment setting, the available acts could be described as the various portfolios available.

States

Uncertainty is described in terms of a set of mutually exclusive and collective exhaustive possible occurrences (or events) called *states*. A description of each state is sufficiently rich so that no uncertainty about consequences is implied by that state.

Consequences

A set of consequences to the decision maker is associated with each state. In general, the description is sufficiently rich to capture all aspects of the states that are of importance. In a simple investment setting, the consequences are often described in terms of the future cash flows (such as interest, dividends, cash proceeds from the sale of the security) received.

Preferences

The desirability of each set of outcomes is described in terms of the decision maker's preferences. Decision making is characterized as if the investor were maximizing a preference function. It is further assumed that the preference function can be divided into two elements—a belief function and a preference function for certain (as opposed to uncertain) consequences. The preference function is denoted U(·), to represent the investor's *utility function.*

Beliefs

The decision maker's beliefs refer to a set of probabilities assigned to each state. Beliefs are personal and subjective. They are based on the cumulative experience of the investor, including training, education, and prior investment experience. Beliefs are also influenced by what information the investor has. This information could not only include financial reports, but also analysts' reports, newspaper articles, and other publicly available information. *Beliefs are the critical element of the decision process, because the role of information is its potential to alter beliefs and hence alter decision-making behavior.*

The Objective Function

The objective function typically is characterized as the maximization of the expected utility, where expected utility is the "average" utility associated with the consequences of each state weighted by the probability of occurrence of each state. Maximization merely implies the decision maker chooses the act that is associated with the highest or "best" expected utility. Under fairly general conditions decision-making behavior under uncertainty can be characterized *as if* the decision maker were choosing the act that maximized expected utility. The theory does not imply that the decision maker literally forms probability assessments and preferences for outcomes. It merely states that if the decision maker obeys some general axioms of consistency, choice behavior can be described *as if* the decision maker were solving such an optimization problem.

The investor will select the portfolio and current consumption that has the greatest expected utility. In general, the optimal portfolio is a function of the investor's wealth, preferences, beliefs, and the securities' prices. Stated in simplest terms, the decision maker chooses that portfolio that is most preferred. The underlying objects of choice are the individual securities, and the choice among different portfolios can be characterized by the amount of each security held.

The investor setting thus far is quite general. Under appropriate additional assumptions, the familiar mean-variance portfolio theory can be derived.[2] In this special setting investor behavior can be described as selecting the portfolio whose combination of expected return and risk (defined as the variance of the portfolio's return) is optimal given the investor's preference function for wealth at the end of one period. The role of information in a two-parameter context is explored in later subsections.

---

[2]The assumptions are: (1) There exists a surrogate preference function for wealth at the end of one period that is state-independent, (2) the relevant attributes of any portfolio are completely described by two parameters, its expected return and its variance, and usually (3) the investor is risk averse.

Illustration of a Simple Investment Setting

Assume that the investor is risk indifferent about end-of-year wealth and further assume that only two securities, A and B, are available. The current price for each is $50. The expected value of the price at the end of the year is $60, as derived in Table 2-1. Assume that the amount to be invested is fixed ($10,000) and the only decision is how much to allocate between the two securities. Given risk indifference, let U equal the market value of the portfolio at the end of the year. Assume that no dividends are paid and ignore income tax considerations. In this case, the investor is indifferent among portfolio strategies in that all strategies offer an expected utility of 12,000 (10,000/50 × 60). However, suppose that earnings per share for the year is not yet known and knowledge of such information could potentially alter the decision.

Role of Financial Information

In this setting the role of information is to alter the probability that future states will occur. This will be illustrated in the context of use of earnings per share (hereafter EPS) in the investment decision setting described immediately above. The value of information is derived in a series of steps.

Step 1: Consider all possible signals.

For simplicity, assume that there are two possible EPS signals for securities A and B. Either firm A will report EPS of $6.00 and B will report EPS of $4.00 (signal 1) or firm A will report EPS of $4.00 and B will report EPS of $6.00 (signal 2).

Step 2: Assess the probability of state conditional on each signal.

The pre-information probabilities of states 1 and 2, as reported in Table 2-1, are .5 and .5, respectively. Conditional on the acknowledge of signal 1, the probabilities of states 1 and 2 are .9 and .1, respectively, as reported in Table 2-2. Similarly, if signal 2 occurs, the conditional probabilities of states 1 and 2 are .1 and .9, respectively. This will lead to revisions in the expected value of end-of-year prices conditional on each signal, as reported in Table 2-2. The probability of each signal is .5.

TABLE 2-1 Simple Investment Setting

STATE	PROBABILITY OF STATE	END-OF-YEAR PRICE	
		SECURITY A	SECURITY B
1	.5	$80	$40
2	.5	$40	$80
Expected End-of-Year Price[a]		$60	$60

[a]$60 = .5($40) + .5($80)

TABLE 2-2 Effect of Information in Simple Setting

SIGNAL	SECURITY A	SECURITY B	CONDITIONAL PROBABILITIES[a]		EXPECTED END-OF-YEAR PRICE	
			STATE 1	STATE 2	SECURITY A	SECURITY B
1	$6.00	$4.00	.9	.1	.9($80) + .1($40) = $76	.9($40) + .1($80) = $44
2	$4.00	$6.00	.1	.9	.1($80) + .9($40) = $44	.1($40) + .9($80) = $76

[a] $p_s = \sum_{y=1}^{2} p(s \mid y)p_y$, where $p(s \mid y)$ is the probability of state s given signal y and p_y is the probability of signal y.

For each state, $p_s = .5 = .9 \cdot .5 + .1 \cdot .5$, where $p_y = .5$.

Step 3: Optimize the portfolio decision for each signal.

Assume that $10,000 is available for investment and that the *current prices of securities A and B remain the same as they were in the pre-information case.*[3] If signal 1 is observed by the investor, the optimal portfolio is to invest 100% in security A, which has an expected utility of 15,200 (10,000/50 × 76). Similarly, if signal 2 is observed, the optimal portfolio is a 100% investment in security B, which also leads to an expected utility of 15,200.

Step 4: Compute the expected value of the conditional expected utilities across all possible signals.

The investor does not know in advance which signal will be reported. Hence, the expected utility of having access to the information system is determined by "averaging" the conditional expected utilities by the probability each signal will be observed. In this particular numerical example it is trivial because *each* conditional expected utility is 15,200 and the expected value across signals is also 15,200 regardless of the probability of each signal. However, in general, the conditional expected utility will vary across signals.

In this simple setting, in which prices are invariant to the signals, the expected utility associated with a *costless* information system can never be less than the expected utility associated with the pre-information setting. Moreover, expected utility associated with the information system can be higher, as it is in the numerical illustration. In such a case, access to the information system is valuable. In fact, the value of the information system (for example, access to EPS data) can be defined as the difference in the level of expected utility in the post- and pre-information decision setting. More generally, the value to the investor of having one information system versus another can be defined in terms of the level of expected utility associated with each. Thus, expected utility conditional on an information system will rank alternative information systems according to their value to the investor. *The investor will always prefer that information system that is associated with the highest expected utility. Such an information system is "best" for that investor.* Although the illustrations have been specific, the latter point is quite general.

The nonnegative value of costless information arises because the decision maker is able to adjust the optimal choice to the revision of beliefs caused by the signal. In the pre-information case, the action must be taken before the receipt of the signal and hence the same action must be taken regardless of the signal. In effect, the post-information case represents a less constrained optimization problem. In particular, the decision is taken after the receipt of a signal. Because the action chosen is "optimal" given the signal, it can never be worse than the pre-information action and it can be better. This nonnegativity holds for each possible signal. In other words, the expected utility of the post-information action based on the conditional probabilities must be at least as great as the expected utility of the pre-information action based on those same conditional probabilities. Because the nonnegativity holds for each signal, it also holds for any average across signals. In particular, it holds for the expected value of the differences in utility.

---

[3]This assumption can be motivated in at least two ways. (1) The EPS figures are privately revealed to the investor. (2) The EPS figures are publicly announced. Due to heterogeneous interpretations of the data, there is no effect on the price.

The demand for information, such as financial reporting, is inherently personal and subjective, depending on the personal attributes of the investor.[4] There is no "intrinsic value" of an information system existing apart from the user and a specific decision context. Moreover, personal value can vary across individual investors. Hence, the demand for financial information can also vary across investors and decision contexts.

Portfolio Theory and Financial Reporting

Portfolio theory provides one decision context within which to view financial information. If the purpose of financial reporting is to provide information for investor decision making, the investor decision context is a critical aspect of financial reporting. One-period, mean-variance portfolio theory is one such decision context. As indicated earlier, it is a special case of a more general investor setting in the sense that sufficient restrictions are placed on the preferences and beliefs of the investor so that the decision behavior can be described as if the investor were choosing among portfolios based solely on two parameters, the expected one-period return and the variance of that return. However, it is still general in the sense that it can embrace a variety of types of investors. For example, diversified, nondiversified, active, and passive investors are all consistent with this theory. In other words, the theory is sufficiently general so that it can be used to illustrate the role of financial information in an individual investor setting broader than the previous illustration. Moreover, portfolio theory enjoys considerable usage in the investment community (Sharpe 1995).

Implications of Portfolio Theory

The mechanics of portfolio theory will not be discussed, but several excellent descriptions are available.[5] Instead, the discussion will focus on implications of portfolio theory for financial reporting. Three aspects of portfolio theory are worth noting. (1) The consequences of concern of the investor are characterized as the expected return (also called reward) and the variance of return (also called risk) of the portfolio. The attributes of the returns of individual securities are relevant only insofar as they contribute to the expected return or risk of the portfolio. (2) A portion of the variance of individual securities' returns can be diversified away, and therefore the variance of the portfolio return is not merely an average of the variances of the securities' returns that comprise it. (3) The security-specific parameters of interest to the investor, and the investor's demand for security-specific information (for example, financial reporting) will vary in a manner related to the portfolio strategy chosen.

---

[4]For example, there is no notion of an objective or "true" set of probabilities. Information can be said to be "false" or "misleading" only in terms of the beliefs and behavior it induces, relative to that induced by a finer information system.

[5]Excellent discussions appear in FASB (1976), Sharpe (1995), and Foster (1986).

Role of
I

The role of financial information is to alter the beliefs of the investor. In this setting the relevant investor beliefs are the expected return and variance of return for each of the portfolios.[6] These two parameters are in turn a function of the expected return on the individual securities, the variance of return on the individual securities, and the covariance or correlation among returns of the individual securities.[7] The role of information is potentially to alter these parameters of the investor's beliefs.

A convenient characterization of a security's return is the market model. Here a security's return is viewed as the sum of a systematic and an unsystematic component. The systematic component reflects that portion of security return that is linearly related to the return on a "market" portfolio.[8] The unsystematic return is a "residual" portion of the security return that remains after taking out the systematic component.[9] Under this construction, the systematic and unsystematic components will be uncorrelated with one another. The systematic portion of the security return is perfectly correlated with the return on the market portfolio because it is a linear function of the market portfolio. The unsystematic portion, by contrast, is uncorrelated with the return on the market portfolio. Hence, the systematic portion of returns across securities is perfectly correlated. The unsystematic portion of returns may be correlated across securities due to factors such as common industry effects.

An intuitive motivation for the market model is that a portion of securities returns is commonly affected by economy-wide events, such as inflation, interest rate changes, and changes in GNP, among other factors. Under this description, the relevant investor beliefs are the expected return on the market portfolio, the variance of return on the market portfolio, the intercept and slope terms of the security's linear relationship with the market return (called alpha and beta, respectively), the variance of unsystematic returns (called unsystematic risk), and the covariance or corre-

---

[6]The one-period return is defined as the dividends received during the period plus any price appreciation (or less any price decline) divided by the market value at the beginning of the period. More formally, the expected return and variance of return of the portfolio are denoted $E(R_p)$ and $\sigma^2(R_p)$, respectively.

[7]The security-specific parameters are expected return, $E(R_i)$, variance of returns, $\sigma^2(R_i)$, and the covariance among returns, $\sigma(R_i, R_j)$, and the correlation among returns, p_{ij}, respectively. The correlation can be viewed as the covariance "standardized" by the standard deviations of two securities' returns [in other words, $p_{ij} = \sigma(R_i, R_j)/\sigma(R_i)\sigma(R_j)$]. Both concepts reflect the extent to which the returns of two securities are affected by common events (for example, economy-wide or industry events). These events cause the prices of the securities to move together.

[8]Conceptually, this could include all capital assets. Operationally, the return on the market portfolio is usually the percentage change in an index reflecting a comprehensive group of stocks (for example, *Standard and Poor's Composite Index*).

[9]More precisely,

$$R_i = \alpha_i + \beta_i R_m + u_i$$

where

R_i = return on security i;

R_m = return on a market portfolio;

u_i = unsystematic or residual portion of return (or simply unsystematic return on security i);

α_i = intercept of linear relationship;

β_i = slope of linear relationship; and

$\alpha_i + \beta_i R_m$ = systematic portion of return.

lations among the unsystematic returns.[10] Beta is also known as the systematic (relative) risk of the security. In this setting the role of financial information is to alter these parameters of the investor's beliefs. The first two are economy-wide parameters; the remaining are security-specific parameters.

Financial Information in a Portfolio Theory Context[11]

The role of financial reporting information is to alter investor beliefs about security-specific parameters. An investor's ability to diversify out of unsystematic risk has potentially dramatic implications for the investor's *direct* demand for security-specific information, such as financial reporting data. Although the undiversified investor has a demand for assessing unsystematic risk, the well-diversified investor does not. The role of security-specific financial information reduces to altering assessments of the parameters, alpha and beta.[12]

In general, portfolio theory does not assume that alpha and beta bear any necessary relationship to one another. However, investor behavior is likely to be affected by the relationship perceived between these two parameters. For example, suppose that the investor perceives the expected returns on securities have the property that alpha is directly related to beta such that securities with the same beta also have the same alpha and hence the same expected returns.[13]

For the investor who has such beliefs and who considers only diversified portfolios, the portfolio choice problem reduces to choosing the beta level of the portfolio. In this context, the only security-specific parameter of interest is beta, the sys-

---

[10]More precisely, the relevant parameters are $E(R_m)$, $\sigma^2(R_m)$, α_i, β_i, $\sigma^2(u_i)$, and $\sigma(u_i, u_j)$, respectively. Note that

$$\beta_i = \frac{\sigma^2(R_i, R_m)}{\sigma^2(R_m)}$$

[11]These comments are being made from the perspective of a single investor. They are offered as intuitively plausible implications in this setting.

[12]Why an investor would be motivated to prefer only well-diversified portfolios will be discussed shortly. For a diversified portfolio,

$$E(R_p) = \alpha_p + \beta_p E(R_m)$$
$$\sigma^2(R_p) \simeq \beta_p^2 \sigma^2(R_m)$$

where

$$\alpha_p = \sum_{i=1}^{N} w_i \alpha_i$$

w_i = proportion of portfolio invested in security i;

$$\beta_p = \sum_{i=1}^{N} w_i \beta_i.$$

[13]For example, $\alpha_i = E(R_z)(1 - \beta_i)$, where $E(R_z)$ is the expected return on the minimum variance zero-beta portfolio. See Sharpe (1995) for further discussion.

tematic risk of the securities. In the most extreme form, the investor may consider only holding an index fund combined with borrowing and lending. In other words, the index fund is the only common stock portfolio considered and the desired beta level for the entire portfolio is attained by levering the portfolio up or down by borrowing or lending.[14] For this class of portfolio strategies, there is no direct demand for security-specific information.

Why does an investor choose to be undiversified? Given the apparent effectiveness of diversification in reducing a major source of risk (unsystematic risk), what would lead an investor to perceive that an undiversified portfolio is best? There are many possible reasons, such as transactions costs. However, one reason is the investor's beliefs regarding the structure of security returns. An investor may choose to be undiversified because of the perception that a few securities offer an expected return sufficiently high to compensate the investor, not only for the systematic risk (which is not diversifiable) but also for the unsystematic risk (which is potentially diversifiable).

The investor may be motivated to incur unsystematic risk when "mispriced" securities are perceived. A security is perceived to be mispriced when it is felt that the price of the security does not "fully reflect" the beliefs of the investor. In particular, the investor may perceive that the information on which the investor's beliefs are based is not fully reflected in the price of the security. The extent to which information is fully reflected in prices is known as *market efficiency.* Alternatively stated, the optimal portfolio chosen by the investor will depend on the investor's perceptions of market efficiency. This perception can also influence the investor's demand for financial information, and the financial reporting system can influence the investor's perceptions of market efficiency. The definition and the implications of the concept will be discussed at greater length in Chapter 6.

The perceived relationship between financial information and security prices can be a major source of diversity among investors with respect to the direct demand for financial information. However, once we focus on the relationship between information and security prices, it strains the discussion to keep the level of analysis confined to the single-person setting.

The portfolio chosen is a function not only of the investor's beliefs and information but also of the beliefs and information the investor perceives as implicit in the *consensus* beliefs and information reflected in prevailing security prices. The prevailing price depends on the beliefs and information of other investors. By contrast, the illustration provided earlier assumes that the current security prices remain the same before and after the receipt of the signal. In particular, the example assumes other investors' behavior, at least as reflected in stock prices, is unaffected by the public availability of those signals or is unaffected by other investors' knowl-

---

[14]An "index" fund is a portfolio whose return is highly correlated with percentage changes in the stock price indexes. It consists of a comprehensive diversified group of securities and is intended to be a cost-effective substitute for literally holding the market portfolio. The riskless security version of the Capital Asset Pricing Model represents one situation in which investors would consider such a strategy.

edge that a particular investor has asymmetrical access to some information.[15] Neither assumption is plausible. Prices arise in a multiperson setting in which securities are issued and traded, which naturally leads to a multiperson perspective.

2-2 INFORMATION IN A MULTIPERSON EXCHANGE SETTING

Financial information is not produced in a setting in which there is only one investor. Additional aspects of financial information arise when a multiperson setting is considered. To separate the consequences of providing information, initially it is assumed that financial data are being used in an exchange economy. Later the consequences of information on production are introduced.

Analysis of the role of information in a multiperson setting is an important, but a relatively recently explored, area.[16] As a result, many aspects of the issue are still not well understood. This research offers considerable promise for increasing our insight into financial reporting, and for this reason, some aspects of this literature are presented here. However, because of the embryonic nature of the work, discussing the implications is a tenuous process. The discussion in this section is intended to illustrate some of the possible effects of financial reporting in a multiperson environment. The discussion gives a flavor for the richness and complexity of the problem and provides a framework within which to view the potential consequences of financial reporting.

Information Asymmetry

The discussion of information in a multiperson setting initially focuses on the predecision role of information. Although some interesting issues arise when everyone has the same information, a primary concern of regulators, among others, arises under conditions of *information asymmetry.* Two situations are relevant: (1) information asymmetry among investors, and (2) information asymmetry between management and investors.

More Informed Versus Less Informed Investors

A more general setting is provided by describing the information asymmetry in terms of *more* informed and *less* informed investors. The exchange market for securities provides a ready example. In this setting the more informed investors may be either holders or nonholders of the security and may be either potential sellers or buyers. In other words, at some price (a bid price) an investor is willing to buy

---

[15]For example, others' willingness to trade is not affected by the information decisions of the investor. Similarly, there is no attempt by others to infer what information the investor may have from the investor's behavior. Obviously, however, others' behavior must be affected by the investor's actions in the sense that the securities must be purchased from someone.

[16]An excellent review of this literature appears in Hirshleifer and Riley (1979).

shares and at some price (an ask price) is willing to sell shares. The distinction is based on the information possessed by the individual, not whether the individual is a holder or nonholder, a buyer or a seller.

In this setting the more informed have incentives to engage in "active" trading to reap expected abnormal returns from trading with the less informed. However, the less informed investors have other options available.

1. They can refuse to trade with the more informed and insulate themselves from the more informed via a buy-and-hold portfolio strategy. This passive policy will minimize trades and thereby reduce the ability of the more informed to extract benefits of their information via abnormal returns.[17]

2. The less informed can attempt to infer information from the behavior of the more informed. For example, the less informed may attempt to infer the information of the more informed from the prices the more informed are willing to pay for the securities. This constitutes a form of "learning from prices" and has been studied by Grossman (1976) and Grossman and Stiglitz (1980), among others. In other words, the actions of the more informed may reveal some of their information to the less informed. As a result, prices may partially reflect and in the limit fully reflect the information.

3. The less informed can attempt to obtain the information of the more informed by hiring information intermediaries either directly or through a financial intermediary.

However, the investors may have incentives to want to remove the information asymmetries, which leads to the preemptive role of public disclosure.

Preemptive Role of Public Information

Information asymmetries among investors provide another role for the provision of publicly available information, namely, preempting the opportunity for abnormal returns due to inside information. In the Hirshleifer analysis, potentially there are enormous gains from private access to information. Hence, the private value and the demand for private information can be enormous. However, in the setting described above the social value of publicly disclosing that information might be zero or negative. Costless private search for information is a zero-sum game in terms of real resources from the viewpoint of the entire set of investors. If the private search for information is costly, such as fees paid to financial analysts for private search, in terms of real resources it is a negative-sum game for investors (due to the wealth accruing to those paid for the private search). Hence, investors might prefer to mutually agree not to privately search for information to save the expenditure of real resources consumed in the private search process. However, such a contract would be difficult (costly) to enforce and there would be natural incentives to cheat. In this

---

[17]This leaves the "more informed" to trade among themselves. Treynor (1979) has developed a trading model whereby prices are solely determined by "active" investors, each of whom possesses some inside information. The less informed investors effectively play no role in the price-setting process because they follow a "passive" buy-and-hold portfolio policy designed to insulate themselves from trading with the more informed investors.

context one potential role for the regulation of financial reporting is to effect such a contract. This could be accomplished by inducing a penalty (liability) for obtaining private information, which itself is a costly process involving detection and litigation cost. Alternatively, private search activities might be preempted by placing the data in the public domain. This rationale will be discussed further in Chapter 7.

More Informed Management and Less Informed Investors

It is often assumed that management is more informed about the firm than the investors are. In this situation, two phenomena can occur, *adverse selection* and *moral hazard.*

Adverse Selection

A related aspect of asymmetrical information among investors is the self-selection that may occur on the part of those offering securities for sale, a phenomenon known as *adverse selection.* It has been illustrated in the market for used cars in a seminal article by Akerlof (1970). In a security market setting, information asymmetry means that securities of different "quality" can sell for the same price. To maintain the analogy with the used car market, assume that security holders (for example, potential issuers and sellers) have superior information (a strictly finer information system) than nonholders (for example, potential buyers). The superior information can be thought of as inside information (known only to holders) plus what is publicly known. The inferior information system is simply what is publicly known to buyers and seller alike. There are several potential consequences.

1. The holders of the higher-quality securities may be "forced" to hold a greater amount of those securities than would be the case if the information asymmetry were removed. Such investors may hold a less diversified portfolio and hence incur more unsystematic risk than they would if the superior information were publicly available. In general, this can lead to nonoptimal risk sharing relative to the more complete information setting.

2. Holders of high-quality securities will attempt to alleviate the information asymmetry by some form of "signaling" behavior.[18] In general, signaling involves undertaking some action that would be irrational unless they were in fact holders of higher-quality securities. Specifically, they have incentives to publicly disclose the information to potential buyers that leads them to believe that their securities are underpriced. It may be costly to do so, and there is the question of the credibility of the evidence. For example, the effectiveness will be affected by the ability of holders of lower-quality securities to imitate the signaling behavior (for example, lie about the information they have).

3. Effectiveness could also be affected by the ability to have the information "certified" in some sense and hence improve the credibility of the information. Other options include offering insurance or warranties, under which the holders promise to pay a penalty or reimbursement to the buyer if in fact the security is judged

---

[18]Ross (1979) examines the implications of the signaling literature for financial reporting.

subsequently to be of lower quality. However, certification and warranties are costly and the latter can also lead to an "excessive" shifting of risk.

4. The prospective purchasers are aware of the information asymmetry and will not act in a naive fashion (for example, as if no information asymmetry existed). They know that the prospective sellers have access to a superior information system, but they do not know which signal from the system has been observed. They may attempt to infer the "average" quality of the securities offered for sale and to reflect it in their offering price. However, at any offering price, there will be some degree of adverse selection, unless there is a natural floor on the quality. In the limit, the information asymmetry may lead to no trading at all (in other words, the market simply shuts down). In fact, the meaning and existence of equilibrium in a market with asymmetrical information are open issues and the subject of extensive current research.

This example has assumed that potential issuers and sellers of the security have access to a superior information system. The markets for used cars and the issuance of new securities provide possible examples. The Securities Act of 1933, which provides for disclosure regulation in connection with the issuance of securities, is motivated by concern that the issuer (such as management) may possess superior information relative to the potential buyers.

Stewardship, Moral Hazard, and Agency Theory

One of the consequences of information is its effect on the relationship between management and investors. Previously, this relationship has been described in terms of the stewardship theory. The economics literature treats this as a problem of moral hazard and is of primary concern to agency theory.[19]

In an agency setting a moral hazard problem arises because of an informational asymmetry. Typically, the agent is assumed to have access to superior information. In particular, it is assumed that the principal cannot observe the agent's behavior. Hence, there is a general concern that the agent will use the position of superior information to maximize the agent's self-interest at the expense of the principal. This is the moral hazard problem. Moral hazard not only includes such acts as fraud and shirking, but also includes other actions that are not in the best interests of the principal, such as risk-reward trade-offs made in project selection. The parallel to the management-shareholder relationship is direct and obvious, and several responses to the moral hazard problem are possible.

1. One response is to provide an incentive contract for management so as to more closely align the interests of management and the shareholders. Profit-sharing agreements and stock options are examples of incentive schemes that could play this role. However, such schemes can also have some potentially undesirable properties. In such a setting management may become not only insurers against deficiencies in their own behavior but also insurers of unfavorable outcomes due

---

[19]Studies that have applied agency theory to the relationship between managers and owners include Stiglitz (1974), Jensen and Meckling (1976), Watts and Zimmerman (1986), Harris and Raviv (1979), and Demski and Feltham (1978).

to environmental factors beyond the control of management. Hence, management becomes involved in risk sharing with the principal in a way that may be nonoptimal, relative to the risk sharing that would occur in the absence of a moral hazard problem.

2. Another option to alleviate the moral hazard problem is to provide for public disclosure of the firm's information so as to remove the superior information position of management. Hence, the information asymmetry that leads to the concern over moral hazard is removed. Further, one can imagine hiring an independent "monitor" to come into the firm and inspect the information system and to render a "certification" that no material information has been withheld by management in its reporting to shareholders.[20]

This approach, therefore, gives rise to a demand for auditing services, and it offers a potentially rich area for future research into the demand for audit services. One of the intriguing aspects of the agency research is its recognition that it can be mutually beneficial to both parties to have public disclosure and an audit. The merits for the shareholder have long been acknowledged in the accounting literature. However, the agency approach highlights the fact that management benefits as well. The absence of public disclosure or an audit may require the use of an incentive scheme that induces an undesirable risk sharing. In the limit, if the concern over moral hazard is sufficiently great, the principal may be unwilling to enter into a contract with the agent. Hence, the demand for the agent's service may increase with the agreement to provide the additional information. As a result, management may be willing to pay for audits.

Alleviating the moral hazard problem via disclosure is one aspect of the investors' demand for financial information. The agency theory perspective is consistent with the FASB (1976) position that the stewardship role of financial information is part of the general investor informational approach.

Contracting Perspective

The discussion of adverse selection and moral hazard has suggested that the less informed investor would have a demand for information that would *monitor* the behavior of the more informed manager. Audits would be one form of such information. A demand would also exist to have the contract between the investor and management defined in terms of some observable aspects of the state. Management incentive contracts defined in terms of net income is a prominent example.

The issue of information asymmetry can be more comprehensive than those issues involving management and investors. One class of capital suppliers (for ex-

---

[20]Signaling behavior may also arise. In this setting, managers signal they have nothing to hide by undertaking certain acts that would be nonoptimal for them otherwise. This is discussed in greater detail in Chapter 7. Examples of the signaling literature are discussed in Ross (1979) who applies the signaling literature to financial reporting issues. Obviously, the strategies, similar to those discussed in the adverse selection situation, may also be considered in an analysis of the moral hazard problem.

ample, bondholders) may be concerned about information asymmetries with respect to another class (for example, common stock investors whose interests are represented by management). In this case, contracts between these classes of suppliers of capital, such as bond covenants, can be structured in terms of accounting data. A bond covenant that imposes a minimum times interest earned ratio (income before interest divided by interest payments) is a prominent example. If our laws are viewed as forms of explicit or implicit contracts between the government and the firm's owners, these "social contracts" are also often defined in terms of accounting data. Explicitly, the provisions of the federal tax rules are defined in terms of accounting data. More subtly, the antitrust provisions of our law can be thought of as implicit contract; accounting data may be used by the Anti-Trust division of the Department of Justice to detect violations of the law. In regulated industries, regulators impose constraints on firm behavior that is defined in terms of financial data. Capital adequacy ratios imposed by federal banking regulators would be one prominent example. Watts and Zimmerman (1986) develop in depth the notion that many of the firm's contracts are defined in terms of financial reporting data.

The contracting perspective has at least two important implications. First, it provides a basis for understanding why management and regulators, among others, regard the choice of accounting method as a substantive issue, even in situations where there would be no difference in information provided from an investor, pre-decision perspective. The reason is that the *form* of the disclosure can affect some of the contracts and have an economic impact on the parties involved. Wyatt (1983) provides several excellent examples. Second, the contracting perspective helps explain why management spends a firm's resources lobbying before the financial reporting regulators on behalf of one form of accounting versus another, and why management contends that a financial reporting regulation can have adverse economic consequences on the value of the firm.

For the contracting perspective to be plausible, the costs of contracting (or re-contracting) must be material. Much of the motivation for adopting this perspective arises because explicit, private contracts are not only defined in terms of accounting numbers, but also define those numbers subject to *generally accepted accounting principles* (GAAP). When the FASB proposes to change GAAP, it is tantamount to altering the terms of the private contracts. At least two questions arise. (1) Why don't the parties, at the outset, define the contract in terms of an explicit set of accounting methods, rather than be subject to the regulator risk induced by changing GAAP after the inception of the contract? (2) Why don't the parties simply recontract when GAAP is changed to restore themselves to the original position? In both cases, the answer must be that the costs of doing so are large, relative to the "costs" imposed by having the terms of the contract changed.

These contracting costs involve not only the direct out-of-pocket costs of negotiating and drafting the contract, but also the indirect costs that include effects on the production and financing decisions of management. These latter costs are often alleged to be substantive and systematic across firms.

2-3 SUMMARY OF ECONOMIC CONSEQUENCES OF FINANCIAL INFORMATION

1. Financial information can affect the distribution of wealth among investors. This consequence involves issues of equity or fairness. Differential access to the information may permit more informed investors to increase their wealth at the expense of the less informed. Information asymmetry is perceived by Congress and the SEC to be unfair and is one motivation for the securities legislation governing disclosure.

2. Financial information can affect the aggregate level of risk incurred and can affect the distribution of the risk among the constituencies. For example, the incentive contracts between investors and management, in response to concern over moral hazard, also determine how risk is shared between them. Similarly, legal liability imposed on management for unfavorable outcomes can influence the risk-reward trade-offs made by management in project selection and can affect the aggregate level of risk taking in the economy.

3. Financial information can affect the rate of capital formation in the economy with a resulting reallocation of society's wealth between consumption and investment.

4. Financial information can also affect how investment is allocated among firms. Disclosure may alter investors' beliefs about the relative rewards and risks associated with particular securities. Consider the recent analyses of the effects of inflation on corporate profits. Failure to disclose the effects of inflation, among other things, may be contributing to a misallocation of resources toward industries or groups of firms showing illusory profits. To the extent that disclosure does alter investor perceptions of relative rewards and risks, investors will shift toward more desirable investment opportunities. In general, this shift may be reflected in the manner in which new capital is allocated among firms.

5. Financial information can affect the amount of resources devoted to the production, certification, dissemination, processing, analysis, and interpretation of disclosures.

6. Financial information involves the use of resources in the development, compliance, enforcement, and litigation of disclosure rules. These will be termed the costs of regulation because they exist in addition to the direct costs of disclosure.

7. Financial information can alter the amount of resources used by the private sector to search for nondisclosed information. Corporations have an incentive to provide such information, and analysts have an incentive to search for and to disseminate such information. This activity constitutes private-sector information production and permits the investment activity, as well as the resulting security prices, to reflect a broader information set than the formal documents of the corporation.

8. Information could alter the incentives of management to undertake certain projects. Disclosure could reduce the ability of the firm to reap the benefits of innovative activities, such as oil exploration, product development, and research and development. This is often called the *competitive disadvantage* aspect of disclosure. Similarly, disclosure of information can alter the risk-return trade-offs that management is willing to make. Consider the requirement to publicly disclose management's forecasts of earnings. If management perceives that greater legal liability is associated with forecasts that have large forecast errors, it may alter the nature of the projects accepted so that earnings will be more stable and more predictable. Hence, the risk-return trade-offs may be affected. Obviously, manage-

ment may also alter its forecasting behavior to reduce the risk of legal liability of an incorrect forecast. Disclosure of financial information may also deter undesirable forms of management behavior, such as fraud—one form of the moral hazard problem. However, effects such as competitive disadvantage and legal liability (often viewed as "costs" of disclosure) as well as the deterrence of fraud can be described as having an impact on one or more of the seven categories listed above.

Furthermore, the list of potential consequences does not include security price effects. Financial information can affect security prices. These security price effects in turn can result in one or more of the consequences listed above. For example, the security prices determine the wealth of the investor and the command the investor has over consumption goods and other investments. Security prices affect the terms on which new securities are offered, and as a result they are related to the rate of capital formation and resource allocation. The importance of prices will be discussed in greater detail in Chapter 6. At present, the purpose is to provide a description of primitive consequences of financial information, rather than a description of intermediate effects on security prices, which may be related to these consequences.

2-4 SOCIAL VALUE AND FINANCIAL INFORMATION

A major implication of a multiperson view of financial reporting is that a lack of consensus may exist among individuals on the value of any particular financial reporting system. The discussion has brought out a number of potential consequences of information. The constituencies can be affected in diverse ways by particular financial accounting standards or corporate disclosure requirements.

As the previous chapter indicated, financial accounting theory has long had a predominantly normative flavor (oriented toward which accounting method is "best"). The multiperson viewpoint suggests that it may be difficult to pursue that perspective by staying strictly within the bounds of technical accounting expertise. Because these various constituencies may be affected by the consequences of information in different ways, there may be no consensus on what the "best" accounting method is.

A standard approach to such an issue is to assess the cost and the benefits of a policy decision requiring the provision of additional information. The notion is that the policy maker (the FASB or the SEC) should select those policies in which the benefits exceed the costs. However, whether a particular consequence is a benefit or a cost will depend on which constituency's perspective is adopted. The setting for choosing among financial reporting systems is thus a political one in the sense that it involves an issue of social choice. A choice among financial reporting systems inevitably involves a choice among which set of consequences is most desirable. This in turn involves value judgments or trade-offs among the welfare or interests of the various constituencies affected. Such judgments can certainly be made. However, they typically involve considerations of a normative nature, which are beyond the purview of technical aspects of accounting. Social choices involve issues of equity, such as altering the distribution of wealth among individuals in our society. No amount of accounting expertise alone is going to resolve such an issue, because such an issue also involves value judgments.

To reinforce this point, consider only the investor interests in information production. It has already been noted that professional investors may differ from non-professional investors in their assessments of the value of an information system. Similarly, the interest of a well-diversified investor may differ from that of an undiversified investor. Generally, the demand for financial information will naturally differ across investors. As indicated earlier, the private demand for information by any given individual will depend on its costs and personal attributes of the investor, such as wealth, tastes, and beliefs. It is reasonable to suspect heterogeneity in the preferences for information. When exchanges among investors are introduced, other aspects arise in the form of redistributional effects that induce a further source of divergence among investors regarding the value of an information system.

A direct extension of a political, social choice view of selecting financial reporting systems is to predict what position the various constituencies will take on various financial accounting proposals. Watts and Zimmerman (1978) predict which groups will support or oppose financial accounting standards based on an analysis of the groups' self-interests.

Viewing the selection among financial reporting systems as a social choice does not necessarily imply that some form of regulation of financial reporting is called for. Markets offer one mechanism for social choice, and an issue is whether some form of market failure is present that could be remedied via regulation. The regulation of financial reporting systems is dealt with in greater detail in Chapter 7.

2-5. CONCLUDING REMARKS

The chapter has focused on a number of potential consequences of financial reporting. These effects are diverse and affect various groups in diverse ways. Hence, the search for the "best" method of financial reporting is inherently a social choice issue. This is an inevitable conclusion if one adopts the view of treating financial reporting information in a multiperson setting.

However, little has been said about the exact content of financial information. The treatment has been intentionally general. It has focused on the potential economic consequences of information, where financial disclosures and financial statement data are but two sources of information among the total available to investors in making their decisions. The next chapter turns to the concept of earnings, the primary output of an accrual accounting system, and explores the concept of economic income in some detail. The analysis begins with the case of certainty (Chapter 3) and then moves to uncertainty (Chapter 4). To better appreciate the implications of such a movement, it is critical to have first explored the general nature of financial information.

BIBLIOGRAPHY

Akerlof, G. "The Market for 'Lemons': Quality Uncertainty and the Market Mechanism." *Quarterly Journal of Economics* (August 1970), 488–500.

Demski, J., and G. Feltham. "Economic Incentives in Budgetary Control Systems." *Accounting Review* (April 1978), 336–359.

Financial Accounting Standards Board (FASB). *Tentative Conclusions on Objectives of Financial Statements of Business Enterprises.* Stamford, Conn.: FASB, October 1976.

————. *Statement of Financial Accounting Concepts No. 1.* Stamford, Conn.: FASB, November 1978.

Foster, G. *Financial Statement Analysis.* 2d ed. Englewood Cliffs, N.J.: Prentice-Hall, 1986.

Grossman, S. "On the Efficiency of Competitive Stock Markets Where Traders Have Diverse Information." *Journal of Finance* (May 1976), 573–585.

———— and J. Stiglitz. "On the Impossibility of Informationally Efficient Markets." *American Economic Review* (June 1980), 393–408.

Harris, M., and A. Raviv. "Optimal Incentive Contracts with Imperfect Information." *Journal of Economic Theory* (April 1979), 231–259.

Hirshleifer, J., and J. Riley. "The Analytics of Uncertainty and Information—An Expository Survey." *Journal of Economic Literature* (December 1979), 1375–1421.

Jensen, M., and W. Meckling. "Theory of the Firm: Managerial Behavior, Agency Costs and Ownership Structure." *Journal of Financial Economics* (October 1976), 305–360.

Ross, W. "Disclosure Regulation in Financial Markets: Implications of Modern Finance Theory and Signaling Theory." *Key Issues in Financial Regulation* (1979), 177–201.

Securities and Exchange Commission. *Report of Advisory Committee on Corporate Disclosure.* Washington, D.C.: U.S. Government Printing Office, 1977.

Sharpe, W. *Investments.* 5th ed. Englewood Cliffs, N.J.: Prentice-Hall, 1995.

Stiglitz, J. "Risk Sharing and Incentives in Sharecropping." *Review of Economic Studies* (April 1974), 219–255.

Treynor, J. "Trading Cost and Active Management." *Proceedings of Seminar on Investment Management: The Active/Passive Decisions.* Menlo Park, Calif.: FRS Associates, September 23–26, 1979, iv–94 through iv–107.

Watts, R., and J. Zimmerman "Towards a Positive Theory of the Determination of Accounting Standards." *Accounting Review* (January 1978), 112–134.

————. *Positive Accounting Theory.* Englewood Cliffs, N.J.: Prentice-Hall, 1986.

Wyatt, A. "Efficient Market Theory: Its Impact on Accounting." *Journal of Accountancy* (February 1983), 56–65.

3

Certainty

Chapters 3 and 4 explore the relation between accounting numbers and the value of the firm and its common stock. As indicated in the introductory chapter, accounting earnings are a primary product of the accrual process. No other figure in the financial statements receives more attention by the investment community than earnings per share. The relationship between accounting earnings and security prices is probably the single most important relationship in security analysis, and its prominence is reflected in the attention given to price-earnings ratios.[1] A considerable amount of empirical research has been conducted on the relationship between accounting numbers and security prices. This research will be the topic of Chapter 5.

The setting in this chapter is perfect, complete markets and certainty. The setting of uncertainty and incomplete markets will be examined in Chapter 4.

3-1 PERFECT, COMPLETE MARKETS AND CERTAINTY: THE PRESENT VALUE MODE

The concept of *perfect markets* means that (1) trading of commodities and claims take place at zero transactions cost, (2) no firm or individual has any special advantage or opportunity to earn abnormal returns on its investments, and (3) prices are invariant to the actions of any individual or firm. The concept of *complete markets* means that

---

[1]The terms *earnings* and *net incomes* are used interchangeably throughout. However, it is important to distinguish between *economic* earnings and *accounting* earnings, assuming the former is well-defined. Usually the context of the discussion will make it clear which concept is being referred to. However, often the distinction will be made explicit to reinforce the importance of the distinction.

markets exist for *all* commodities or claims, and hence the market price for any commodity or claim is publicly observable. Of particular interest here is the valuation of "cash flows" over time. Two critical aspects are the completeness of the market with respect to claims to future cash flows (hereafter intertemporal claims) and the ability to costlessly trade in these claims in any desired combination.[2] For example, consider a simple economy in which there are three points in time: now ($t = 0$), one period from now ($t = 1$), and two periods from now ($t = 2$). A complete market for claims to future cash flows would permit the opportunity to (1) invest now and receive $1 at $t = 1$, (2) invest now and receive $1 at $t = 2$, (3) invest now and receive $1 each at $t = 1$ and $t = 2$, (4) contract now to invest at $t = 1$ and receive $1 at $t = 2$ (a futures market exists), and (5) know now that at $t = 1$ a market will open for one-period claims to $1 to be received at $t = 2$ (future spot markets will be available). Moreover, claims can be traded in any multiple, and fractions of claims are available. In other words, a complete market for claims to future cash flows is simply a very "rich" market that permits whatever trading that is desired by investors.[3]

The assumption of certainty means that all expectations are realized and investors know that they will be realized. Hence, the future prices of any claim are known with certainty. Given the assumption of zero transactions costs, the setting implies that certain relationships exist between the prices of intertemporal claims. These relationships give rise to the familiar present value formulation. Perfect and complete markets permit a costless, riskless arbitraging of intertemporal claims and hence require the pricing of the claims to behave such that a present value formulation is attainable.

In the most general case, both interest rates and amounts to be received will vary over time. However, without loss of insight and with the added convenience of illustration, the interest rate (r) is hereafter assumed to be constant over time. Let C_t denote the cash flow to be received at time t for $t = 1$, T. $_0P_t$ is the present value (or price) as of now ($t = 0$) for a claim to receive $1 at time t. Then,

$$_0PV_T = \sum_{t=1}^{T} \frac{1}{(1+r)^t} C_t = \sum_{t=1}^{T} {}_0P_t C_t$$

where $_0PV_T$ is the present value or price of the compound claim as of now ($t = 0$) for a T-period compound claim of nonconstant amounts. The compound claim can be viewed as a bundle of simple claims, and the price of the bundle is the sum of the prices of the simple claims that comprise the bundle. Each T-period compound claim represents T valuable claims. The analogy to commodities in an atemporal setting is obvious. In perfect and complete markets the value of any bundle of claims (commodities) is merely the sum of the value of claims (commodities) it represents. This value additivity property follows from the fact that arbitrage profits

---

[2]The chapter will adopt the terminology of claims to "cash flows" to ease the transition to traditional valuation theory, which is typically characterized in terms of future cash flows.
[3]Although the text refers to investment (lending opportunities), analogous borrowing opportunities are also implied. Default risk is not an issue here because of the certainty assumption.

must be zero in this setting. If value additivity did not hold, arbitrage profits could be earned, as illustrated earlier for the two-period simple claim.

The present value characterization permits a vector of future cash flows $(C_1, C_2, \ldots, C_T)$ to be converted into a scalar, the present value of those cash flows. Moreover, this single number has several important properties. The cash flow stream that has the highest present value is the most preferred by investors. This statement can be made regardless of the personal characteristics of investors, such as the exact nature of their initial endowment of intertemporal claims or their preference function for intertemporal cash flows. It merely requires that they prefer (or at least do not oppose) more cash flow to less in any given time period. Because of the richness of the market for intertemporal claims, any two streams can be evaluated regardless of their individual cash flow patterns. Obviously, cases in which one stream strictly dominates another are simple to evaluate. For example, consider the case in which the cash flow for stream A is at least as large as the cash flow for stream B at each and every point in time and is strictly larger for at least one point. However, the present value mechanism permits a comparison of cash flow streams that initially cannot be evaluated by a strict dominance criterion. The market assumptions underlying the present value model (perfect and complete markets) permit any arbitrary cash flow stream to be expressed as an infinite number of other cash flow streams of equivalent present value ("alter ego" cash flow streams). This flexibility guarantees that any cash flow stream that has a higher present value than another cash flow stream has at least one "alter ego" cash flow stream that strictly dominates the cash flow stream with the lower present value. Hence, as long as the marginal utility of additional cash flows is nonnegative (positive), the cash flow stream with the higher present value will be at least as good as (strictly preferred to) the cash flow stream with the lower present value.

The present value of future cash flows strictly ranks all simple and compound claims to future cash flows in spite of investors' diversity with respect to initial endowments and preferences. In equilibrium, ranking claims according to their present values is equivalent to ranking them according to the preferences of each and every investor. Moreover, this unanimity of preference is fully reflected in the price. The price of any compound claim to future cash flow *is* the present value of that claim. Finally, the present value rule gives the management of firms a basis for project selection. Management can select capital investments that maximize the firm's present value and hence maximize the utility of each of the owners.

3-2 ECONOMIC EARNINGS UNDER CERTAINTY

This section explores economic income under conditions of certainty of future cash flows. It is the simplest setting and approximates the setting accounting theorists had in mind in their early developments of accounting earnings concepts. Moreover, the economic concept of earnings in this setting is well defined. As a result, it is a natural starting point for the discussion of the economic earnings concept. Throughout this section the illustrations will refer to an all-equity firm. The firm's net income will also be the earnings available to common shareholders. Because there is no debt, the total assets of the firm will equal shareholders' equity at any point in time. The concept of earnings is explored in two contexts: (1) a single-asset firm in which the cash flows have a finite life, and (2) a multiasset firm in which the cash flow stream is treated as having an infinite life. The assumptions about the economy and the firm are summarized in Table 3-1.

Single-Asset Firm

Consider the simple setting of a single-asset firm, as illustrated in Table 3-2. The assumptions about the asset are summarized in Table 3-1. The asset has a two-year

---

TABLE 3-1 Assumptions

I. Assumptions About the Economy
  A. Certainty
    1. All expectations are realized
    2. All future prices of assets and claims are known
  B. Perfect and complete markets
    1. Zero transactions costs
    2. No abnormal earnings opportunities
    3. No arbitrage profits
    4. Prices are invariant to actions of individuals or firms
    5. Markets are very "rich"
  C. Interest rate is 10% per year
    1. It is constant over time
    2. It is also the earnings rate (internal rate of return) on all multiperiod assets and claims
II. Assumptions About the Firm
  A. Single-asset firm
  B. All equity—no debt
  C. Cash flows occur discretely at end of each year
  D. All cash flows from operations are paid out as dividends
    1. No cash is retained in firm
    2. At each balance sheet date only the single asset is shown (in other words, there is no cash balance)
III. Assumptions About the Asset
  A. Useful life is two years
  B. Salvage value is zero
  C. Cash flow pattern:
     Year   1   2
     Amount $600 $550
  D. Acquisition price at end of year 0 (now) is $1,000
  E. Economic depreciation is used
  F. Depreciation is recorded at end of year

TABLE 3-2 Economic Earnings for a Single-Asset Firm

	YEAR	
	1	2
Net Cash Flow	$ 600	$ 550
Present Value (PV) of Asset, Firm, and Equity at Beginning of Each Year[a]		
PV of year 1 flow	$ 545	
PV of year 2 flow	455	$ 500
	$ 1,000	$ 500
Economic Depreciation		
Beginning present value	$ 1,000	$ 500
Ending present value	500	0
Decline in present value	$ 500	$ 500
Economic Net Income of Asset and Firm	$ 600	$ 550
Net cash flow		
Less: economic depreciation	(500)	(500)
Economic net income	$ 100	$ 50
Return on Investment	$\frac{\$\ 100}{\$\ 1,000} = 10\%$	$\frac{\$\ 50}{\$\ 500} = 10\%$
Economic Net Income of Shareholders		
Dividends received	$ 600	$ 550
Decline in present value of equity	(500)	(500)
Net income	$ 100	$ 50
Permanent Earnings		
Present value at beginning of year	$ 1,000	$ 500
Times: interest rate	.10	.10
Permanent earnings	$ 100	$ 50
Beginning Market Value of Asset, Firm, and Equity[b]	$ 1,000	$ 500
Beginning Market Price per Share[c]	$ 10	$ 5
Earnings per Share[c]	$ 1	$ .50
Price-Earnings Ratio	10X	10X

[a] $\$545 = \dfrac{600}{1.1}; 455 = \dfrac{550}{(1.1)^2}; 500 = \dfrac{550}{(1.1)}.$

[b] *Because of assumptions about the economy, present value equals market value. In other words, net value equals entry value equals value in use.*

[c] *100 shares are outstanding.*

life, an estimated salvage value of zero, and an acquisition cost of $1,000. The after-tax cash flows are $600 and $550, and the discount rate is 10%.[4]

The present value of the asset at the time of acquisition is $1,000, as shown in Table 3-2. The present value of $1,000 represents the present value of $600 to be received in one year (at the end of year 1) and of $550 to be received in two years.

[4]The assumption of perfect and complete markets implies that the earnings rate on all assets will be equal to the cost of capital, which is the interest rate. The definition of the *earnings rate* (r^*) is that rate which

Because of the assumptions made about the economy, the present value must be equal to the market value at the time of acquisition. One year later, the present value of the asset is only $550, representing the present value of $550 to be received in one year (at the end of year 2). Of course, at the end of year 2 the present value is zero. All cash flows received are immediately paid out as dividends (see Table 3-1), and the present value of the two-year asset is also the present value of the cash flows of the firm. Because the firm is all-equity, the present value of the asset's remaining cash flows is equal to the present value of the cash flows of the equity.

Economic depreciation is defined as the change in the present value of the remaining cash flows at two points in time. The present value of the asset will decline by $500 per year. Hence, economic depreciation is $500 per year in this example, which happens to be equal to the amount of depreciation that would have been recorded using a straight-line method.

From the perspective of the firm, economic income in any given year is defined as the cash flows received in that year less the reduction in the present value of the asset's remaining cash flows (cash flow less economic depreciation). This would produce economic earnings of $100 and $50 respectively for each of the two years, as shown in Table 3-2.

From the perspective of the shareholders, economic net income is the amount of cash dividends received in that year less any change in the market value of their holdings (any capital gain or loss). As Table 3-2 shows, this also produces the same net income figures. Hence, economic net income for the firm is equal to the economic net income to the shareholders. Further, the present value of the asset is equal to its market value at any point in time.[5] Moreover, the market value (present value) of the asset is equal to the market value (present value) of the firm, which is equal to the market value (present value) of the firm's equity.

With 100 shares outstanding, the market price per share is $10 as of the beginning of year 1, an the earnings per share (EPS) is $1. The price-earnings ratio is 10 times. In year 2 the beginning market price would be $5 and the EPS would be $.50. Again the price-earnings ratio would be 10 times, and it is equal to the reciprocal of the interest rate of 10%.

---

will discount the asset's future cash flows to a present value equal to the acquisition cost of the asset. It is also known as the *internal rate of return* or the *time adjusted rate of return*. More formally, $r*$ has the property that

$$\text{acquisition cost} \equiv \sum_{t=1}^{T} \frac{C_t}{(1+r*)^t}$$

In the example,

$$\$1,000 = \frac{\$600}{(1+.10)} + \frac{\$550}{(1+.10)^2}$$

[5]The entry price of the assets (what it would cost to purchase the asset) is equal to its exit price (what it could be sold for), which in turn is equal to its value in use (its present value). Hence, there is no ambiguity about the definition of the market value of the asset at any point in time.

In this simple context there would be little dispute about the attributes of this measure of net income, and it would have the "desirable" properties discussed in Chapter 1. In any given time period, more net income is preferred to less. In evaluating management's stewardship function, a more preferred management action will result in a higher net income than a less preferred management action. In year 1 the implications for management's stewardship with respect to this asset are reflected in the cash flows of year 2 and in their present value. Hence, the net income of year 1 reflects the impact of management's actions in the subsequent year. Not only is this measure of net income virtually unassailable in the context of this simple setting, but no notions of accrual accounting were required to generate this number. Economic earnings is a valuation concept, not an accounting concept, as has been eloquently argued by Treynor (1972), among others. It could have been generated with a modicum of knowledge about the present value model, but it does not require knowledge of financial accounting.

However, various financial accounting proposals on how to measure *accounting* net income have been evaluated in terms of their proximity to the measure of economic net income. For example, if straight-line depreciation were applied to the asset described above, accounting net income would be equal to economic net income. The book value of the asset at any point in time (its acquisition cost less accumulated depreciation) would be equal to the market value of the asset and to the present value of its remaining cash flows. This is illustrated in Table 3-3. Extensive literature exists in

TABLE 3-3 Financial Statements for a Single-Asset Firm

	YEAR	
	1	2
Cash Flows	$ 600	$ 550
Less: Straight-Line Depreciation	(500)	(500)
Accounting Net Income	$ 100	$ 50
Book Value of Asset at Beginning of Year:		
Original cost	$1,000	$1,000
Less: accumulated depreciation	0	500
Net book value of asset	$1,000	$ 500
Book Value of Firm and Equity	$1,000	$ 500
Accounting Return on Investment:		
$\dfrac{\text{Accounting Net Income}}{\text{Beginning Book Value of Firm}}$	$\dfrac{\$\ 100}{\$1,000}=10\%$	$\dfrac{\$\ 50}{\$\ 500}=10\%$
Accounting Return on Equity:		
$\dfrac{\text{Net Income Available for Common}}{\text{Beginning Book Value of Equity}}$	$\dfrac{\$\ 100}{\$\ 1,000}=10\%$	$\dfrac{\$\ 50}{\$\ 500}=10\%$
$\dfrac{\text{Market Value of Equity}}{\text{Accounting Net Income}}$	$\dfrac{\$1,000}{\$\ 100}=10X$	$\dfrac{\$\ 500}{\$\ 50}=10X$

financial accounting called *depreciation theory* that evaluates the relative merits of various depreciation schemes in precisely this manner.[6] In this setting, net income is a well-defined concept and is a byproduct of the valuation process.

A Multiasset (Infinite-life) Firm

Now consider a firm that purchases an asset identical to the one described in the previous illustration once each year. In a "steady state" the firm will report the financial results depicted in Table 3-4. The financial results will be the same for each year in perpetuity. For simplicity, the financing of the additional investment in assets of $1,000 per year is assumed to be provided via internal equity financing (in other words, via the retention of a portion of cash flows from operations).

In this simple "no-growth" case, the annual net cash flow from operations is $1,150, the sum of the cash flows from the two assets held. At the beginning of each year the firm is assumed to have just purchased a new asset. As a result, at the start of each year the firm has one asset new (with a two-year life) and one asset one-year old (with one year remaining). At the end of that year the new asset will produce cash flows of $600 and the one-year-old asset will produce cash flows of $550. Each asset has an economic depreciation of $500, as illustrated in the single-asset example, and total depreciation for both assets is $1,000. Economic net income is $150 ($1,150 less $1,000).

Each year the firm purchases an additional asset with an acquisition cost of $1,000, which is financed out of the cash flows from operations. As a result, each

---

TABLE 3-4 Multiasset Firm (No-Growth)

Net Cash Flows ($600 + $550)	$1,150
Less: Economic Depreciation ($500 + $500)	($1,000)
Economic Net Income ($100 + $50)	$ 150
Dividend ($1,150–$1,000)[a]	$ 150
Present Value of Dividend	$\dfrac{\$\ 150}{.10} = \$1,500$
Stream (PV of Equity)	
Market Value of Firm and Equity	$1,500
Permanent Earnings	$1,500 × .10 = $150
Market Price per Share	$ 15
Economic Earnings per Share	$ 1.50
Price-Earnings Ratio	10X
Dividend per Share	$ 1.50
Payout Ratio	
$\dfrac{\text{Dividend per Share}}{\text{Earnings per Share}}$	$\dfrac{\$\ 1.50}{1.50} = 100\%$

[a]*Cash flows of* $1,150 *less the additional investment required to keep the firm in "steady-state."*

---

[6]This literature is discussed and bibliographic references are given in Beaver and Dukes (1973, 1974).

year the firm pays out a dividend of $150 ($1,150 less $1,000). The present value of the perpetuity of $150 (assuming an interest rate of 10%) is $1,500 ($150/.10).[7] Of course, the market value of the firm and its equity will equal the present value of that perpetual dividend stream and hence also is $1,500. With 100 shares outstanding, the market price per share will be $15 and the economic net income per share is $1.50. The ration of market price to economic earnings per share will be 10 times, the reciprocal of the interest rate of 10% (1/.10 = 10 times). The payout ratio with respect to economic earnings is 100% ($1.50/$1.50).

The analysis can be easily extended to a "growth" case by the retention of a portion of economic earnings (in other words, by paying a smaller dividend than economic earnings). Consider a second firm identical to the one above, except that the second firm follows a policy of paying out dividends equal to 60% of its economic earnings. Specifically, at the beginning of a year in which its economic earnings are $150, the payout ratio is 60% (instead of 100%) of $150 (and subsequent economic earnings). This implies an amount invested of $60 more than if all of economic earnings are paid out. As a result, economic earnings will grow by 4% per year. For example, the additional $60 available for investment will earn at a rate of 10%, which means that next year's economic earnings will be higher by $6. Economic earnings will increase from $150 in one year to $156 in the next year, which is a growth rate of 4%. The dividend paid out in the next year will be $93.60 (156 times .60), which is 4% higher than the previous dividend of $90. In this situation, both economic earnings and dividends will grow at 4% per year.

But does this alter the present value of the dividend stream and hence the price of the common stock relative to a no-growth case? The answer is no. Although the initial dividend is lower ($.90 per share rather than $1.50 per share), it will grow at 4% per year, while there will be zero growth in the 100% payout. It can be easily shown that, *as of the beginning of the year,* the present values of these two streams are both equal to $15. It is implied by the constant dividend growth model of Williams (1938), among others.[8] The formula states:

$$P_0 = \frac{D_1}{r - g}$$

where
P_0 = price per share at the *beginning* of the year ($t = 0$);
D_1 = dividend paid at the end of the year ($t = 1$);
r = interest rate (assumed constant); and
g = growth in dividends (assumed constant).

---

[7]The present value of a perpetual annuity of X per year at a discount rate of r is X/r.
[8]The formula follows directly from the equation for the sum of an infinite geometric progression and is discussed further in Sharpe (1995). More generally, the term *discount rate* is used rather than the interest rate. However, under certainty, the discount rate is the interest rate, which has been assumed to be constant over time.

For the no-growth case,

$$P_0 = \frac{\$1.50}{.10 - 0} = \frac{\$1.50}{.10} = \$15$$

For the growth case,

$$P_0 = \frac{\$.90}{.10 - .04} = \frac{\$.90}{.06} = \$15$$

Of course, subsequently a growth in price per share will occur to reflect the retention policy. In the no-growth case, not surprisingly, the price per share remains constant. In the growth case, the price (per share) will grow at the same rate as dividends (per share) and economic earnings (per share). In the example this growth rate was 4%. In particular, with 100 shares outstanding, the market value (per share) of the equity will increase from $1,500 ($15) at the beginning of the year ($t = 0$) to $1,560 ($15.60) at the end of the year ($t = 1$). However, because price (per share) and economic earnings per share are growing at the same rate, the price-earnings ratio will be constant and will be the same regardless of the growth assumption. In the example the ratio of price to economic earnings is 10 times in both the no-growth and growth cases.[9] Given the assumptions of this example, the growth rate in dividends and earnings bears a direct relationship to the payout policy of the firm. In particular, the growth will equal the product of the earnings rate on additional investment (here, the interest rate) times the retention ratio, where the retention ratio is defined as that percentage of earnings not paid out in dividends (for ex-

---

[9]In the constant divided growth model the price-earnings ratio P_0 / E_1^* is

$$\frac{P_0}{E_1^*} = \frac{K^*}{r - g}$$

For the no-growth case,

$$\frac{P_0}{E_1^*} = \frac{1}{.10 - 0} = \frac{1}{.10} = 10$$

For the growth case,

$$\frac{P_0}{E_1^*} = \frac{.6}{10 - .04} = \frac{.6}{.06} = 10$$

This formula follows from the one introduced above by noting that the payout ratio (K^*) is defined here as the ratio of dividends to *economic* earnings. Divide both sides of the expression by E_1^* (economic earnings) and

$$P_0 = \frac{D_1}{r - g}$$

becomes

$$\frac{P_0}{E_1^*} = \frac{K^*}{r - g}$$

ample, one minus the payout ratio).[10] In the numerical example the growth rate of 4% is the product of the interest rate of 10% times the retention ratio of .40. More elaborate forms of financing, such as debt financing and external equity financing, could be introduced, and price per share would still be characterized by the simple dividend growth formula.[11]

3-3   PERMANENT EARNINGS

In the multiasset example, economic earnings in a certainty setting is equal to permanent earnings. Permanent earnings are equal to that constant (no growth) dividend, which if received in perpetuity would have the same value as that of the dividend stream that will actually be paid out.[12] Economic earnings equal permanent earnings and are $1.50 per share in both the no-growth and growth examples. Of course, this is obvious for the no-growth case. However, economic earnings have the same property in the growth case as well. As indicated earlier, the investor would be indifferent between receiving a constant dividend of $1.50 in perpetuity or receiving a dividend stream that started at $.90 and grew by 4% per year. Hence, the concept applies to growth situations. Permanent earnings can be computed by multiplying the beginning price per share times the interest rate ($15 times .10 = $1.50).[13]

---

[10]There are no abnormal earnings opportunities (because the earnings rate equals the interest rate). Both growth and no-growth cases have the same price-earnings ratios. There are no "growth premiums" here, and the price-earnings ratio equals $1/r$ regardless of the growth rate.

[11]Obviously, this statement is being made in the context of the economy-wide assumptions of certainty as well as perfect and complete markets. In this context, the distinction between debt and equity as well as the distinction between external and internal equity financing is trivial. Hence, the emphasis on an all-equity firm is not restrictive in this setting.

[12]More formally, at $t = 0$,

$$\frac{\text{permanent earnings}}{r} \equiv \sum_{t=1}^{\infty} \frac{D_t}{(1+r)^t} = P_0$$

$$\text{permanent earnings} \equiv r \cdot \left[\sum_{t=1}^{\infty} \frac{D_t}{(1+r)^t} \right]$$

$$\equiv rP_0$$

where

r = interest rate;
P_0 = price per share;
D_t = dividend in period t.

[13]Specifically, in the growth case,

$$\frac{\$1.50}{.10} \equiv \frac{.90}{(1+.10)} + \frac{.90(1+.04)}{(1.10)^2} + \ldots = \$15$$

or

$$\$1.50 \equiv .10 \cdot \$15 = .10 \left[\sum_{t=1}^{\infty} \frac{.90(1+.04)^{t-1}}{(1+.10)^t} \right]$$

TABLE 3-5 Summary of Concepts of Earnings[a]

I. Economic Earnings

Cash flows received plus change in present value of remaining cash flows

II. Permanent Earnings

That constant cash flow which if received in perpetuity would have the same present value as that of the remaining cash flows and computed as the present value at the beginning of the period times the interest rate

---

[a]*Note that, under the assumptions of this chapter, the market value of an asset or a claim is equal to the present value of the future cash flows. Hence, the term* market value *can be substituted for the term* present value *in the definitions. Obviously, consideration must be made for deposits and withdrawals in defining the earnings of the firm.*

The concept of permanent earnings is central to security analysis and security valuation (Cottle, Murray, and Block 1988). In security analysis, accounting earnings are used to form assessments of the *permanent earnings* of the firm and its common stock. However, as defined here, the concept of permanent earnings, as well as the concept of economic earnings, is essentially a valuation concept. Permanent earnings are equal to the present value of the remaining cash flows times the interest rate; neither component is an accounting concept.

These earnings properties are summarized in Table 3-5. The key feature is that *value and earnings are two sides of the same coin.*

3-4 EARNINGS VERSUS CASH FLOWS AS AN INDICATOR OF FUTURE DIVIDEND-PAYING ABILITY

In this context, the FASB's emphasis on earnings as the primary focus of financial reporting can be examined. The FASB's contention is that dividend-paying ability is better measured by accounting earnings than by current cash flows. The FASB's point is difficult to understand in the no-growth case because cash flows from operations less investment equal earnings. However, consider the single-asset example. The FASB's contention can be interpreted as saying that the *economic* earnings in year 1 of $100 is a better measure of the dividend-paying capacity of the firm than is the cash flow of $600 that was paid out in dividends. The reason is that a dividend of $600 could not be paid out in perpetuity and as a result reduces the present value of the remaining cash flows.

Also consider the growth case in the multiasset example. The dividends paid out are only $90, but the economic earnings are $150. The dividend of $90 "understates" the future dividend-paying ability of the firm, because the $90 dividend permits a growth of 4% in future dividends. This is reflected in an increase in the present value of the dividend stream from $1,500 (at the beginning of the period) to $1,560 (at the end of the period). The $60 reflects the present value of the increased dividend-paying ability. The sum of $90 plus $60 ($150) reflects the total dividend-paying ability and is equal to the economic earnings.

In the security analysis literature a motivation for using accounting earnings as parameters of the security valuation model stems from the belief that accounting earnings ("properly" interpreted and adjusted) provide a measure of the dividend-paying capacity of the firm. In this sense, the security analysis literature is interested in the permanent earnings property of economic earnings. Permanent earnings reflect the dividend stream that could be paid out in perpetuity. *Hence, the vector of actual future dividends, regardless of their pattern or length of life, is reduced to a scalar, a single number, called permanent earnings.* The definition of permanent earnings clearly shows how an "earnings" concept can measure the "dividend-paying" capacity (cash flow concept). However, the relationship between accounting earnings and permanent earnings (economic earnings) is less clear.

3-5 ACCOUNTING EARNINGS AND ECONOMIC EARNINGS

Security analysis often uses accounting earnings as an input to a valuation formula, such as the constant dividend growth model. For example, growth in earnings per share is often used rather than growth in dividends per share. Moreover, the ratio of stock price per share to accounting earnings per share (hereafter P/E ratios) can be characterized by the following formula, which is a direct extension of the formula cited earlier.

$$\frac{P_0}{E_1} = \frac{K}{r - g}$$

where P_0, r, and g are defined as before; E_1 equals the *accounting* earnings per share reported for the year; and K equals the ratio of dividends per share for the year (D_1) to *accounting* earnings per share for the year (E_1).

What definitions of accounting earnings are consistent with such an expression for price-earnings ratios? Initially, one would speculate that if accounting earnings equal economic (or permanent) earnings, the expression would be correct. However, as the equation now stands, *any* definition of accounting earnings is consistent because the equation was derived from the constant dividend growth model by merely dividing both sides of the equation by accounting earnings per share (E_1). The result is a P/E ratio on the left-hand side and a payout ratio (K) on the right-hand side. It provides one characterization of the determinants of price-earnings ratios, and it will hold for *any* definition of accounting earnings because it is tautological. If the constant dividend growth model is valid, then the derived expression for the P/E ratio must follow. In fact, if the constant dividend growth model is valid, then we can divide both sides of the equation by *any arbitrary constant* and the resulting equation will still hold. If accounting earnings measure economic earnings with error, this will be merely reflected in the payout ratio. Although such a representation is logically valid, it is devoid of any substance or additional insight.

Note, however, that growth in dividends is still used in the denominator of the right-hand side. Suppose that the growth in accounting earnings is used in place of the growth in dividends. This implicitly assumes that the payout ratio will be constant over time. If the payout ratio is not constant over time, the growth in earnings will not equal the growth in dividends, and hence the former cannot be used to measure the latter. If the payout ratio is constant over time, the growth in earnings equals the growth in dividends, and hence the growth in earnings can be used to measure the growth in dividends.

3-6 ANALYSIS OF ALTERNATIVE ACCOUNTING METHODS

The impact of alternative accounting methods can be analyzed in two respects. (1) An analysis can be conducted of the relationship between economic income and accounting net income under various alternatives. The difference between economic income and accounting income can be thought of as the extent to which accounting income measures economic income with error. Obviously, this requires a setting in which economic income is well defined. The context of this chapter (perfect and complete markets and certainty) provides one such setting. Alternative accounting methods can be analyzed in terms of the *measurement error* that occurs under specified conditions. (2) An analysis also can be conducted of the *descriptive differences* induced by alternative methods under specified conditions. This requires no notion of economic income. Both types of analyses will be illustrated here in the context of alternative depreciation methods.

Measurement Error in Accounting Earnings

Accounting earnings may not be equal to the economic earnings of the firm. The difference between accounting earnings and economic permanent earnings can be called the measurement error in accounting earnings. One reason for an error is that a firm can use different accounting methods (for example, straight-line or accelerated depreciation methods) that can affect the level of accounting earnings. This can induce a difference in the level of earnings that is unrelated to the future dividend-paying ability of the firm. Price-earnings ratios of firms that use different depreciation methods would also differ.

For example, consider a firm that grows by 4% per year. If the asset acquisition cost was $1,000 in the previous year, this year's asset acquisition cost is $1,040. At the beginning of the year the firm holds a one-year-old asset (with one year remaining) and a new two-year asset. The assets purchased are identical to the one illustrated in Tables 3-2, 3-3, and 3-4 *per dollar of acquisition cost.* However, the dollar amount of the asset purchased is assumed to grow by 4% per year (from

$1,000 to $1,040). The financial results, assuming straight-line (SL) and sum-of-the-years-digits (SYD) depreciation, are reported in Table 3-6.

Note that the economic depreciation on this asset is equal to straight-line depreciation. As a result, accounting net income under straight-line depreciation is equal to *economic income*. The book value of the asset, firm, and equity under straight-line is equal to the present value of the remaining cash flows and is equal to the market value of the asset, firm, and equity. The price-earnings ratio is 10 times, which is the reciprocal of the interest rate. The accounting rate of return is 10%, which is the earnings rate (here, the interest rate).[14] This is hardly surprising and would be expected to occur in this growth case as it did in the single-asset (negative-growth) and no-growth case.

TABLE 3-6 Differences in Financial Statement Results
Due to Depreciation Differences

| | DEPRECIATION METHOD[a] | |
	SL	SYD
Cash Flows (550 + 624)[b]	$1,174	$1,174
Depreciation	$1,020	1,027
Net Income	$ 154	$ 147
Beginning Book Value of Asset, Firm, and Equity		
Original cost (1,000 + 1,040)	$2,040	$2,040
Less: accumulated depreciation	500	667
	$1,540	$1,373
Market Value and Present Value of Assets, Firm, and Equity	$1,540	$1,540
$\dfrac{\text{Market Value of Equity}^c}{\text{Net Income}}$	$\dfrac{\$1,540}{\$\ 154} = 10X$	$\dfrac{\$1,540}{\$\ 147} = 10.48X$
Return on Equity: $\dfrac{\text{Net Income}}{\text{Beginning Book Value}}$	$\dfrac{\$\ 154}{\$1,540} = 10\%$	$\dfrac{\$\ 147}{\$1,373} = 10.71\%$

^{a}*SL = straight-line depreciation*
SYD = sum-of-the-years-digits depreciation
^{b}*Cash flows = $550 + (1 + g)$600 = $1,150 + g$600*
Depreciation (SL) = $550 + (1 + g)$500 = $1,000 + g$500
Net income (SL) = $150 + g$100
Depreciation (SYD) = $333 + (1 + g)$667 = $1,000 + g$667
Net income (SYD) = $150 - g$67
Original cost = $1,000 + (1 + g)$1,000 = $2,000 + g$1,000
Accumulated depreciation (SL) = $500
Accumulated depreciation (SYD) = $667
Market value = present value = book value under SL
Growth Rate = g = .04
^{c}*This is also the price-earning ratio (market value per share divided by earnings per share).*

[14]The term *earnings rate* is defined in footnote 4.

TABLE 3-7 Effect of Growth on Financial Statement Results[a]

GROWTH RATE	RATIO OF NET INCOME UNDER SL VS. SYD	RATIO OF MARKET VALUE OF EQUITY TO NET INCOME		RETURN ON EQUITY		RATIO OF MARKET VALUE TO BOOK VALUE OF EQUITY	
		SL	SYD	SL	SYD	SL	SYD
0%	1.00	10X	10X	10%	11.25%	1.00	1.125
4%	1.048	10X	10.48X	10%	10.71%	1.00	1.122
6%	1.068	10X	10.68X	10%	10.48%	1.00	1.119
10%	1.119	10X	11.19X	10%	10%	1.00	1.119
20%	1.241	10X	12.41X	10%	8.94%	1.00	1.109

[a]*Firm assumed to be purchasing an asset with a two-year life and in which straight-line is economic depreciation. The earnings rate and the interest rate are assumed to be 10%. These cases assume that the firms are in "steady state" (in other words, the firms are "mature"). In general, for an asset with a useful life of N years, the firm must be at least N years old. Here, N = 2.*

However, the net income under SYD is lower ($147 versus $154). As a result, the price-earnings ratio is higher (10.48 versus 10 times). Moreover, the accounting return (10.71%) does not equal the earnings rate (10%). The difference in depreciation methods can be called the measurement error in depreciation under SYD, and the net income under SYD can be said to measure economic income with error. Obviously, the absolute difference in earnings will change over time as the firm grows. However, the proportional difference in net income, the price-earnings ratio, and the accounting rate of return are a constant for a given level of (constant) growth.

As a result, the values of the ratio of net income, the price-earnings ratio, and the accounting rate of return can be specified as a function of the growth rate. These variables are reported in Table 3-7 for growth rates ranging from 0% to 20%.[15]

1. Accounting income under straight-line equals economic income, and hence the measurement error is zero.
2. As a result, the price-earnings ratio under straight-line depreciation remains a constant with respect to the assumed growth rate and is equal to the reciprocal of the interest rate (10 times).
3. As a result, the accounting rate of return under straight-line depreciation remains a constant regardless of the assumed growth rate and is equal to the earnings rate (10%).
4. Accounting income under SYD depreciation is less than income under straight-line depreciation and, as a result, understates economic income for all positive

[15]Throughout, the firm is assumed to be purchasing a two-year asset whose cash flows are identical to the one illustrated in Tables 3-2 and 3-4 *per dollar of acquisition cost*. The amount (in dollars) of the asset purchased is assumed to grow at the indicated rate.

growth rates, and the proportional difference is greater the higher the assumed growth rate. For the special case of zero growth, accounting income under both depreciation methods and economic income is equal.

5. The price-earnings ratio under SYD depreciation exceeds the price-earnings ratio under straight-line depreciation and, as a result, exceeds the reciprocal of the interest rate for all positive rates of growth. The price-earnings ratio is greater the higher the assumed growth rate.

6. The accounting rate of return in general does not measure the earnings rate. For the special case in which the growth rate equals the earnings rate, the accounting rate of return will also equal the earnings rate. At growth rates below the earnings rate, the accounting return will overstate the earnings rate; the reverse is true for growth rates below the earnings rate.

It is important to sort out the features that are particular to the illustration from inferences that are applicable in more general settings. In this illustration the economic depreciation is equal to straight-line depreciation. As a result, SYD measures economic depreciation with error and is "too accelerated" for this asset. However, other assets could be constructed whose cash flow pattern implied different patterns of economic depreciation. For example, constant cash flows imply an economic depreciation equal to the annuity or sinking fund method, some forms of linearly declining cash flows are consistent with straight-line depreciation, and some forms of quadratically declining cash flows are associated with SYD depreciation.[16] These are summarized in Figure 3-1.

Therefore, the properties exhibited by straight-line depreciation in Tables 3-2 through 3-7 arise out of the assumption on the pattern of the asset's cash flows. For other types of assets, straight-line depreciation can lead to either an overstatement or understatement of economic income. Hence, the major point of the illustration is *not* the superiority of straight-line depreciation. However, three generalizations do emerge.[17]

1. When economic income is well-defined, the measurement error associated with alternative accounting methods, such as alternative depreciation methods, can be examined.

2. The nature of the measurement error in general will be a function of (a) the cash flow pattern of the assets (including useful life), (b) the acquisition cost of the assets, (c) the accounting alternative chosen, (d) the growth rate, and (e) the earnings rate.

3. When accounting depreciation exceeds economic depreciation, the ratio of the market value to the book value of equity will exceed one, as illustrated in Table 3-7. The ratio is inversely related to the growth rate. As the growth rate increases, a higher proportion of the assets are "newer" assets where the difference between book value and economic values are smaller. As a result, the ratio declines toward one and approaches one as the growth rate becomes infinitely large. The example represents a case of *conservative* accounting or *biased recognition*. For higher

---

[16]This approach is discussed in greater detail in Beaver and Dukes (1974), which examines a comprehensive class of depreciation methods. A bibliography of earlier research is also summarized there.
[17]Obviously, these generalizations are made within the context of a setting in which economic income is well-defined, such as perfect and complete markets and certainty.

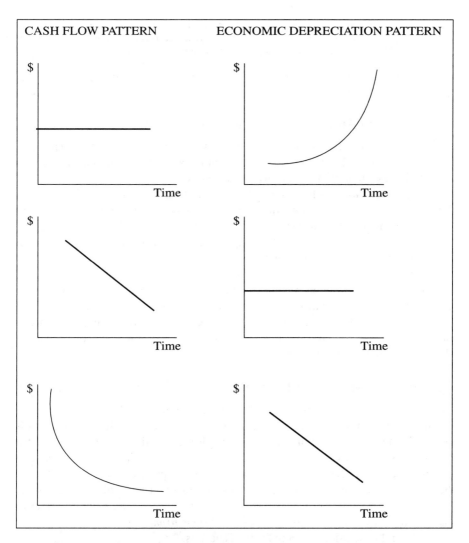

Figure 3-1   Cash flow and economic depreciation. This figure is not to be interpreted literally in the sense that depreciation methods treat time as discrete while the graphs are drawn as if time were continuous.

growth rates, the effects on the price-earnings ratios become more accentuated (departs farther from 10 times), because the effects on net income become greater. The effect on return on equity is smallest (zero) when the growth rate is equal to the earnings rate. For lower growth rates, the return on equity overstates the earnings rate, whereas the reverse is true for higher growth rates. Conservative accounting policies are also discussed in Chapter 4.

Extensions of Analysis of Measurement Error

The illustration thus far has focused on alternative depreciation methods. The same type of analysis can be applied to other accounting alternatives. In principle, any set of alternatives would be amenable to such an analysis.

The discussion this far has also focused on the impact of alternative accounting methods applied to the *same* firm. However, measurement errors can also be induced by applying uniform methods to different firms. For example, applying the same depreciation methods (such as straight-line) to firms with differing patterns of cash flows can induce measurement errors in one or both firms.

In this context, measurement errors in accounting income can occur under (1) the application of different methods to the same set of events (for example, the same firm) or (2) the application of the same method to different events (for example, firms with different types of assets). These constitute two major reasons that accounting earnings may not equal economic earnings and may not reflect the dividend-paying ability of the firm.

Analysis of Descriptive Differences

An analysis can also be conducted of the descriptive differences induced in various financial results by the use of alternative accounting methods. Such an analysis is less ambitious in the sense that it does not require any notion of economic income. If the market value of the firm, asset, and equity is invariant to the accounting method used, the effects of accounting alternatives on price-earnings ratios can also be examined. Alternatively stated, the analysis of descriptive differences can be viewed as examining the extent to which alternative accounting methods affect financial measures *when they are applied to the same firm.*

Several conclusions emerge from an analysis.[18]

1. In general, accounting net income, price-earnings ratios, and accounting rates of return systematically vary as a function of the accounting method used. Moreover, the impact on these variables of different accounting methods in general is a function of the growth rate. In other words, in general, for a given firm (for *given* cash flows and acquisition cost), accounting net income, price-earnings ratios, and accounting rate or return will depend on not only the accounting method used but also the growth rate.

2. For a given firm, the difference in accounting net income and in price-earnings ratios under alternative accounting methods is *zero* when the growth rate is *zero* for

---

[18]A bibliography of analyses that produce these conclusions appears in Beaver and Dukes (1974).

a mature firm, where the age of the firm is at least as great as the useful life of the assets. In general, the difference will vary directly with the growth rate. The difference in net income will be of opposite sign when the growth rate is positive versus negative.

3. For a given firm, the difference in the accounting rate of return will also be a function of the growth rate. No difference will exist when the growth rate equals the earnings rate. The absolute value of the difference will become proportionately larger as the absolute value of the difference between the growth rate and the earnings rate becomes larger. The difference in accounting rate of return will be of opposite sign when the growth rate is above versus below the earnings rate.

3-7 CONCLUDING REMARKS

In the perfect and complete markets and certainty setting, the concept of economic earnings is well-defined. Moreover, it has several properties. (1) More earnings are better than less in any given year, holding earnings constant in other years. (2) Earnings reflect the stewardship of management and multiperiod effects of management's decisions. (3) Unanimity exists among investors regarding shareholder wealth maximization, which can be characterized in terms of a unanimous preference for projects with greater earnings. Measuring economic earnings is straightforward.

However, in this setting, economic earnings fall out of the analysis as a byproduct of the valuation process. Earnings and valuation are two sides of the same coin. This is readily apparent in the permanent earnings property of economic earnings, where earnings are computed as the present value (or market value) times the interest rate. Value and earnings are linked via the interest rate. One is a stock concept, the other is a flow, and the interest rate is used to make the transition from one to the other. Both are scalars representing a vector of intertemporal future cash flows. The assumptions about the markets ensure that nothing is lost in representing a vector of cash flows in terms of a single member.

In this setting, earnings are redundant and can be derived from the valuation of the firm and its equity. In other words, the notion of earnings is a valuation concept. To measure economic earnings requires a modicum of knowledge of the present value model. However, no knowledge of financial accounting is required. Value and hence economic earnings can be measured directly from an observation of the market values of assets and claims. Alternative accrual methods can be evaluated in terms of their ability to produce accounting earnings numbers that approximate economic earnings. Also analyses of the descriptive differences in earnings induced by alternative accounting methods can be examined.

These conclusions have been drawn in a special setting. In a different setting the accounting earnings may take on additional roles. For example, the assumptions of perfect and complete markets would be regarded as unrealistic.

This naturally leads to the next topic—earnings under uncertainty in imperfect, incomplete markets.

BIBLIOGRAPHY

Beaver, W., and R. Dukes. "Interperiod Tax Allocation and Delta Depreciation Methods: Some Empirical Results." *Accounting Review* (July 1973), 549–559.

—— and R. Dukes. "Delta-Depreciation Methods: Some Analytical Results." *Journal of Accounting Research* (August 1974), 205–215.

Cottle, S., R. Murray, and F. Block. *Security Analysis.* New York: McGraw-Hill, 1988.

Sharpe, W. *Investments.* 5th ed. Englewood Cliffs, N.J.: Prentice-Hall, 1995.

Treynor, J. "The Trouble with Earnings." *Financial Analysts Journal* (September–October 1972), 41–43.

Williams, J. *The Theory of Investment Value.* Cambridge: Harvard University Press, 1938.

4

Uncertainty

Chapter 3 examined financial statements under assumptions of perfect and complete markets and certainty. This chapter extends the discussion of financial statements to a more general setting of uncertainty. The chapter begins with the setting of perfect and complete markets and then moves to imperfect and incomplete markets. An information perspective with respect to financial statements is introduced. Key features of financial statements, such as accrual accounting, delayed recognition, conservatism, and discretionary behavior, are discussed.

4-1 PERFECT AND COMPLETE MARKETS UNDER UNCERTAINTY

With perfect and complete markets, the introduction of uncertainty involves a simple extension of the analysis of the previous chapter. The notion of a perfect market is the same as it was in the certainty setting. The meaning of a complete market in an uncertain setting requires some elaboration. In the multiperiod certainty setting the claims of interest are the future cash flows, and complete markets imply that a rich set of markets exists with respect to the trading of claims to future cash flows. These markets potentially include futures markets and *spot* markets that could open in the future. In an uncertain setting the claims of interest are future, state-contingent cash flows.

As indicated in Chapter 2, uncertainty is characterized by a set of states that could occur in the future. The return from holding a security is uncertain because the cash flow it yields will depend on which state occurs. For example, a common stock represents a complex claim to a bundle of future, state-contingent dividends. The price of the common stock will be some function of those dividends. The dividends that common stock will actually pay will depend on which state occurs.

Under certainty, the present value of a claim is characterized by the following expression:

$$_0PV_t = {_0}P_t C_t$$

where $_0PV_t$ is the present value or price as of now ($t = 0$) for a claim to receive future cash flows at time t. $_0P_t$ is the price or present value of a claim to \$1 at time t valued as of now, and C_t is the cash flow to be received at time t. Under uncertainty but retaining perfect and complete markets, a similar characterization of the present value of a claim is possible:

$$_0PV_t = \sum_{s=1}^{S} {_0}P_{st} C_{st}$$

where $_0PV_t$ is the present value or price as of now for a claim to receive future uncertain cash flows at time t. $_0P_{st}$ is the price of a primitive claim to \$1 at time t *if state s occurs*. Each of the prices, $_0P_{st}$, reflects a combination of (1) investors' preferences for cash flows if state s occurs, derived from the underlying preference for state-contingent consumption, and (2) investors' beliefs about the probability that state s will occur. The price of the simple claim, $_0P_{st}$, jointly represents investors' beliefs about the probability that state s will occur *and* their preferences for an additional \$1 of cash flow *if state s occurs*. C_{st} is the cash flow to be received from the complex security at time t *if state s occurs*. Hence a complex security is merely a collection of primitive claims.

Valuation under uncertainty is a simple extension of a similar expression under certainty and merely requires an additional indexing of claims to reflect the states as well as the time periods.[1]

Discounting Under Uncertainty

A common approach to valuation of complex claims under uncertainty is to take a valuation model derived from certainty, such as the discounted cash flow model, and to replace each variable in that formula with the expected value of that variable

---

[1]Remember that the concept of a state involves conditional certainty. If state s occurs, then there is no remaining uncertainty about what will happen. Therefore, the dividends a stock will pay in state s is certain. Moreover, this assessment does not change over time for this reason. Although the arrival of information may lead investors to alter their probability that state s will occur, the amount paid at time t if state s occurs remains unchanged. Costless arbitrage, as described in Chapter 3, guarantees that value additivity is preserved (in other words, the price of a complex claim is equal to the sum of the prices of the primitive claims it represents).

to reflect the uncertainty. For example, consider the valuation of a common stock. In the numerator of each term the dividend in period t would be replaced by the expected value of dividends in period t. In the denominator the interest rate would be replaced by a "risky" discount rate. Typically, this is viewed as the expected value of the rate of return on other investments of identical risk.[2]

In a multiperiod setting, characterizing the present value or price of a complex claim in terms of discounting expected cash flows at expected rates of return is not possible in general. However, special cases can be derived. A key assumption is independence. between the *ex post* past rates of return and the future expected rates of return at any point in time.[3]

A case of discounting at expected values will be illustrated by an extension of the single-asset, all-equity firm discussed in the previous chapter. The possible cash flows are described in Figure 4-1. At $t = 1$, a cash flow of either $660 or $540 will be received. Hereafter, the state in which $660 is received will be called state A, and the receipt of $540 will occur in state B. The expected cash flows for $t = 1$, assessed as of $t = 0$, is $600 because each state has an equal chance of occurring. Conditional on state A occurring, the *expected* cash flow for $t = 2$, assessed as of $t = 1$, is $605, whereas the conditional *expected* cash flow for $t = 2$ for state B is $495.[4] As of $t = 0$, the expected cash flow for $t = $ is $550, which can be computed either as the expected value of $605 and $495 or by weighting each of the four possible outcomes, $655 through $445, by the probability of their occurrence (.25 in each case). Note that $600 and $550 were the *known* cash flows for the firm in the certainty illustration of Table 3-2. Hence, this illustration extends the asset of the previous chapter to an uncertain setting in which the *expected* cash flows are $600 and $550, respectively. As of $t = 0$, the *expected* rate of return is assumed to be 10% for both the first and second period. Moreover, as of $t = 1$, the expected rate of return for the second period is still 10% regardless of whether state A or B has occurred.

The independence of the rate of return distributions permits the present value of the firm's assets and the firm's equity to be characterized as if it involved discounting the expected value of future cash flows at the expected value of the rate of return. This is illustrated in Table 4-1. This table begins with the "correct" computation, which involves computing the value of the firm and its equity at $t = 1$ for states A and B and then computing the value as of $t = 0$. The computed market value as of $t = 0$ is $1,000. However, the alternative computation in Table 4-1 demonstrates that

---

[2]One model of equilibrium prices that derives expected returns is the familiar capital asset pricing model (hereafter CAPM). See Sharpe (1995) for further discussion. The "risky" discount rate is also often referred to as the *cost of capital* (or *cost of equity capital* in the case of common stock).

[3]Equilibrium rates of return are influenced by the investors' preferences for future wealth (for example, cash flows), such as the degree of risk aversion. Also preferences for cash flows may be state-dependent, either because prices of consumption goods are state-dependent or because the preferences for consumption goods are state-dependent.

[4]$600 = (.5 \times \$660) + (.5 \times \$540)$

$605 = (.5 \times \$655) + (.5 \times \$555)$

$495 = (.5 \times \$545) + (.5 \times \$445)$

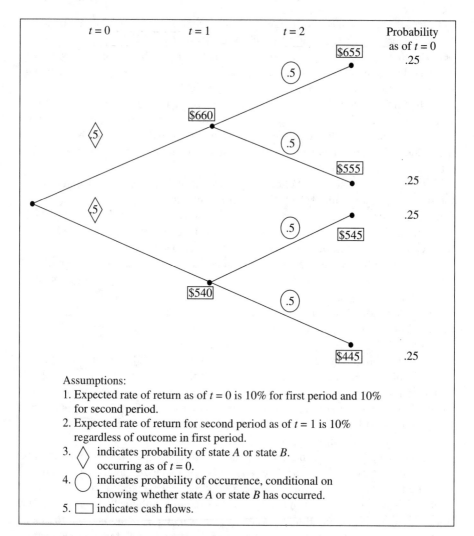

FIGURE 4-1 Cash flows of single-asset firm.

the market value could also have been computed by simply discounting the expected cash flows at $t = 1$ and $t = 2$ at the expected rate of return.

Economic Value of Equity Under Uncertainty

The economic value of equity is equal to the present value of the remaining cash flows, which is also equal to the market value of the asset. If state A occurs, the economic value of equity is $1,210 (before the year 1 dividend) and $550 (after the dividend) as of $t = 1$. If state B occurs, the economic value of equity is $990 (before the dividend) and $450 (after the dividend). If the accounting model used market values

TABLE 4-1 Computation of Market Value of Firm and Its Equity

If State A Occurs:		
Cash flow received at $t = 1$		$ 660
Value of remaining cash flows		
Expected cash flow at $t = 2$		$ 605
Market value of remaining cash flow at $t = 1$[a]		$ 550
If State B Occurs:		
Cash flow received at $t = 1$		$ 540
Value of remaining cash flows		
Expected cash flow at $t = 2$		$ 495
Market value of remaining cash flow at $t = 1$[a]		$ 450
Market Value at $t = 0$:		
Value at $t = 1$ if state A occurs		
Cash flow	$660	
Market value	550	$1,210
Value at $t = 1$ if state B occurs		
Cash flow	540	
Market value	450	$ 990
Expected value at $t = 1$[b]		$1,100
Market value at $t = 0$[a]		$1,000
Alternative Computation:		
Expected cash flows as of $t = 0$		
At $t = 1$		$ 600
At $t = 2$		$ 550
Present value		
$600 \div 1.1$		$ 545
$550 \div 1.21$		$ 455
Total		$1,000

[a] $\$550 = \dfrac{\$605}{(1+.10)}$; $\$450 = \dfrac{\$495}{(1+.10)}$; $\$1,000 = \dfrac{\$1,100}{(1+.10)}$

[b] $\$1,100 = (.5 \times \$1,210) + (.5 \times \$990)$

to measure the book value of the asset, book value of equity would equal the market value of equity. The ratio of the market value of equity to the book value (the market-to-book ratio) would be one. This example will now be used to illustrate the concepts of earnings under uncertainty.

Economic Earnings in Perfect and Complete Markets Under Uncertainty

Under certainty, there is no difference between what is expected and what actually occurs. As a result, economic earnings can be defined in a number of ways, all of which are equivalent under certainty. Such definitions were summarized in Table 3-5. Under uncertainty, a distinction must be made between *ex ante* or expected economic earnings and *ex post* economic earnings. The hypothetical, all-equity firm is used as an illustration. From the perspective of the firm, the *ex ante (ex post)* earnings can be defined as the expected (actual) cash flows received during the period plus the expected (actual) change in the market prices (present value) of the assets held by the firm. As in the certainty case, appropriate adjustments would be made for deposits and withdrawals by suppliers of capital. From the perspective of the shareholders, *ex post* earnings are the cash received (dividends) plus the change in the market price of the common stock. *Ex ante* or expected earnings for the shareholders are equal to the *expected* dividends received during the period plus the *expected* change in the market price of the common stock.

Alternatively, expected earnings can be computed in a manner analogous to the computation of permanent earnings in the certainty case. In an uncertain setting, expected or permanent earnings can be defined as the current market price at the beginning of the period times the expected rate of return for the period. The concepts of *ex post* and *ex ante* earnings are illustrated in Table 4-2. A single-asset, all-equity firm is assumed, as in Chapter 3. But, in this case, the risky asset illustrated in Table 4-1 is held. Also, state A is assumed to have occurred in the computation of *ex post* earnings. *Ex post* earnings for year 1 are $210. Assessed as of $t = 0$, *ex ante* earnings for years 1 and 2 are $100 and $50, respectively. Assessed as of $t = 1$, *ex ante* earnings are $55 for year 2, given that state A has occurred.

There are several aspects of these earnings concepts worth noting.

1. *Ex post* earnings can be readily measured from observable cash flow data and from observable market prices of assets and securities. The role of accrual accounting is not obvious. Moreover, the key items of interest are the cash flows and the market values, and it is not obvious what further insight is added by measuring net income, once valuation is known.

2. Actual earnings can differ from expected earnings for several reasons. (a) The cash flow in that period may differ from what was expected. In the illustration, a cash flow of $600 was expected in $t = 1$, yet a cash flow of $660 occurred. (b) The occurrence of the state (state A or B) may lead to a revision in the distribution of future cash flows. This is apparent in the illustration in which originally a cash flow of $550 for $t = 2$ was expected as of $t = 0$, whereas the expectation as of $t = 1$ is $605, given that state A occurred. (c) There may also be a revision in the expected rate of return for the second period. This source of *ex post* earnings was not illustrated here, and the original expectation of 10% for the second period, assessed as of $t = 0$, was not revised at $t = 1$.

3. So far the discussion has treated the expected rate of return as a given. For any individual, expected earnings are equal to the observed market price times the individual's expected rate of return. However, if market behavior is being characterized, the notion of the expected rate of return requires some elaboration. One possibility is to posit some composite or consensus belief among investors. Where heterogeneous beliefs prevail, each individual will have a personal perception of the "expected" or "permanent" earnings of the firm and its securities, and this perception will vary across individuals. *Hence, although market prices and* ex post *earnings are publicly observable and known by all, expected (or permanent) earnings are generally not observable.*

4. By introducing uncertainty, valuation and the earnings concept become less well-defined in at least two respects. (a) The valuation of multiperiod, uncertain cash flows may not admit to any simple characterization, such as discounting expected

TABLE 4-2 Economic Earnings for Single-Asset Firm (Assuming State *A* Occurs)

	YEAR[a]	
	1	2
Expected cash flows as of $t = 0$	$ 600	$ 500
Cash flows as of $t = 1$		
Actual	660	
Expected		605
Market price of asset at *beginning* of year:		
Actual	1,000	
Expected as of $t = 0$		500
Actual as of $t = 1$		550
Ex Post Earnings		
From the perspective of the firm:		
Cash flow	660	
Depreciation[b]	(500)	
	160	
Holding gain[c]	50	
Ex post economic earnings	$ 210	
From the perspective of the stockholders:		
Dividend paid[d]	660	
Change in present value of equity[e]	(450)	
Ex post economic earnings	$ 210	
Ex Ante or Expected Earnings		
As of $t = 0$		
Expected cash flow	600	550
Expected depreciation[b]	(500)	(500)
Expected earnings	$ 100	$ 50
As of $t = 1$		
Expected cash flow		605
Expected depreciation		(550)
Expected earnings		$ 55
From the definition of permanent earnings:		
As of $t = 0$		
Beginning market price	1,000	500
Expected rate of return	.10	.10
Permanent earnings	$ 100	$ 50
As of $t = 1$		
Beginning market price		550
Expected rate of return		.10
Permanent earnings		$ 55

[a]*The beginning (end) of year 1 is* t *= 0* (t *= 1). The beginning (end) of year 2 is* t *= 1* (t *= 2).*
[b]*Depreciation based on expected market value of asset at beginning of year 2 assessed as of* t *= 0 ($500).*
[c]*The holding gain could also be included in depreciation, which would equal $450.*
[d]*As in the certainty case, the firm is assumed to pay out all cash received.*
[e]*$450 = $1,000 − $550 (where $550 is the actual market price as of* t *= 1).*

cash flows at the expected (risky) rate of return. (b) Concepts of *ex ante* earnings depend on the expected rate of return, which is not directly observable and may vary across individuals.

5. Nevertheless, valuation and earnings under perfect and complete markets are still well-defined concepts in the sense that individuals will unanimously prefer market value maximization. Prices are "rich" in reflecting the preferences of individuals, and prices are "rich" in reflecting the multiperiod implications of managerial decisions (stewardship).

6. Both the *ex post* and *ex ante* concepts of earnings are derived from the valuation process. If the valuation process is ill-defined, then so is the concept of earnings.

Relation Between Economic Earnings and Accounting Earnings: Delayed Recognition

As indicated earlier, the concepts of *ex post* and *ex ante* earnings are measures of economic earnings. They are byproducts of the valuation process, and accrual accounting plays no obvious role. However, this framework can be used to examine the relation between economic earnings and accounting earnings in an uncertain setting. For example, if the firm illustrated in Table 4-2 used straight-line depreciation, at $t = 0$ the expected accounting earnings would be equal to the expected economic earnings. At $t = 1$, either state A or B will have occurred, and the actual accounting earnings will not equal the expected accounting earnings. Moreover, assuming that the depreciation figure is not revised (in other words, historical cost is used), the actual accounting earnings will not in general equal the actual economic earnings. For example, if state A occurs, the accounting earnings will be $160 ($660 − $500), whereas *ex post* economic earnings are $210. The difference of $50 is the holding gain, which reflects *unanticipated* change in the value of the asset as of $t = 1$ ($550 − $500). In this illustration, historical cost accounting earnings can be viewed as a mixture of *ex post* and *ex ante* earnings. The unanticipated portion of the cash flows ($60) are reflected in the accounting net income, based on an actual cash flow of $660. However, the depreciation expense here reflects the anticipated year-end market value as of $t = 0$, not the actual market value of the asset at $t = 1$.

Similarly, under historical cost, the book value of the asset at $t = 1$ is $500, instead of its economic value of $550. The market-to-book ratio is 1.10, reflecting the unexpected gain on the asset's value that is unrecognized by the historical cost model as of $t = 1$. Of course, the $50 gain will eventually be recognized over the remaining life of the asset. In the two-year asset, the $50 will be implicitly recognized in year 2 via lower depreciation. Historical cost depreciation in year 2 is only $500, rather than the $550 economic depreciation. As a result, the expected net income in year 2 under historical cost is $105 ($605 − $500), which reflects the $55 of expected economic income (see Table 4-2) and $50 of deferred unrecognized gain of $50 from $t = 1$. The expected rate of return on equity in year 2 is 21%, in excess of the assumed discount rate of 10%. However, the difference is entirely due to the *delayed recognition* feature of historical cost accounting. In year 1, the *ex post* economic rate of return was 21% ($1,210/$1,000), whereas the historical cost rate of return was only 16%. The lower rate of return reflects the fact that the recognition of the gain was delayed until year 2. In general, for an asset with a remaining life of N years, the unrecognized gain (or loss) will be spread over those remaining N years. Ryan (1995) has formally developed a model of delayed recognition.

As a result, this hybrid nature of accounting earnings has led to criticism of historical cost accounting. In this setting a movement to market value accounting would make accounting earnings equal to economic earnings. Remember, perfect and complete markets ensure that the asset's entry price equals its exist price equals its value in use. Moreover, the market value of the asset will equal the market value of claims against the assets. This perspective provides a rationale for those who advocate the introduction of market value accounting systems. In a setting of perfect and complete markets such arguments have obvious appeal because economic earnings have the "desirable" properties usually associated with "ideal" income. For example, with respect to the stewardship motivation for financial reporting, earnings under a market value accounting system will reflect the impact of managerial decisions on the future multiperiod state-contingent cash flows of the firm. In this vein, the proposals of Edwards and Bell (1961), Chambers (1966), and Sterling (1970) can be viewed as proposals for accounting models that better measure the economic value and earnings of the firm.

Because economic earnings are well defined, the "measurement error" associated with alternative accounting methods can be examined. Historical cost versus market value accounting provides a ready example. For example, the depreciation analyses discussed in Chapter 3 can be extended to an uncertain setting, such as the use of straight-line versus accelerated depreciation methods. The discussion now turns to incomplete markets. In this setting, a role of accounting data, such as earnings, is an informational one in which earnings are used as an *input* into the valuation process rather than as some output derived as a byproduct of the valuation process. This setting helps to explain how accounting earnings are used in security analysis.

4-2 VALUATION IN IMPERFECT OR INCOMPLETE MARKETS

Imperfect markets and their implications are familiar from elementary economics. However, incomplete markets may be less familiar. A complete market is one in which *primitive* claims can be traded. A primitive claim is a claim to receive $1 if state s occurs and receive nothing otherwise. A complex or compound claim is simply a collection of primitive claims. In a complete market one can directly observe the prices of primitive claims or infer them from the prices of complex claims. In an incomplete market some primitive claims are not tradable. Therefore, prices may exist on complex or compound claims, such as a common stock, but one cannot infer the implied prices for primitive claims from the prices of complex claims.

In a complete market, prices of complex securities can be determined from the prices of the primitive securities they represent. Alternatively, the prices of primitive securities can be inferred from the prices of complex securities. In an incomplete market the prices of at least some of the primitive securities cannot be inferred from the complex securities. This follows from the meaning of an incomplete market. Moreover, in an incomplete market setting some complex claims may not be valued to future cash flow because no market exists in which that claim or claims identical to it are traded and because the value of such a claim cannot be inferred from observing the value of other complex claims.

The market for many assets of a firm may be incomplete. A market for the results of research and development expenditures may be incomplete because revealing the results of the research and development project may destroy its value (in other words, a potential buyer need no longer pay to obtain the information), although patent rights may partially alleviate this concern. The market for intangible assets is another example. Incompleteness makes it difficult to value those assets.

Another reason valuation of a firm's assets may be difficult is imperfection in the markets. Under such imperfections, such as transactions costs, the entry price of the asset (its replacement costs), the exit price (its liquidation value), and its value in use (the present value of the future cash flows) may not be the same.

In a setting of imperfect or incomplete markets, market values no longer necessarily have the properties they did under perfect and complete markets. For example, market value maximization may not be unanimously preferred by shareholders. In general, a lack of consensus will exist because the markets are no longer rich enough to sort out the individual heterogeneity of preferences and beliefs. In some cases, shareholder consensus may exist, but the decision not to maximize market value may be unanimous. Market value no longer is rich enough to capture the value of all the attributes of a particular project or asset. A project may have non-marketable aspects that override those aspects reflected in market prices. In this sense, valuation is no longer a well-defined process. In other words, it is no longer clear what properties prices possess. *An important implication is that any concept of earnings that is valuation based is no longer a well-defined concept.* Hence, the properties of earnings are no longer clear.

It is important to make clear what is meant by saying valuation is ill-defined in an incomplete or imperfect market setting. Prices of complex claims, such as common stocks, can still be observed. Moreover, the valuation process giving rise to those prices may very well be capable of a simple characterization. For example, prices of common stocks may admit to a characterization in terms of expected values of future cash flows discounted at an expected rate of return. Whether they do depends in part on the independence of rates of return. In this sense, the valuation process may be well-defined. Moreover, *ex post* earnings may be measured by dividends and market price changes for a security that is traded. However, in an incomplete market the prices of some of the firm's claims cannot be valued because of the incompleteness, and the observed market prices of claims for which markets do exist may no longer have the same "optimality" properties because of imperfection or incompleteness.[5]

This leads to a different perspective within which to view financial statement data, such as accounting earnings. This perspective is called an *informational perspective,* which was discussed in Chapter 2.

In particular, in this setting asymmetric information may exist between management and shareholders. This asymmetry of information allows accounting data to reduce the information asymmetry via disclosure in the financial statements. The reduction of the asymmetry can mitigate some of problems induced by adverse selection and moral hazard, as discussed in Chapter 2. However, information asymmetry affords the opportunity for discretionary behavior in financial reporting.

Earnings from an Informational Perspective

Securities such as common stocks possess value because they possess certain attributes that are valued by investors, such as claims to future dividends. Prices can be characterized in general as dependent on investors' expectations regarding these attributes. The role of information is to alter investors' beliefs about the attributes, and hence information can alter stock prices. In particular, a role of earnings is to alter beliefs about the firm's ability to pay future dividends, and it is consistent with the belief that earnings are an indicator of future dividend-paying ability.

A conceptual relationship can be developed between accounting earnings and the price of common stocks by introducing three critical links: (1) a link between security price and future dividends, (2) a link between future dividends and future earnings, and (3) a link between future earnings and current earnings.[6]

Prices and Future Dividends

Future dividends and price are linked via a valuation model. In general, the valuation model will depend on the amount of the dividend to be received in each state in each time period, the beliefs of the investors regarding the probability of each state, and the value of receiving $1 in state *s* in period *t.* As indicated earlier, a typical approach to valuation under uncertainty is simply to extend the model under certainty by replacing each of the valuation parameters, which were known with certainty, with the expected value of the analogous variables under uncertainty. In this special case, price can be characterized as if it were a function of the expected value of future dividends.

If the earnings and dividends are assumed to be dependent, prices can also be viewed as a function of the expected value of future earnings. For example, any level of expected dividends is associated with a level of expected earnings, and the

---

[5]As a result, the rationale for market value accounting discussed above is no longer unassailable.
[6]A formal treatment of the set of relationships appears in Ohlson (1995).

two are linked by a payout ratio.[7] This link between dividends and earnings is the second component in the price-earnings relationship.

The dividend-earnings link is a key assumption. One view is that earnings represents a primitive variable that reflects the underlying source of dividend-paying ability. In particular, it can be viewed as reflecting the underlying operating cash flows of the firm. It is assumed that nothing is lost in the earnings representation.[8] In fact, arguments on behalf of accrual accounting imply earnings provide a better indictor of expected cash flows relative to directly using cash flows. However, this latter contention is an open issue. Evidence is discussed in Chapter 5 on earnings, cash flows, and accruals.

Future Dividends and Future Accounting Earnings

For earnings to have informational content, there must be a perceived relationship between earnings and the attributes that are assumed to give rise to a security's value. In this context, a perceived relationship between future earnings and future dividends (the attribute that causes a security to have value) is assumed.

Future earnings are relevant to the extent that they are perceived to be statistically dependent with future dividends. This is one interpretation of the assertion that earnings are an indicator of future dividend-paying ability. Although it enjoys widespread usage, the concept of "future dividend-paying ability" is not well-defined. In perfect and complete markets the price of the security would be a measure of the security's perceived future dividend-paying ability, and an earnings measure derived from price presumably would also be an indicator of dividend-paying ability.

In a setting of imperfect or incomplete markets the concept of dividend-paying ability is not necessarily reflected in a readily available market price statistic. The concept of dividend-paying ability and the perceived relationship between earnings and dividends are primitive assumptions in this setting. At one level, empirical evidence indicates that earnings changes are correlated with dividend changes.[9] Hence, the assumption of a statistical dependence between future earnings and future dividends appears to be a reasonable one. One of the most common and simplest assumptions is that future earnings and future dividends are linked via a payout ratio that is constant over time.

However, sole reliance on the empirical findings is tenuous without a deeper conceptual basis for this relationship. Concluding that the observed dependency arises because of management's perceptions of the ability of earnings to reflect

---

[7]Alternatively stated, associated with each state is a known level of dividends and earnings, and hence associated with the expected value of dividends in period *t* is an expected value of earnings in period *t*. A payout ratio in period *t* can be defined as the ratio of the two expected values.

[8]Under the assumption of the clean surplus relation, to be discussed shortly, nonearnings information must be reflected in earnings at some point. As a result, the earnings formulation is not as restrictive as it might appear.

[9]Leftwich and Zmijewski (1994) provide a brief summary of the research that examines the earnings-change–dividend-change relation.

dividend-paying ability may be intuitively appealing. However, this begs the deeper question: Why do managers hold such a perception?

Future Accounting Earnings and Current Accounting Earnings

The relationship between past earnings and future earnings is expressed in the stochastic process that is perceived to be describing earnings over time. From this perspective, events occurring within a particular period may be atypical (transitory) and not expected to have the same impact on earnings in subsequent periods. Strikes and catastrophic events are two examples of this type of event. Accounting earnings can be viewed as two components: *permanent earnings* and *transitory earnings*. Permanent accounting earnings can be thought of as the expected value of future accounting earnings, and as of any point in time, is a vector rather than a single number.[10] Moreover, as time passes, the expected or permanent earnings for a given year may change.

Accounting earnings are relevant because they reflect events that lead to an alteration of beliefs about the future dividend-paying ability of the firm. The prediction of earnings is part of a larger analytical process in which the ultimate concern is the prediction and valuation of the dividend stream. Earnings are an important informational source about future dividend-paying ability. Accounting earnings are *not* a derived valuation concept as are economic earnings. Accounting earnings are not necessarily a surrogate for valuation. Relevance arises out of earnings' perceived relationship to future dividend-paying ability.

Future earnings can be described as the revenue and expense components that comprise earnings. Earnings forecasting can involve forecasting those income statement items on an item-by-item basis. The earnings forecast would then be an aggregation of the forecasts of the individual components. Moreover, each income statement item can be further decomposed. For example, each item could be described as the product of a future price times a future quantity. For example, future sales are the product of future selling price times future quantities (of output) sold; future cost of goods sold is the product of future prices of inputs times the quantity of inputs required to produce the quantity of output sold. Of course, each of these variables is uncertain and must be forecasted as well. Future depreciation expense is a function of the future price of the depreciable assets to be purchased and the quantity of such assets. From this perspective, the forecasting of future accounting earnings includes (1) an assessment of the distribution of (a) future quantities of outputs, (b) future prices of output, (c) future quantities of inputs, and (d) future prices of in-

---

[10]More formally, permanent earnings are a vector $[E(X_{t+1}), E(X_{t+2}) \dots E(X_{t+k})]$ where $k > 0$ and where $E(X_{t+k})$ is the expected earnings for time $t + k$ assessed as of time t. Either an individual or marketwide perspective can be taken here, as long as a given perspective is consistently maintained throughout. In the former case, the beliefs are those of a particular individual; in the latter case, the beliefs are a composite or consensus across investors.

puts and (2) the accounting methods used to transform these raw data into earnings numbers.

Forecasting Future Earnings from Current Earnings

Needless to say, the above forecasting approach is extremely ambitious. Typically, the problem of forecasting earnings is viewed somewhat more modestly. In a more limited setting the question becomes one of how to use past and current earnings so as to best forecast future earnings. This section provides a simple example and it illustrates permanent versus transitory components of accounting earnings.[11]

The information content of current and past earnings for future expected earnings will depend on how much of the current and past earnings is expected to persist. For example, suppose that current earnings are larger or smaller than expected because of certain events that originated in the current year. These events will be called the *unexpected component* of this year's earnings or *shocks* to the earning series. The implications of these shocks for the permanent (expected) accounting earnings depend on the process perceived to govern the time series behavior of accounting earnings. Alternatively stated, the importance of these shocks depends on the extent to which they are expected to have an impact on future earnings.

A numerical example is provided in Table 4-3. Earnings per share changed from $1.50 for the year ending at $t = 0$ to $2.00 for the year ending at $t = 1$. As of $t = 0$, the expected future earnings are also assumed to be $1.50.[12] In other words, for sim-

---

TABLE 4-3 Relationship Between Current Earnings and Permanent Earnings

Actual Earnings:	
For the year ending at $t = 0$	$1.50
For the year ending at $t = 1$	$2.00
Permanent (or Expected) Earnings:	
As of $t = 0$	$1.50
As of $t = 1$	
Case 1 (100% sensitivity)	$2.00
Case 2 (0% sensitivity)	$1.50
Case 3 (intermediate case)	$1.50 to $2.00
Case 4 (greater than 100% sensitivity)	More than $2.00

---

[11]The study of the relation of current earnings to future earnings has a long history and is known as the time series of earnings literature. The research examines not only the forecasting ability of statistically based naive models but also the properties of earnings forecasts by analysts. A brief summary of this literature appears in Brown et al. (1987).

[12]To simplify the discussion, it is assumed that expected earnings are the same for all future periods as of any given point in time (*no growth in earnings per share is expected*). More formally, $E(X_{t+k}) = E(X_{t+1})$ for all $k > 1$, where $E(X_{t+k})$ is defined in footnote 10.

plicity, the change in earnings is equal to the unexpected portion of earnings. What is the expected future earnings as of this year, given that this year's earnings were $.50 above the expected? The importance of this short-run change in earnings depends in a large part on the earnings process. For some earnings processes, it is relatively unimportant. For other processes, it is critical because changes in near-term earnings (for example, changes in current earnings) can have implications for *permanent* earnings, *future* dividends, and hence *current* stock price. Four cases are illustrated in Table 4-3.[13]

In the first case, if the events that caused this year's change in earnings are expected to persist (in other words, have a permanent effect on the level of future expected earnings), all of the earnings change can be regarded as "permanent" in the sense that it is a measure of the change ($.50) in expected earnings. All of current earnings are permanent (expected earnings are $2.00 for all future periods). The transitory component is zero. This is the so-called *random walk* case, and there is a one-to-one relationship between percentage changes in current earnings and percentage changes in expected earnings. A 33% change in earnings ($2.00 − $1.50/$1.50) implies a 33% change in expected earnings.

By contrast, consider the second case in which the events that caused this year's earnings change are expected not to persist (in other words, to have no effect on the level of future expected earnings). All of the earnings change can be regarded as "transitory" and will lead to no revisions in expectations regarding future earnings. Here there is a zero relationship between percentage changes in current earnings and percentage changes in expected earnings. A 33% change in current earnings would lead to *no* change in expected earnings ($.150 − $1.50/$1.50). Of the current earnings of $2.00, the permanent earnings are $1.50 and the transitory component is $.50.

In a third, intermediate case, the current period events are such that only a portion of the earnings changes the level of future expected earnings. In this case, the change in earnings contains both a "permanent" and a "transitory" component. Here there would be less than a one-to-one relationship between percentage changes in current earnings and percentage changes in future expected earnings. In other words, the 33% change in current earnings implies a change in permanent earnings of less than 33% but greater than 0%.

Finally, in the fourth case, the current period events are such that the events are expected to have an even greater impact on future years' earnings than they did

---

[13]In general, expectations regarding future earnings will be conditional on both past and current earnings, as well as nonearnings information. However, to simplify the discussion, the role of current earnings is illustrated. From this perspective, the illustration assumes that earnings are generated by an Integrated Moving Average [IMA (7,1)] process. For this class of processes,

$$X_t - X_{t-1} = a_t - \theta a_{t-1}$$

where X_t is the earnings for period t, a_t is the unexpected shock in period t, and θ is a coefficient that reflects the effect of a_{t-1} on X_t. $E(X_{t+k}|X_t) = X_t - \theta a_t$ for $k > 0$. In the illustration, $a_0 = 0$, $a_1 = \$.50$. $X_0 = \$1.50$, and $X_1 = \$2.00$. This implies that $E(X_1|X_0) = \$1.50$. The four cases illustrated assume that θ equals 0, 1, between 0 and 1, and less than 0, respectively. $E(X_{t+k}|X_1) - E(X_{t+k}|X_0) = (1 - \theta)a_1 = (1 - \theta)\$.50$ for $k > 0$.

on this year's earnings. This could happen when events have permanent effects on the level of expected earnings but occur randomly throughout the year. Therefore, on the average, an event affects this year's earnings for only 6 months of the fiscal year, but it will affect future earnings for all 12 months of the future fiscal years. In this case, the change in this year's earnings understates the impact on the level of expected earnings. As a result, there is more than a one-to-one relationship between percentage changes in the current year's earnings and percentage changes in the future year's expected earnings. A 33% change in this year's earnings leads to a percentage change in expected earnings of more than 33%. In fact, in the example just cited, there would be about a two-to-one relationship (a 33% change implies a 66% change in expected earnings). The relationships in these four cases can be expressed as sensitivity coefficients. The sensitivity coefficient is the proportion of the earnings change that is permanent and would be 100%, 0%, less than 100%, but greater than 0%, and greater than 100% for cases one through four, as summarized in Table 4-3.

Prices and Earnings: An Illustration

With the three links described, a relationship between current earnings and the current price of the security can be derived. The relationship depends on each of the three links and can be illustrated by making some simple assumptions about each of the three links.

For the first link (between current price and future dividends), an extremely simple valuation relationship is adopted. No growth in dividends is assumed (as of time t, $E(D_{t+1}) = E(D_{t+k})$ for all $k > 1$). It is further assumed that current price is proportional to future expected dividends, and the factor of proportionality (ρ) is constant over time $[P_t = \rho E_t(D)]$.[14]

For the second link (between future dividends and future earnings), a constant payout ratio (K) over time is assumed. The implication is that revisions of expected earnings can be easily translated into revisions of expected dividends. Revisions in future expected earnings lead into identical proportional revisions in expected future dividends.[15]

Because expected earnings are assumed to differ from expected dividends by a constant payout ratio, current price can also be expressed as future expected earn-

---

[14]$E_t(D) = E(D_{t+1}) = E(D_{t+k})$, which are the expected future dividends assessed as of time t.

[15]$E(D_{t+k}) = KE(X_{t+k})$ for all $k > 0$ as of time t. $E(D_{t+k})$ is the expected dividend at time $t + k$ assessed as of time t, and K is the payout ratio. In the no-growth case, $E(D_{t+1}) = E(D_{t+k})$ for all $k > 1$ assessed as of t. Let $E_t(D) = E(D_{t+1}) = E(D_{t+k})$ assessed as of t; then

$$\frac{E_{t+1}(D) - E_t(D)}{E_t(D)} = \frac{E_{t+1}(X) - E_t(X)}{E_t X}$$

where $E_t(X) = E(X_{t+t}) = E(X_{t+k})$ assessed as of t. More compactly stated ($\Delta \equiv$ change from t to $t + 1$):

$$\frac{\Delta E(D)}{E_t(D)} = \frac{\Delta E(X)}{E_t(X)}$$

ings ($P_t = \rho KE_t(X)$). In the spirit of the no growth in dividends assumption, the assumed payout ratio is 100%. Assume further that $\rho=10$. In this setting the perpetual stream of "constant" (no-growth) dividends will have a market price equal to 10 times the expected future dividend and the ratio of price to permanent accounting earnings is also 10 [or $P_t = 10E_t(X)$]. From Table 4-3, the expected earnings at $t = 0$ are \$1.50, the expected dividends are also \$1.50, and the price of the share is \$15.00 (10 × \$1.50). The ratio of price to expected earnings is 10 times (alternatively, price is equal to 10 times expected earnings).

The third and final link is the relationship between current and future earnings. Four cases were discussed earlier and are used here.

With these specific assumptions about the links, the sensitivity of stock price changes to earnings changes can be examined. By the first two links introduced above, *the percentage changes in price, the percentage change in expected dividends, and the percentage change in expected earnings are equal.*[16] In other words, the sensitivity of percentage changes in price to percentage changes in *expected* earnings (permanent accounting earnings) is one to one. For example, a change in expected earnings (for example, of 33%) will lead to an equal change in price (for example, 33%).

However, the sensitivity of a stock price change to change in *current* earnings depends on what process is perceived to be governing earnings. Under case one, percentage changes in current earnings are equal to percentage changes in *expected* earnings. Here the sensitivity of price changes to *current* earnings changes is also expected to be one to one. For example, from Table 4-3, a 33% change in current earnings would lead to a 33% change in stock price (for example, a price change from \$15 to \$20). In case two there is zero sensitivity between current earnings changes and price changes because all shocks are transitory and have no information content about future earnings or future dividends. In this case, the stock price would be expected to remain the same (for example, \$15). If the process of earnings is described by case three, the sensitivity between stock price changes and earnings changes would be less than one. A 33% change in current earnings will imply a percentage change in price of less than 33% (for example, price would be less than \$20 but more than \$15). In case four the price change sensitivity would be greater than one to one. A 33% change in current earnings would lead to a percentage change in price of greater than 33% (for example, price would be greater than \$20).[17]

The preceding discussion provided a simple illustration linking earnings and prices. The general analysis would involve an identification of the events that led to

---

[16]More formally, $E_t(D) = K \cdot E_t(X)$ and $P_t = \rho E_t(D)$. Hence, with k and ρ constant,

$$\frac{\Delta P}{P_t} = \frac{\Delta E(D)}{E_t(D)} = \frac{\Delta E(X)}{E_t(X)}$$

where $\Delta \equiv$ the change from t to $t + 1$.

[17]In all four cases, the new price can be computed by multiplying expected earnings (as reported in Table 4-3) by 10 (the ratio of price to *expected* earnings). Note that the ratio of price to *current* earnings would be 10, 7.5, between 7.5 and 10, and above 10 for each of the four cases, respectively.

the earnings change and an assessment of their permanent versus transitory components. This is obviously a highly judgmental process, and the appropriate case may vary across firms and vary for a given firm over time.

Informational and Measurement Views of Financial Reporting

The preceding discussion reflects two distinct views of financial reporting—an informational view and a measurement view.[18]

From an informational perspective, financial reporting provides value-relevant information incremental to the *total mix of information* (in other words, all other sources of publicly available information). The total mix of information available is rich, and financial reporting data are only a portion of this total. Under this view, to have value financial reporting data must successfully compete against all other sources of information and provide something that is different from those other sources.

Imagine a world in which market prices reacted only to accounting data and only at the announcement dates of such data. In some sense, this would be a world in which accounting data are very important. In this world, large price changes occur at announcement dates with relative calm in price changes at other times. However, the market abhors "surprises" and the participants will attempt to obtain information on a more timely basis. For example, if earnings drives stock price changes, the market will attempt to obtain proxies for accounting earnings (implicitly forecasting accounting earnings) during the quarter. Obtaining such data will cause interim stock price movements and such data will tend to preempt the information content of the earnings announcement.

To the extent that information obtained preempts accounting data, there will be less, and, in the limit, no price reaction at the time of the disclosure. In active markets, the major barrier to complete preemption of accounting data is *information costs,* broadly defined. These costs include not only information search costs but also legal liability that might be associated with attempts to obtain information prior to its formal announcement. As information technology reduces many of these costs, accounting information would be preempted by other, more timely sources.

A measurement perspective takes a different view. Its origins are in the setting of perfect and complete markets. From a measurement perspective, financial reporting measures assets, liabilities, and equity. From this perspective, the financial statements do not need to be the sole or unique measure of that item. The language used by the FASB to describe its objectives is a mixture of informational and measurement perspectives. The FASB has both objectives, which vary in relative importance across standards. Understanding the motivation for many of the FASB standards is difficult without introducing a measurement perspective. For example, even if research were to establish unequivocally that depreciation expense is pre-

---

[18]These issues are discussed in greater depth in Schipper (1994) and Lambert (1996).

empted completely by other information, the FASB would be unlikely to mandate that depreciation expense be omitted from the measurement of net income. Net income is not a partial listing of revenues and expenses based on the criterion of what has or has not been preempted by other information. Similarly, even if research were to establish unequivocally that the amounts reported for depreciable assets on the balance sheet are preempted completely by other information, depreciable assets would probably not be removed from the balance sheet. The balance sheet is a partial listing of assets and liabilities that have not been preempted by other information. At a basic level, the language of accounting—*assets, liabilities,* and *equity*—is the language of measurement. The FASB describes major accounting issues as issues of *recognition* and *measurement.*

The measurement approach arises out of a world of perfect and complete markets, where everything of interest is measured via market prices. Although perfect and complete markets are not necessary conditions for a measurement perspective, measurement is not nearly as well-defined in a setting of imperfect and incomplete markets. The FASB discusses the trade-off between *relevance* and *reliability* in deciding recognition and measurement issues. Under perfect and complete markets, the relevance and reliability of market value reporting is unassailable. In a more realistic setting, both the relevance and reliability of estimated market values is a nontrivial issue. Lack of reliability can be thought of as measurement error in accounting numbers.

The two views are not mutually exclusive. Each raises different issues, and the research designs that reflect each perspective differ. Events studies are a prominent example of the research on the informational approach. Events studies have a rich tradition and provide a great deal of evidence of the relation of security prices and accounting data. Levels studies are a prominent example of the measurement perspective. Both are discussed in Chapter 5.

Feltham–Ohlson Model of Earnings

A third approach to the relation between accounting data and security valuation is the model of Ohlson (1995) and Feltham and Ohlson (1995), which is neither informational nor measurement in its perspective. The model derives important properties of financial statements from one simple accounting relation, the clean surplus relation (CSR). This relation states that the ending book value of equity must equal the beginning balance plus earnings less dividends. From this relation, Feltham and Ohlson (F–O) derive expressions that relate market value of equity to the book value of equity and earnings.

The market value of a firm's equity (MV) is expressed as a function of the current book value of equity (BV) and the present value of future expected "abnormal" earnings ($E\,[NI_{at}]$). In particular,

$$P_0 = BV_0 + \sum_{t=1}^{\infty} \frac{E(NI_{at})}{(l+r)^t}$$

where $E(NI_{at})$ equals expected "abnormal" earnings t periods in the future (period 0 is the current period). In particular, abnormal earnings are the expected net income, $E(NI_t)$, in excess of expected "normal" earnings. Expected normal earnings are defined as equal to the discount rate (r) times the beginning of period book value. In other words, $E([NI_{at}]) = E(NI_t) - E(r \times BV_t - 1)$. Expected normal earnings are the net income that would be expected if the return on equity were equal to the cost of equity capital.

F–O demonstrate that the expression flows from two basic assumptions. The first is a valuation equation that states that the market value is equal to the present value of future expected dividends, where the discount rate is equal to the equity cost of capital (r). The second assumption is CSR. The first assumption is widely used in finance and accounting. The second equation is a familiar accounting identity and states that changes in book value are due to net income and dividends.[19] The clean surplus relation permits net income and book values to be substituted in place of dividends. With appropriate rearrangement and cancellation of terms, value can be represented as a linear combination of current book value and future expected abnormal earnings.[20]

A striking feature of the F–O expression is its apparent simplicity and generality. It characterizes market value solely by book value and expected abnormal net income. Moreover, it applies to any accounting system that obeys the CSR. No specific assumptions are required as to the use of historical cost, accruals, or fair values.

Sources of Abnormal Earnings

What are the sources of abnormal earnings? By definition, they are factors that cause the market value and book value to differ. The differences flow from a combination of the economic conditions and the accounting system used to describe those conditions.

---

[19]More formally, the two conditions state

$$P_0 = \sum_{t=1}^{\infty} \frac{E(D_t)}{(1+r)^t}$$

$BV_{t+1} = BV_t + NI_{t+1} - Dt + 1$, which implies

$$D_{t+1} = NI_{t+1} - BV_{t+1} + BV_t = NI_{t+1} - \Delta BV$$

[20]It is not clear how severe an assumption the clean surplus relation is. It assumes a measure of comprehensive income. Current accounting standards permit some gains and losses to be charged directly to shareholders' equity. Currently, gains and losses from investment securities available for sale and foreign currency translation gains and losses are two examples. However, with sufficient disclosure, earnings can be reconstructed to incorporate these items. Similarly, the concept of dividends is comprehensive as well and includes more than cash dividends paid to shareholders; it also reflects increases in book value due to additional equity issue (negative dividends) and equity repurchase transactions, such as retirement of shares and treasury stock transactions.

Excess Net Present Value Projects

One potential source of abnormal earnings is the ability of firms to make positive net present value (NPV) investments, in which the present value of the future expected cash flows from the investments exceeds the expenditures.[21] Currently accounting systems do not record the excess present value at the time of the investment. If the ability to find such projects is a pervasive phenomenon, then excess present value projects is a major source of market value being in excess of book value. Under the CSR condition, this excess present value is reflected in positive abnormal earnings for one or more future periods.

However, other factors can lead to nonzero abnormal earnings even if no positive NPV projects existed. These factors are due to the features of the accounting system used to record the transactions. One factor is the use of historical costs, which can lead to *delayed recognition* in the accounting system discussed earlier in this chapter.

Another factor is use of accounting methods that lead to book values different from economic values. Accounting depreciation can differ from the economic depreciation, as discussed in Chapter 3. Also inventory costing methods such as LIFO can lead to accounting book values for inventories that are different from their economic values.[22] An extreme form of the depreciation example occurs when an expenditure for an economic asset is immediately and entirely expensed. Intangible assets, such as research and development, are a primary example of the expensing of an asset (100% depreciation or amortization in the year of expenditure).

Abnormal earnings could be either positive or negative. In the Chapter 3 example, sum-of-the-years-digits (SYD) depreciation leads to more rapid depreciation than economic depreciation, and the market value exceeded the book value. Here, future expected abnormal earnings are positive. This occurs because the more rapid expensing of the depreciation asset will be reflected in lower depreciation expense in the remaining years of the asset's life and hence to higher net income. However, if SYD depreciation is less accelerated than the economic depreciation of the assets, the market value would be below book value and future abnormal earnings would be expected to be negative.

Conservatism

However, the general perception is that positive abnormal earnings is more likely than negative. This feature of financial reporting is known as *conservatism* or *biased recognition.* Many of the sources just discussed imply predominantly positive

---

[21]Many introductory courses in finance and management accounting present the capital investment decision in a present value context. In this setting, the firm accepts projects with positive excess present values.

[22]This disparity is widely discussed in the use of the LIFO inventory method. The concern is sufficiently great that disclosure of the "LIFO reserve," the difference between the ending inventory reported under LIFO and the amount under a replacement cost assumption, is a required disclosure for firms using LIFO.

abnormal earnings. Excess present value investments, the use of LIFO, accounting depreciation in excess of economic depreciation, and immediate expensing of economic assets are examples. Also many of the accounting standards, such as lower of cost or market (LCM), are not symmetrical. Losses will be recorded but gains will not. For example, LCM-type rules apply to inventory valuation and to asset impairment standards. The empirical evidence discussed in Chapter 5 indicates that across large samples of firms pooled over several years, on the average the market value of equity exceeds the book value of equity, which implies positive abnormal future expected earnings.

In contrast to delayed recognition, which is expected to produce abnormal earnings for only the remaining life of the assets that give rise to the unrecognized gain (or loss), the effects of conservatism on book value and earnings can be permanent or indefinite for a firm that is in steady-state growth. Chapter 2 illustrates how growth can induce permanent differences in earnings, book values, and return on equity.

Earnings and book value in the Feltham–Ohlson model are neither information nor measurement. Earnings are not an underlying fundamental variable that is the source of dividend-paying ability. Earnings are not a value-derived concept as in the measurement perspective. Instead, earnings simply obey the CSR. Nevertheless, the model does help to structure our thinking about the relation between book value and earnings and about the implications of CSR for financial reporting.

Role of Accruals

The theory of why accruals have an ability to forecast future cash flows has not been well developed. The major premises in the argument are (1) financial reporting is useful to investors; (2) investors have a demand for information that forecasts future cash flows; and (3) if financial accounting is to be informative, it must be useful in forecasting future cash flows. In particular, because accruals are a major feature of financial reporting, accruals must be useful in forecasting future cash flows. However, the last link is not well documented.

Intuitively, an accrual (such as accounts receivable) is expected to be informative about future cash flows (such as collections from credit customers). However, the informational perspective would compare information content of accruals against an alternative, such as cash collections from credit customers from prior time periods. One can imagine situations in which sufficient stability to the operations exists that a past series of cash collections from credit customers provides an informative basis for future collections. In this richer context, it is no longer obvious that the accrual, accounts receivables, is incrementally informative. Further, accruals inherently involve estimation, discretion, and judgment. Depending on the nature of these latter processes, the information content of accruals can be significantly affected and not necessarily for the better. Discretionary behavior is discussed shortly.

Thus far, the comparison has been against a cash flow accounting system, which is only one alternative. Market values are another. To the extent that market values reflect the present value of the future cash flows of an asset or obligation, they possess potential forecasting ability for future cash flows. Of course, estimation, discretion, and judgment are potentially involved here as well. A third alternative is an ambitious set of disclosures that would report detailed information to aid in forecasting cash flows, including the use of nonfinancial information.

A Role of Accrual Accounting: An Illustration

From an informational perspective, a function of a financial accounting reporting system is to provide information that potentially will alter investors' beliefs about the future dividend-paying ability of the firm. As such, accrual accounting can be viewed as a cost-effective compromise between merely reporting cash flows and an ambitious policy of "full" disclosure. The choice then involves selecting that accrual system that provides the most valuable information, subject to cost considerations. The issues that arise in choosing the "best" information system in a multiperson setting were discussed in Chapter 2 and are relevant to the choice among accrual systems.

An accrual can be viewed as a form of forecast about the future, and as such accrual accounting can be viewed as a cost-effective way of conveying forecasts or expectational data. This is illustrated in a simple setting. Consider the financial results reported in Table 4-4. What are the earnings for the year? One possible answer is $50,000 ($1,200,000 − $800,000 − $350,000). However, because this makes no allowance for uncollectable accounts, such a number would be considered optimistic. The aging of the receivables provides one source of information on which to base an estimate or *forecast* of the amount of uncollectable accounts. The bottom panel of Table 4-4 indicates the possible amounts that actually will be collected and the credit manager's assessment of the probability of each state. For simplicity, only four states have been assumed. A second possible measure of net income would be to take a "pessimistic" forecast based on the assumption that nothing will be collected until the cash is actually received. In this case, the estimated uncollectables would be $310,000 with a loss of $260,000.[23] However, neither optimism nor pessimism need be adopted, and some attempt could be made to represent an intermediate situation by choosing some measure of central tendency. If the expected value is chosen, the expected collectables are $292,000, the implied estimated uncollectables are $18,000, and the implied earnings are $32,000. However, the expected value is only one measure of central tendency. The median amount of collectables is $300,000 and the implied estimated uncollectables are $10,000 for a reported earnings of $40,000. If the modal (most likely) value is chosen, the average amount of collectibles is $280,000 for an estimated uncollectables of $30,000 for a reported earnings of $20,000.

---

[23]A less extreme variation of this approach is provided by installment sales accounting, which recognizes no gross margin until the receivable is collected. The realized gross margin would be $296,667 [$400,000 × ($890,000 ÷ $1,200,000)] and the corresponding loss is $53,333.

TABLE 4-4 Accrual Accounting
as a Forecast

The company began operations this year. On December 31 the following selected financial statement items were reported:

Accounts receivable	$ 310,000
Sales (gross)	$1,200,000
Cost of goods sold	$ 800,000
Other operating expenses	$ 350,000

The credit terms to customers are the amounts due within 30 days after billing. An aging of the accounts receivable account reveals the following:

Current	$200,000
30–60 days	$ 50,000
60–90 days	$ 30,000
90–120 days	$ 20,000
Over 120 days	$ 10,000
	$310,000

The credit manager indicates the following:

STATE OF THE WORLD	PROBABILITY
Will collect $310,000	.25
Will collect $300,000	.30
Will collect $280,000	.40
Will collect $250,000	.05

Thus far, six measures of earnings have been derived depending on how the information on collectability is treated. A multitude of earnings numbers arise in part because there is an attempt to capture an entire probability distribution over several states in a single number. Obviously, this can be done in a variety of ways, and these are only a few of the possibilities. For example, perhaps some information should be incorporated on the variability as well as the central tendency of the possible outcomes (for example, a certainty equivalent approach that "risk adjusts" the central tendency measures by some variability measure). Moreover, no allowance has been made for the fact that these amounts will not be received immediately but at some time in the future. There are present value considerations to be considered here.

If perfect and complete markets are assumed, all these considerations would be fully reflected in the "price" at which the firm could sell those receivables. The market price reflects these judgmental factors. In this sense, the accrual could be viewed as an attempt to surrogate the valuation process. In perfect and complete markets the market price of the asset could be used to measure earnings and no reliance on accrual accounting is required.

The premise here is, of course, that accrual accounting plays a role precisely because markets are imperfect or incomplete. For example, in some cases receivables can be sold (for example, receivables can be factored). However, the firm may choose not to sell its receivables because of some perceived imperfection or incompleteness in the market (such as, its "value in use" exceeds its "exit price"). Similarly, the accounting system may not incorporate such information for the same reasons. However, the issue of how to aggregate the underlying data arises. There typically will be a number of alternatives.

Some loss of information can occur via aggregation (for example, the entire probability distribution of the credit manager will not be reported). However, the premise is that the aggregation can be more informative than merely reporting cash flows. Given that the price of a security is a function of what is expected in the future, it is not unreasonable to suppose that accrual accounting, if it provides data on management's expectations about the future, may in fact convey information over and above the cash flows.

However, much of the information arising out of the accruals is of a short-term nature (for example, accruals with respect to current assets such as receivables and inventories). A major long-term accrual is depreciable plant and equipment. However, here the accrual process relies on "boilerplate" allocation rules, such as straight-line depreciation, and estimates of useful lives based on guidelines motivated in part by income tax considerations. Moreover, depreciation under historical cost has been particularly subject to considerable criticism because of inflation. Hence, the area for the greatest potential for accrual accounting is also the area that has been the target of severe criticism. As a result, it is not immediately obvious that accrual accounting accomplishes its purpose, as stated by the FASB. As such, the merits of accrual accounting are still largely an open issue. The next chapter provides some empirical evidence on this issue.

Discretionary Behavior with Respect to Accounting Numbers

Discretionary behavior with respect to accounting numbers is a major financial reporting issue. Opportunities for discretion arise because of uncertainty and the asymmetry of information between management and shareholders. Opportunities for discretion arise in accrual accounting in part because of the difficulty in estimating the accruals.

For example, the FASB standard on loss contingencies calls for the estimation of losses due to receivables or loans where it is *probable* and *reasonably estimable*. The standard and its interpretations provide only general guidelines regarding the estimation. Accounting research has examined four major areas of accounting discretion: (1) voluntary disclosure, (2) earning forecasts (which are a particular type of voluntary disclosure), (3) choices in accounting method, and (4) accruals. Accruals are widespread, are present in almost every firm to some extent, and are a key feature of the financial reporting system.

Discretionary behavior is important because it can affect the effectiveness of the financial reporting system. Traditional forms of discretionary behavior have often assumed that someone was being "fooled" (for example, the early income smoothing literature). Schipper (1989) discusses many of the important issues in discretion. Alternatively, discretionary behavior can be viewed as the natural manifestation of multiperiod contracting in an incomplete market in which management is expected by other parties to take discretionary actions, conditional on finding itself in certain states of the world. As described in Watts and Zimmerman (1986), more recent approaches to discretionary behavior based on contracting do not require that anyone be fooled. Sloan (1996) provides a summary of research on discretionary accruals.

One aspect of discretionary behavior is the effects on the capital markets, and, in particular, the effects on the value of the common equity. The pricing of discretionary components of accounting numbers can affect both the incentives and the economic consequences associated with discretionary behavior. The valuation evidence is of interest in its own right because it can show whether security prices are affected by discretionary behavior, but it can also serve as a proxy for whether other parties are also likely to be able to conduct a similar decomposition. The relation between discretionary behavior and valuation is summarized in Chapter 5.

Opposing Views of Discretion

There are two distinct views of discretionary behavior. The first is the traditional view that discretion is an invitation to mischief. In particular, management will use discretion to manipulate the financial reporting system in ways that enhance management's well-being to the determinant of capital suppliers and others. Often this means discretionary behavior that understates bad news and overstates good news. In the traditional income smoothing literature, it involves adopting accounting policies that make the volatility of reported earnings lower than it otherwise would be in an attempt to provide a less risky picture of the firm's activities. It has also been called the "opportunistic" view of discretion (Watts and Zimmerman 1986) and arises in situations in which adverse selection or moral hazard exists. Although increased monitoring by independent parties such as auditors can mitigate the problem, it in general will not eliminate it.[24]

A second view flows from the signaling literature and states that management will use the discretion and judgment to reveal some of its private information to investors. In this literature for a signal to be credible, it must be costly to imitate. In other words, there must be some cost to "falsely" signaling good news, for example.

---

[24]Even if everyone can infer behavior, from an agency perspective, there still may be "losses" relative to a first-best solution of no information asymmetry. For example, nonoptimal risk sharing may still occur.

In a financial reporting context, Healy and Palepu (1993) have been advocates of this more benign view of discretion.

Motivations for Discretionary Behavior

The exercise of discretion is a timing issue. Reducing the provision for loan losses in the current year implies a higher provision at some time in the future on or before the date when the loan is written off. Generally, in a market in which the total mix is rich and private information search is active, the news can be delayed but not permanently postponed. Motives for discretion must incorporate this timing dimension. Why is it important to report the information either earlier or later? Various explanations include impact on compensation plans and effects on stock price. For stock price, a link between the pattern of stock prices and incentives for discretion must exist. For example, a planned issue of stock, sales of shares by management, or a share repurchase program could affect incentives to alter the short-term pattern of share prices, even if the price at the end of the eventual disclosure is the same.

Several specific motivations for discretionary behavior with respect to accruals are offered by prior research: regulatory, financial reporting, tax factors, legal liability, and signaling. Regulatory motivations arise because of the desire to provide reported numbers that make the firm appear to be less risky and more capital adequate to regulators. Financial reporting motivations reflect a diverse set of factors that arise in part from the fact that many explicit and implicit contracts written by the firm are stated in accounting numbers (for example, compensation contracts and debt convenants) in ways that can affect the economic value of the firm (Watts and Zimmerman 1986). Moreover, some discretionary behavior may be motivated by the perception that capital markets are influenced by the reported numbers (for example, bond rating agencies, analysts, and potentially security prices). In general, tax factors can be quite complex but prior research has typically characterized the desired goal as the minimization of the present value of the tax payments. Legal liability for financial reporting can affect the incentives for discretionary behavior.

The motivation for discretionary behavior is not well formulated. The costs and benefits associated with various magnitudes of discretionary behavior is not well defined. Two types of behavior are postulated for some "target performance" variable. The first type is that the net benefit function causes behavior to have the observed number close to this "target" such that departures either above or below are equally undesirable. This leads to "smoothing" behavior. The other form of behavior typically postulated is that below a certain level of performance the net benefits of discretionary behavior to improve the reported performance variable are zero (or even negative) such that no discretionary behavior (or "big bath" discretionary behavior) is observed. Healy (1985) gives an example of the latter motivated by compensation contracts. Much of the empirical research since Healy is an example of the former in that the estimation models assume a monotonic relation between the discretionary behavior and the chosen performance variable.

In addition, the variables that are used to proxy for these motivations are diverse, generic, and measure with error the underlying motivations. There is no agreement among the prior literature as to whether the discretionary behavior varies as a linear or nonlinear (for example, U-shaped or quadratic) function of the performance proxies. In some cases, there is no agreement as to the sign of the relation between the discretionary component and the proxy because the motives operate in conflicting directions. In addition, the magnitude of the costs and benefits associated with various types of discretionary behavior are not well defined or quantified.

Evidence provides support for both opportunistic (Dechow, Sloan, and Sweeney 1996) and signaling perspectives (Wahlen 1994). Questions have also been raised concerning whether discretionary accrual behavior has been effectively measured (Dechow, Sloan, and Sweeney 1995). Empirical evidence on the relation between security prices and discretionary accruals is discussed in Chapter 5.

4-3 CONCLUDING REMARKS

This chapter has explored earnings under conditions of uncertainty. The initial setting was perfect and complete markets in which earnings and valuation are still well-defined, and conceptually this setting constitutes a modest extension of the certainty case. However, some aspects of introducing uncertainty were worth noting. (1) Economic earnings can still be defined but a distinction must be drawn between *ex post* and *ex ante* (or expected) earnings. (2) Either earnings measure is a byproduct of the valuation process. They cannot be defined until the valuation process has been specified. (3) The merits of measuring earnings, given valuation is known, is not obvious. (4) Neither *ex post* nor *ex ante* earnings involve any obvious reliance on accrual accounting.

Under imperfect or incomplete markets, valuation is no longer a well-defined process in the sense that market prices may no longer fully reflect the preferences of individuals. In some cases, market prices may not simply exist, and in other cases, observed market prices may not fully capture the value of the claim because of some imperfection. As a result, the properties of prices are unknown, as are the properties of any earnings number derived from price. Hence, a price-oriented approach no longer has the obvious appeal it does in a perfect and complete markets setting.

In this setting, accounting earnings can be viewed from an informational perspective. Earnings are a source of information used by investors in assessing the value of securities. However, earnings do not necessarily bear any simple, direct relationship to the valuation process as economic earnings did in the perfect and complete markets case. In particular, the price-earnings process can be viewed as consisting of three elements: (1) a link between current price and future dividends, (2) a link between future dividends and the future earnings, and (3) a link between future earnings and current earnings. With these three elements, it is possible to link conceptually prices and accounting earnings.

In this setting a role of accrual accounting is to provide an information system that is a cost-effective compromise between merely reporting cash flows and a more ambitious disclosure policy. An accrual can be viewed as a forecast about the future. Given that the price and the value of a security is a function of expected future cash flows, accrual accounting may convey information that cannot be extracted from an analysis of past cash flows. However, an inspection of the accruals makes this superiority less than obvious. The efficacy of accrual accounting still remains essentially an open issue. However, this chapter has attempted to present some of the conceptual aspects of this issue and to provide a framework for interpreting accounting earnings in a setting of uncertainty and incomplete markets.

The chapter also discussed major features of the current financial reporting system, including delayed recognition, conservatism, and discretion.

BIBLIOGRAPHY

Brown, L., P. Griffin, R. Hagerman, and M. Zmijewski. "Security Analysts' Superiority Relative to Univariate Time Series Models in Forecasts of Quarterly Earnings." *Journal of Accounting and Economics* (April 1987), 61–88.

Chambers, R. *Accounting Evaluation and Economic Behavior.* Englewood Cliffs, N.J.: Prentice-Hall, 1966.

Dechow, P., R. Sloan, and A. Sweeney. "Detecting Earnings Management." *The Accounting Review* (April 1995), 193–225.

———. "Causes and Consequences of Earnings Management: An Analysis of Firms Subject to Enforcement Actions by the SEC." *Contemporary Accounting Research* (Spring 1996), 1–36.

Edwards, E., and P. Bell. *The Theory and Measurement of Business Income.* Berkeley: University of California Press, 1961.

Feltham, G., and J. Ohlson. "Valuation and Clean Surplus Accounting for Operating and Financial Activities." *Contemporary Accounting Research* (Spring 1995), 689–731.

Healy, P. "The Effect of Bonus Schemes on Accounting Decisions." *Journal of Accounting and Economics* (April 1985), 85–107.

——— and K. Palepu. "The Effects of Firms' Financial Disclosure Strategies on Stock Prices." *Accounting Horizons* (March 1993), 1–11.

Lambert, R. "Financial Reporting Research and Standard Setting." Unpublished working paper, Stanford University, 1996.

Leftwich, R., and M. Zmijewski. "Contemporaneous Announcements of Dividends and Earnings." *Journal of Accounting, Auditing, and Finance* (Fall 1994), 725–762.

Ohlson, J. "Earnings, Book Values, and Dividends in Equity Valuation." *Contemporary Accounting Research* (Spring 1995), 661–687.

Ryan, S. "A Model of Accrual Measurement with Implications for the Evolution of the Book-to-Market Ratio." *Journal of Accounting Research* (Spring 1995), 95–112.

Schipper, K. "Earnings Management." *Accounting Horizons* (December 1989), 91–102.

———. "Academic Accounting Research and the Standard Setting Process." *Accounting Horizons* (December 1994), 61–73.

Sharpe, W. *Investments.* 5th ed. Englewood Cliffs, N.J.: Prentice-Hall, 1995.

Sloan, R. "Do Stock Prices Fully Reflect Information in Accruals and Cash Flows About Future Earnings?" *Accounting Review* (July 1996), 289–315.

Sterling, R. *Theory of the Measurement of Enterprise Income.* Lawrence: University of Kansas Press, 1970.

Wahlen, J. "The Nature of Information in Commercial Bank Loan Loss Disclosures." *The Accounting Review* (July 1994), 455–478.

Watts, R., and J. Zimmerman. *Positive Accounting Theory.* Englewood Cliffs, N.J.: Prentice-Hall, 1986.

5

The Evidence

Few areas of empirical research in finance or accounting have received as much attention as the relation between stock prices and accounting earnings. Prices depend on the individuals' endowments, tastes, and beliefs. From an informational perspective, earnings can be viewed as a signal from an information system. As discussed in Chapter 2, for an information system to have value some of the signals must alter beliefs. If unexpected earnings can alter the beliefs of market participants in a systematic way, increases in stock prices would be associated with favorable unexpected earnings, and conversely for unfavorable unexpected earnings. One class of research that has examined the price-earnings relation is known as the *information content of earnings* studies and often uses an *events study* approach.

Events studies are a major focus of prior research and as a result are a focus of this chapter.[1] However, the evidence summarized here includes not only event studies with short windows of time surrounding the announcement but also the relation between price changes and earnings changes over longer intervals (for example, annually) and are often called *first difference* studies. Another set of price-earnings empirical research also examines the relation between prices and earnings and are called *levels* studies.

[1]Event studies examine the residual price change of a sample of firms for a window of time on either side of an identifiable event, such as announcements of earnings, stock splits, stock dividends, cash dividends, earnings forecasts, and changes in accounting methods. The influence of economy-wide factors and additional factors, such as industry-wide information, on stock prices are extracted via regression to obtain a residual price change. A nontechnical description of events study research design appears in Kritzman (1994).

As in the previous chapters, prices are viewed as dependent on expectations regarding future dividend-paying ability. The three-element framework developed was used to illustrate a specific relationship by adding additional assumptions about each of the three links. This framework provides a basis for interpreting price-earnings relationships and will be used here to interpret empirical research on the observed relationship between prices and earnings. This chapter provides a brief, nontechnical summary of the evidence and will discuss many of its implications. A more detailed discussion of the research appears in Foster (1986), Bernard (1989), and Lev (1989).

Several conclusions are drawn from the empirical research. (1) A significant, positive correlation exists between price changes and earnings changes. (2) Although significant, it is not a simple one-to-one relationship. One reason is that prices behave as if earnings are perceived to possess a transitory component. (3) Security prices act as though investors adjust at least partially for many accounting method differences among firms, such as depreciation method differences. (4) Price changes appear to value both the cash flow and accrual components of earnings changes. (5) Prices anticipate earnings because of more timely sources of information. (6) Prices can be used to forecast earnings, a feature known as the *information content of prices*. (7) Prices behave as if market participants perceive there is a delayed recognition component to earnings and book value of common equity. (8) Prices behave as if market participants perceive there is a *conservative* component to earnings and book value. (9) Book value of equity, as well as earnings, appears to be important in explaining prices. (10) Footnote disclosures are also priced by the market. (11) Discretionary components of accounting numbers are priced by the market differently from the nondiscretionary components. (12) Measures of systematic risk in security prices are significantly positively correlated with measures of systematic volatility in accounting earnings.

5-1 PRICE CHANGES AND EARNINGS CHANGES— THE INFORMATION CONTENT OF EARNINGS

Research by Benston (1966) and Ball and Brown (1968) explored the relationship between security price changes and earnings changes.[2] Ball and Brown found a significant association between the sign of the price changes and the sign of the earnings changes.[3] For the years in which a firm experiences positive residual earnings

---

[2]Throughout, the term *security prices* will refer to the prices of common stock securities and the term *earnings* will refer to accounting earnings available for common shareholders.

[3]The security price variable is *unsystematic return* (in other words, *u*, as defined in footnote 9 of Chapter 2). This variable is the residual percentage change in price (adjusted for dividends) after taking out the effects of marketwide movements, measured by the percentage change in price index (adjusted for dividends) of a market portfolio. Similarly, the changes in accounting earnings are measured relative to some earnings benchmark, such as previous changes in earnings or marketwide changes in earnings. Some studies use analysts' forecasts of earnings as the benchmark. Ball and Brown called the difference

change, there tends to be positive residual price change and, conversely, for the years in which there is a negative residual earnings change. Good earnings news is associated with annual residual price increases of about 7%, whereas bad earnings news is associated with residual price declines of about 9% (see Figure 5-1). A hypothetical $10,000 invested 12 months prior to the earnings announcement rises to approximately $10,700 for the firms that 12 months later announce a positive residual earnings change ("good news"), whereas a hypothetical $10,000 declines to $9,100 for the firms reporting "bad news" in earnings.

Beaver, Clarke, and Wright (1979) extend the Ball and Brown study by incorporating the magnitude of the earnings change. Table 5-1 reports the average residual percentage change in earnings and the residual percentage change in price for 6 of 25 portfolios. The 25 portfolios were constructed based on their residual percentage change in earnings. Portfolio 1 (the earnings losers) consists of those securities that experienced the greatest residual decline in earnings (a mean decline of 154.8%), whereas portfolio 6 (earnings winners) consists of those securities that experienced the greatest residual increase in earnings (a mean increase of 185.1%). Portfolios 2 through 5 represent securities that experienced intermediate residual changes in earnings. The mean residual percentage change in earnings and the mean residual percentage change in price for the portfolios are reported in Table 5-1.

TABLE 5-1 Relationship Between Residual Percentage Changes in Price and Percentage Changes in Earnings

PORTFOLIO	RESIDUAL PERCENTAGE CHANGE IN EPS	RESIDUAL PERCENTAGE CHANGE IN PRICE	BETA[a]
1	−154.8	−17.5	1.23
2	−12.7	−9.0	.98
3	0.4	−2.1	.88
4	9.0	2.0	.98
5	23.4	10.4	1.01
6	185.1	29.2	1.15

[a]*The beta is based on a return on a "market" portfolio, with equal weights assigned to securities. The betas originally reported were based on a "market" portfolio return with market value weights. The relative behavior is identical under either definition of beta. The market protfolio consists of all New York Stock Exchange securities, and the beta of the market portfolio is one, by construction.*
Source: Beaver, Clarke, and Wright (1979), Table 3.

between the actual earnings change and the benchmark earnings the *forecast error*. Positive forecast errors are also called favorable earnings changes or "good news," whereas negative forecast errors are called unfavorable earnings changes or "bad news." The forecast error has been interpreted as a measure of unexpected changes in earnings. Hereafter, the unsystematic return will be referred to as the *residual percentage change in price*, and the earnings forecast error will be referred to as the *residual percentage change in earnings*.

The relationship is positive and significant, and the magnitude of the differences in security price changes is sizable.[4] The residual percentage change in price ranges from −17.5% for portfolio 1 to 29.2% for portfolio 6. The magnitudes residual price change is much larger than the 7 and −9%, which incorporated only the sign of the residual earnings change.

To better understand the importance of these magnitudes, consider two hypothetical portfolios, each of which starts with $10,000 at the beginning of the year. By the end of the year the terminal value of portfolio 1 would decline to $8,250, whereas the terminal value of portfolio 6 would increase to $12,920. The terminal value of portfolio 6 (earnings winners) is 157% of the terminal value of portfolio 1 (earnings losers). The relationship is not only statistically significant, but also large enough to be economically important. The difference in price performance is well in excess of transactions or management fees on managed investment portfolios.

What are the implications of these findings? A modest interpretation is that accounting earnings changes are correlated with the events that induce changes in security prices. The evidence is also consistent with a more ambitious interpretation that prices behave as if investors perceive that accounting earnings convey information about the value of a security. In the context of the framework developed in Chapter 4, security prices behave as if investors perceive that current earnings provide information about future earnings and the future dividend-paying ability of the firm. Hence, prices act as if current earnings changes possess a *permanent* component. Under this more ambitious interpretation, prices behave as if investors perceive earnings as information (in other words, altering their beliefs) about future earnings and future dividend-paying ability. Evidence presented in section 5-5 will shed further light on these two interpretations.

5-2 SENSITIVITY OF PRICE CHANGES TO EARNINGS CHANGES

Given the results reported in Table 5-1, one might conclude that percentage changes in security prices are associated with percentage changes in earnings on a simple one-to-one basis. The relation is not a simple one-to-one relation in two respects.

First, the correlation between price changes and earnings changes is less than one. At the individual security level, the average correlation is .38. This is hardly surprising for two reasons: Some factors or events affect price changes but not current earnings changes, and other factors affect current earnings changes but not price changes. Some examples are; (1) Sources of information other than current earnings are available about future dividends and future earnings. Even though current earnings is one important source of information, it is not the only source of in-

---

[4]A significant, positive correlation exists between the residual percentage change in earnings and the residual percentage change in price. The rank correlation among the 25 portfolios is .74 and is statistically different from zero. If the data were aggregated into fewer portfolios, the correlation would approach one (Beaver, Lambert, and Morse 1980).

formation. Announcements of litigation, contract awards, petroleum discoveries, future capital expenditures, and anticipated strikes are examples of events that may affect future earnings but may not be reflected in current earnings. (2) Other sources of changes in stock prices are not related to changes in future earnings or future dividends. For example, consider economy-wide events that alter the discount rate applied to future earnings or dividends, such as changes in interest rates or risk premiums. (3) Some changes in earnings per share are not expected to alter the dividend-paying ability of the firm. Changes in depreciation methods and reliance on historical cost basis of accounting are two among many possible examples. (4) The "wrong" benchmark has been chosen for measuring the expected change in earnings. As a result, residual earnings change measures unexpected earnings with error. (5) A portion of the current earnings changes is affected by factors that are expected not to alter the level of future expected earnings, in which case a portion of earnings change contains a *"transitory"* component.

Second, although price changes move in the same direction as earnings changes, they typically do not move as far. For example, in Table 5-1, the percentage change in price is smaller than the percentage change in earnings for the same portfolio. Whereas the "earnings losers" (portfolio 1) decline by 154.8%, the residual price decline is only 17.5%. Although the "earnings winners" (portfolio 6) increase by an average of 185.1%, the residual price increase is only 29.2%. A similar behavior is observed for the other portfolios. Beaver, Lambert, and Ryan (1987) estimate a linear regression in which price changes are the dependent variable and earnings changes are the independent variable. The earnings sensitivity averaged only .31, which was significantly different from both zero (no sensitivity) and one (a one-to-one sensitivity).[5] Hence, a 33% earnings changes on the average is associated with approximately a 10% change in prices.[6] The sensitivity of price changes with respect to earnings changes is less than one for several reasons. Reasons 3 through 5 discussed above are examples. The next section summarizes evidence for the fifth reason, a portion of the current earnings changes is perceived to contain a *transitory* component.

Transitory Components in Earnings

The price-earnings ratios of securities behave as if investors perceive that a component of earnings contains of a transitory component. Table 5-2 reports findings from a study of price-earnings ratios by Beaver and Morse (1978). The study finds that

---

[5]The slope coefficient on the earnings variable is known as the earnings sensitivity coefficient or as the earnings response coefficient (ERC). The resulting slope coefficient can be thought of as an elasticity measure obtained by regressing percentage changes in price on percentage changes in earnings. As indicated in Chapter 4, it is expected to be between zero and one for a broad class of earnings behavior. An alternative earnings measure is to divide the difference between the earnings forecast error by lagged security price (the same denominator used in the price change variable). Here the resulting slope coefficient is also a measure of earnings sensitivity but no longer scaled to be between 0 and 1. It can be thought of as the price-earnings multiple applied to each dollar of additional earnings forecast error.

[6]The evidence indicates that the relation is nonlinear in the very extreme earnings changes (for example, greater than 100% in absolute value) such that price changes become incrementally less sensitive to earnings changes in these extreme values.

TABLE 5-2 Relationship Between Price-Earnings Ratios and Earnings Growth

PORTFOLIO	MEDIAN PRICE EARNINGS	MEDIAN EARNINGS GROWTH IN SAME YEAR	MEDIAN EARNINGS GROWTH NEXT YEAR
1	50.0	−4.1%	95.3%
2	20.8	10.7%	14.9%
3	14.3	9.6%	12.9%
4	11.1	10.0%	8.8%
5	8.9	10.8%	5.2%
6	5.8	26.4%	−3.3%

Source: Beaver and Morse (1978), Tables 3 and 5.

stocks that have high price-earnings ratios at the end of a year have experienced low earnings growth in that year and high earnings growth in the subsequent year. Similarly, low price-earnings ratios stocks experience high growth in the year just ended and low growth in the subsequent year. This is exactly the behavior that would be expected if (1) earnings are perceived by investors to contain a transitory component and (2) earnings behave as if they contain a transitory component.

The Beaver and Morse study constructed portfolios based on year-end price-earnings ratios for a sample of firms with a December 31 fiscal year-end. The price-earnings ratio was computed as the ratio of price on December 31 divided by earnings per share (before extraordinary items). The study then examined the behavior of one-year earnings growth in the year just ended and the one-year growth in the subsequent year. Table 5-2 reports the pooled results for the 19 years covered by the study. Portfolio 1 consists of those securities with the highest price-earnings ratios (a median of 50 times earnings), whereas portfolio 6 consists of those securities with the lowest price-earnings ratios (a median of 5.8). Portfolios 2 through 5 represent intermediate portfolios with respect to price-earnings ratios, and the median values of the price-earnings ratios of these portfolios are also reported in Table 5-2. For portfolio 1, the median earnings growth in earnings in the year just ended relative to the earnings of the previous year was −4.1%, whereas for portfolio 6, the median earnings growth in the year just ended was 26.4%. It may seem anomalous that high price-earnings stocks would have poor earnings growth and conversely for low price-earnings stocks. However, as will be shown shortly, this is exactly what would be expected if earnings are perceived to contain a transitory component. In the next year the median earnings growth of portfolio 1 was 95.3%, whereas the median earnings growth for portfolio 6 was −3.3%. Again, this is consistent with earnings actually behaving as if they contained a transitory component.

TABLE 5-3 Effect of Transitory Component in Earnings

	YEAR 1	YEAR 2	YEAR 3
Expected earnings per share (EPS)	$ 1.00	$ 1.00	$ 1.00
Price per share	$10	$10	$10
I Negative Transitory Component			
Actual earnings per share	$ 1.00	$ .75	$ 1.00
Price-earnings ratio	10	13.2	10
Growth in EPS	—	−25%	+33%
II Positive Transitory Component			
Actual earnings per share	$ 1.00	$ 1.25	$ 1.00
Price-earnings ratio	10	8	10
Growth in EPS	—	+25%	−20%

Effect of Transitory Component on Price-Earnings Ratios and Earnings Growth

The purest example of a transitory item in earnings in one in which the unexpected earnings in a given year does not alter expectations about expected future earnings. The effect of a transitory component in earnings on price-earnings ratios and earnings growth can be demonstrated by the simple illustration shown in Table 5-3. Suppose that expected earnings per share is $1.00 for all years.[7] Also assume that actual earnings per share in years 1 and 3 was $1.00 and in year 2 is $.75. Price per share is $10 and remains $10 throughout because expected earnings have not changed. In year 2 the price-earnings ratio is 13.3 times ($10/$.75), whereas the growth in earnings is a minus 25% [($.75 − $1.00)/$1.00)]. As of the end of year 2, the expected growth in earnings in year 3 is 33% [($1.00 − $.75)/$.75)].

The first case had a negative transitory component to earnings of $.25. Conversely, assume the same facts as before except that there is a positive transitory component to earnings in year 2 of $.25 (in other words, the earnings per share in year 2 is $1.25). The price-earnings ratio at the end of year 2 would be 8 times ($10/$1.25), and the growth in earnings is a positive 25% [$1.25 − $1.00)/$1.00)]. However, as of the end of year 2, the expected growth in earnings per share in year 3 is −20% [$1.00 − $1.25)/$1.25)]. A high price-earnings ratio (13.3 times) is associated with low contemporaneous growth (−25%). A low price-earnings ratio (8 times) is associated with high contemporaneous growth (+25%). In other words, a

---

[7]This expectation holds as of the beginning of each of the three years, even though there is unexpected earnings in year 2.

negative correlation exists between price-earnings ratios and earnings growth in that year, as was reported in Table 5-2.

Similarly, a high price-earnings ratio (13.3 times) is associated with high expected growth in the next year (+33%), and low price-earnings ratios (8 times) is associated with a low expected growth in the next year (−20%), as reported in Table 5-2. In other words, the transitory component in earnings is expected to induce a positive correlation between price-earnings ratios in the current year and growth in earnings in the subsequent year. This can be explained by observing that both the price-earnings ratio and the next year's subsequent growth in earnings contain the same denominator ($.75 in the first case and $1.25 in the second case). Therefore, when earnings per share is temporarily low, both price-earnings ratios and next year's growth will be temporarily high. Conversely, when earnings contain a positive transitory component, both price-earnings ratios and next year's expected growth will be temporarily low. Hence, price earnings and subsequent growth will be positively correlated.[8]

In sum then, market prices act as if earnings are perceived to contain a transitory component. Moreover, the actual behavior of earnings confirms this perception. In other words, earnings per share behaves as if earnings have a transitory component, which is caused by events that have an impact on current earnings but affect expected future earnings only partially or not at all. Research by Hayn (1995) shows that the earnings sensitivity coefficient is lower for firms reporting losses rather than positive net income. Losses are not as permanent as positive net income. Also, special charges in earnings (such as restructuring charges, divestitures of a division, asset sales) can have a large impact on one quarter or one year's earnings. Yet the stock prices respond in a highly contextual manner to the special charges. In many cases, there is no stock price reaction at all, because the charge represents "old news." In some cases, announcement of large losses are accompanied by price increases. On the average, earnings sensitivity coefficients based on earnings that include special charges show a much lower sensitivity than those based on earnings before the inclusion of such charges (Collins, Maydew, and Weiss 1996). The earnings sensitivity coefficient varies across firms. Kormendi and Lipe (1987), Easton and Zmijewski (1989), and Collins and Kothari (1989) show that the earnings response coefficient varies not only with persistence but also with growth, risk, and the level of interest rates.

5-3 SECURITY PRICES AND DIFFERENCES IN ACCOUNTING METHODS

Changes in accounting methods are another reason for a less than one-to-one relationship between price changes and earnings changes. These events may permanently affect the level of accounting earnings but not in a way that implies a change in the value of the security. The nature of the financial accounting system is a major contributor to

---

[8]The transitory component in earnings has also been documented by Penman (1996).

such events. For example, a firm may change its method of accounting for depreciation. This can produce a change in earnings that is "permanent" in the sense that the level of earnings is expected to be permanently affected as long as the firm continues to grow, but it may not be an event that alters the firm's dividend-paying ability.

Firms are permitted to use different accounting methods (for example, straight-line or accelerated depreciation methods) that affect the level of accounting earnings. For example, firms with net growth in asset acquisitions will report higher net income under straight-line depreciation than under accelerated depreciation. This induces a difference in the level of earnings across firms that is unrelated to the future dividend-paying ability of the firm. Price-earnings ratios of firms that use different depreciation methods would be expected to differ, after taking into account other reasons for differing price-earnings ratios. Empirical evidence by Beaver and Dukes (1973) suggests that price-earnings ratios systematically differ as a function of the depreciation method used for annual report purposes. The results are summarized in Table 5-4. The method used for tax purposes is accelerated depreciation, and the difference refers to the depreciation method used for annual reports purposes only. In particular, firms that use accelerated depreciation would be expected to have lower earnings and hence higher price-earnings ratios than firms that use straight-line depreciation, assuming risk, growth, and other things are equal.

The evidence indicates that firms using accelerated depreciation, on the average, do in fact have higher price-earnings ratios (16.61 versus 15.08). Moreover, an analysis of other factors indicates that there were no differences between the two groups with respect to risk or earnings growth. In fact, on the average, the firms using accelerated depreciation had essentially the same risk and growth as firms

TABLE 5-4 Differences in Price-Earnings Ratios, Risk, and Earnings Growth for Firms Using Accelerated Versus Straight-Line Depreciation

| | DEPRECIATION GROUP | | | |
| | ACCELERATED | | STRAIGHT-LINE | |
VARIABLE	MEAN	STANDARD DEVIATION	MEAN	STANDARD DEVIATION
Market beta[a]	1.003	0.25	1.009	0.33
Average price earnings ratio[b]	16.61	6.72	15.08	3.82
Earnings growth[c]	0.043	0.11	0.045	0.10

[a]*Computed from a time series regression of monthly security return data from January 1950 through December 1967.*
[b]*Computed as the median of the ratio of price per share divided by earnings per share at fiscal year-end based on annual data from 1950 through 1967.*
[c]*Computed as annual rate of growth in earnings available for common stockholders assuming continuous compounding over the 18-year interval from 1950 through 1967.*
Source: Beaver and Dukes (1973), Table 2. Reprinted with permission.

using straight-line depreciation. Moreover, when the earnings of the firms using straight-line depreciation were converted to the earnings that would have been reported had accelerated depreciation been used, the differences in price-earnings ratios essentially disappeared. The average price-earnings ratio increased to 16.2 when the earnings of the straight-line group were computed under accelerated depreciation. In other words, when the earnings of the firms using straight-line depreciation were converted to an accounting basis equivalent to that of the firms using accelerated depreciation, the price-earnings ratios of the two groups of firms were essentially the same. This is consistent with a security price formation process that adjusts for differences in the level of earnings induced by accounting method differences. If prices are not dependent on the method of accounting used but accounting earnings are, the ratio of price to earnings will be dependent on the method of accounting used. Price-earnings ratios computed under differing accounting methods will also differ, even though price-earnings ratios computed under a consistent, uniform method of accounting would show no difference in price-earnings ratios.

Archibald (1972) has examined the security price behavior at times when firms changed their method of depreciation for annual report purposes from accelerated to straight-line. Prices behave as if the change in methods has no favorable impact on security prices, even though earnings are greater under the new method than they otherwise would have been. Hong, Kaplan, and Mandelker (1978) conclude that the use of the pooling treatment of accounting for business combinations produced no apparent superior stock price performance relative to that of firms that used the purchase treatment of accounting for their business combinations, even though pooling will lead to higher reported earnings than the purchase treatment. Dukes (1976) finds that security price behaves as if investors implicitly regard research and development expenditures as assets, even though the firm entirely expensed these expenditures for annual report purposes. Lev and Sougainnis (1996) reach a similar conclusion, although they also offer evidence that the market may not fully adjust.

This evidence is consistent with the contention that prices behave as if investors "look beyond" reported accounting earnings and attempt to make adjustments for the effects of events on earnings that do not imply altered dividend-paying ability. The adjustment process appears to include adjusting for differences in earnings among firms induced by using different accounting methods (for example, depreciation method differences and purchase versus pooling), using the same accounting method (for example, research and development), and changing methods of accounting (for example, depreciation method).

Choice of Accounting Method: A Contracting Perspective

The changes in accounting methods discussed previously were treated as if they had no effect on the dividend-paying ability of the firm and hence no effect on the price of common equity. Clearly not all accounting changes would have that property.

For example, changes in accounting methods for financial reporting purposes that were accompanied by similar changes for tax purposes could well be expected to affect the after-tax cash flow of the firm and hence future dividend-paying ability. The switch of inventory valuation methods from FIFO to LIFO is often cited as an example of such an accounting change. The choice of accounting method may constitute a signal, which permits the firm to distinguish itself from firms that choose other methods. Under this signaling interpretation, the event could have informational value and affect security prices. More generally, a change in accounting methods can affect stock price if it is perceived to alter the production or financing activities of the firm in such a way as to alter the expected after-tax future cash flows.

The contracting hypothesis focuses on particular ways in which changes in accounting methods can alter the production and financing activities. The contracting hypothesis argues that the firm is affected by a number of "contracts" that are defined in terms of accounting numbers. As a result, a change in accounting method can be expected to alter the numbers in such a way that the economic impact of that contract is affected. Compensation plans and debt covenants are two major examples. More subtle, yet potentially important, effects can be induced by implicit, social contracts that in turn permit changes in accounting methods to induce changes in "political costs" borne by the firm.

Watts and Zimmerman (1986, 1990) describe the contracting hypothesis and summarize the empirical evidence with respect to stock price effects. They view the evidence as generally consistent with all three hypotheses, but acknowledge the desirability of more powerful tests and for the desirability of treating the choice as one among many endogenous factors. To the extent that choice of accounting method is a natural evolution of multiperiod contracting, the valuation implications are often not clear.

5-4 EARNINGS, CASH FLOW, AND ACCRUALS

Several studies have examined the price reaction to the cash flow and accrual components of earnings changes. The accrual component is the difference between earnings and cash flow.

Ball and Brown (1968) analyze residual "cash flow" changes and found that they were not as successful as residual earnings changes in predicting the sign of residual price changes.[9] One difficulty in interpreting these results is that earnings and cash flow variables tend to be highly correlated and, as a result, distinguishing differences in information content is difficult. Wilson (1986, 1987) examines a sample of firms where cash flow data were announced subsequent to earnings. Wilson finds that these data do have an incremental impact over and above that provided by

---

[9]The definition of "cash flow" varies across studies. For example, some studies define it as cash flows from operations, whereas others adopt a more comprehensive measure that includes cash flows from investment and financing activities.

earnings. Bernard and Stober (1989) find that the information content of cash flow and accrual numbers varies with economic conditions. Sloan (1996) concludes that the market does not assign significantly different sensitivity coefficients to the accrual and cash flow components of a residual earnings change, even though the cash flow component appears to contain a more permanent component than the accrual component does.

5-5 PRICES ANTICIPATE EARNINGS— TIMELINESS OF EARNINGS

The studies by Benston (1966) and Ball and Brown (1968), among others, indicate that much of the price reaction associated with earnings occurs prior to the announcement of annual earnings, and they provide important evidence on the issue of the timeliness of earnings.

This "anticipatory" effect is consistent with the notion that prices reflect earnings expectations and is illustrated in Figure 5-1. The Ball and Brown study is based on annual earnings announcements. The set of lines in the upper half of Figure 5-1 shows the cumulative, residual price change in the months surrounding the announcement of positive residual earnings changes (month 0). The positive slope indicates that residual price changes are positive for several months prior to the announcement. In fact, only a small proportion of total price movement occurs in the month of the announcement. The announcements of negative residual earnings change as shown in the bottom half of Figure 5-1. Of course, here the slope is negative. Again, much of the downward drift has occurred by the month of the announcement. Overall, only 10% of the cumulative price movement occurs in the month of the announcement.

This effect is not surprising because there is other information being publicly released during the year that permits investors to revise their predictions of annual earnings. Quarterly earnings, quarterly dividends, and earnings forecasts by analysts and management are examples. This evidence, among others, has led to the interpretation (Benston 1976) that annual earnings are not timely information and are preempted by alternative, more timely sources.

Although a portion of earnings information may be preempted by earlier, more timely announcements, a significant price reaction does occur in the week of the announcement of annual earnings (Beaver 1968). The study focuses on price movements without attempting to specify the direction of the price changes, as the Benston and the Ball and Brown studies do. Figure 5-2 reports the magnitude of the residual price change, ignoring its sign, in the week of the announcement relative to other weeks during the year. There is an obviously large "spike" at week 0 (the week of the announcement). This finding means that large price changes (in either direction) are more likely to occur during the week of the annual earnings announcement than at other times during the year. Roughly speaking, the average

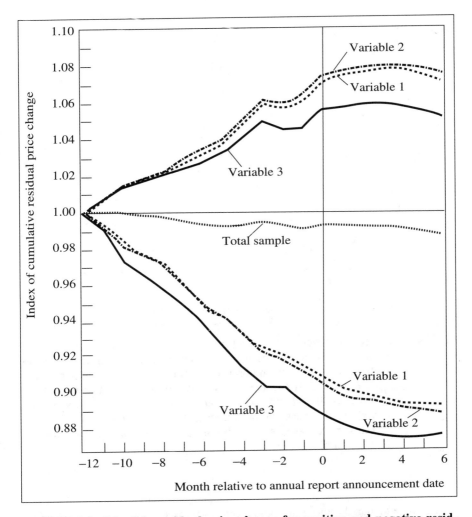

FIGURE 5-1 **Monthly residual price change for positive and negative residual earnings changes. The top set of lines represents the cumulative residual price change associated with positive residual earnings changes measured three ways (variables 1 through 3). The bottom set of lines represents the cumulative residual price changes associated with negative residual earnings changes measured three ways. The cumulative residual price changes start with a hypothetical portfolio of 1.00 (for example, $1) 12 months prior to the announcement. The graph shows the value of that portfolio over time.**

Source: Ball and Brown (1968), Figure 1, p. 169.

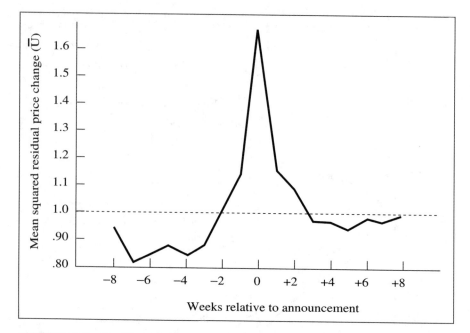

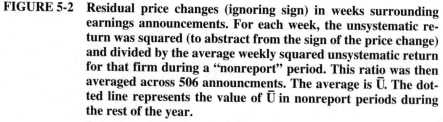

FIGURE 5-2 **Residual price changes (ignoring sign) in weeks surrounding earnings announcements. For each week, the unsystematic return was squared (to abstract from the sign of the price change) and divided by the average weekly squared unsystematic return for that firm during a "nonreport" period. This ratio was then averaged across 506 announcments. The average is $\bar{U}$. The dotted line represents the value of $\bar{U}$ in nonreport periods during the rest of the year.**
Source: Beaver (1968), Figure 6, p. 91.

price change (squared) during the announcement week is approximately 167% of a "normal" or average price change (squared) during other weeks in the year.[10]

Later studies have examined these relationships using daily data. Applying the Ball and Brown research design to the days surrounding the annual (and quarterly) earnings announcements, Foster (1978) finds a small, but statistically significant residual price change the day before and day of the earnings announcement. This price movement is illustrated in Figure 5-3. Applying an approach similar to Beaver, Morse (1981) also finds a statistically significant price reaction the day before and day of the earnings announcement. As illustrated in Figure 5-4, the price

---

[10]Beaver (1968) examined the number of shares traded as well as price volatility surrounding earnings announcement dates. A formal treatment of information, price changes, and trading volume appears in Holthausen and Verrecchia (1990).

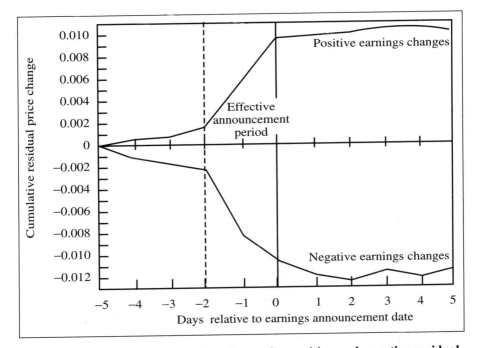

FIGURE 5-3 **Daily residual price change for positive and negative residual earnings changes. The graph represents a composite across all four quarters. The results for the annual earnings and for each of the other three quarterly announcements are similar to the composite. The graph uses zero as the initial value and sums the residual percentage price changes.**

Source: Financial Statement Analysis by Foster, G., © 1978. Reprinted by permission of Prentice-Hall, Inc., Upper Saddle River, NJ.

reaction on each day is approximately 40% larger than during an average day when no earnings are reported.

Morse and prior studies used the day the earnings announcement appeared in the *Wall Street Journal* as the announcement day. Many earnings announcements are released over the Dow-Jones newswire the day before the article appears in the *Wall Street Journal*. Patell and Wolfson (1984) have examined stock price reactions to earnings on an intraday (transaction-by-transaction) price data. They find that a significant reaction to the earnings announcement as it is released over the broad tape. The frequency of extreme price changes is over five times greater during the hour of the earnings announcement than during nonreport hours.

A major portion of the reaction occurred within two hours of the announcement, but with detectable traces for an additional two hours. Some price effects continue into the next day and are more likely on announcements made late in the trading day. An important implication is that the earnings announcement itself does

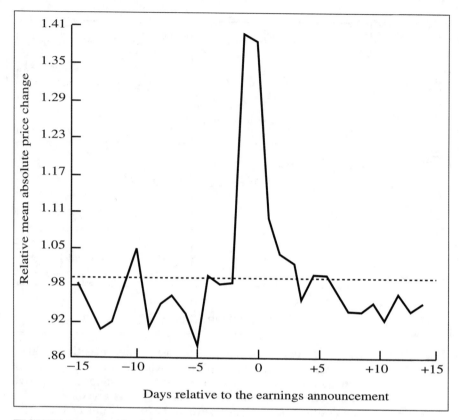

FIGURE 5-4   **Residual price changes (ignoring sign) in days surrounding earnings announcements. Mean absolute price change is similar to $\bar{U}$ as described in Figure 5–2, except the absolute value, rather than squaring, is used to abstract from the sign. The dotted line represents the sample average, which has been indexed to 1.0.**

Source: Morse (1981), Figure 1.

provide information to the market—the preemption is not complete.[11] The Patell and Wolfson study and its implications for market efficiency are discussed in greater length in Chapter 6.

Measurement Error in the Earnings Forecast Error

Prices act as if earnings announcements alter investors' beliefs in such a way as to alter the price of the security. These results may appear paradoxical when compared

[11]Even over small windows of time, it cannot be assumed that the only announcement made is the earnings announcement. Newswires announcing earnings often contain other information as well.

with the Ball and Brown findings. However, the resolution of the paradox is relatively simple. The anticipatory price movements indicate that earnings expectations are being revised as other information is being disseminated. For example, this involves an incorporation of quarterly earnings, as well as earnings forecasts by management and analysts, announcements of litigation, contracts awarded, and in principle all information reflected in prices. This more timely information naturally preempts some of the information content of earnings.

However, there is a byproduct that affects a researcher's measured reactions of prices to earnings. The market is constantly updating its forecast of earnings conditional on the prior information. If the researcher does not update the earnings forecast, an out-of-date benchmark is being used and the forecast error is measuring unexpected earnings with error. For example, predicting the direction of the price change in the *month* of an earnings announcement involves an inclusion of information available up to the beginning of the *month* of announcement. Predicting the direction of the change in price in the *week* of an earnings announcement involves a consideration of information on which earnings expectations were based as of the beginning of the *week* of the announcement. Similarly, predicting the direction of the change in price in the *day* of an earnings announcement involves a consideration of information on which earnings expectations were based as of the beginning of the *day* of the announcement. By contrast, a measure of price changes ignoring sign does not require an earnings expectation model to be used.

If the earnings expectations models were not updated for information coming onto the market during the year, the earnings expectations models are becoming increasingly misspecified as the announcement month approaches. A residual earnings change, defined relative to a benchmark in which the most recent firm-specific information is last year's earnings, has limited ability to predict the direction of the price change in the final month of the announcement.

In sum, earnings are one source of information that alters security prices, although they are only one of many such sources. How important are earnings? The answer depends on the perspective taken. One way to view the relative importance of earnings is to consider a pie chart such as that in Figure 5-5. The pie represents all the sources of information that alter or affect security prices. Earnings represent one small slice of the pie. However, the pie consists of many small slices (indicated by dashed lines), and no one slice is very large. In one sense, earnings are not important because they represent only a small portion of the total. But in another sense, earnings are very important, in that their slice may be at least as large as any other slice in the pie, particularly if the price reaction to a type of announcement is considered in terms of the frequency of occurrence of that type. Moreover, the other data may be sources of information about earnings. If earnings are viewed as important information, investors naturally would attempt to obtain other information that would permit them to predict earnings. It would be somewhat anomalous if earnings were deemed to be unimportant merely because investors were obtaining other data that permitted them to successfully predict earnings.

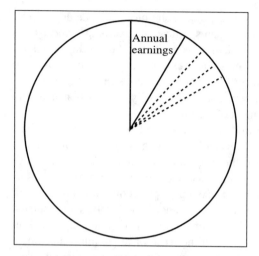

FIGURE 5-5   **Earnings relative to all
other information.**

5-6   SECURITY PRICES AS PREDICTORS
OF ACCOUNTING EARNINGS—
THE INFORMATION CONTENT OF PRICES

The empirical evidence regarding the relation between security prices and earnings presented thus far has treated earnings as a predictor (an explanatory variable) for prices. This is a natural way to view the relationship because earnings are typically viewed as one source of information used in assessing dividend-paying ability, which in part determines security price. However, recent research has turned around the familiar price and earnings relation and has used price as a predictor of accounting earnings.

As discussed in Chapter 4, prices at any given time can be viewed as if they are a function of future, expected earnings. Prices reflect investors' expectations regarding value-relevant factors, including future earnings. If prices are based on an information system with many signals other than current and past earnings, prices can potentially reflect information about future earnings that is not reflected in current and past earnings. For example, prices may respond before earnings to certain events or information. A mineral discovery and news about an anticipated strike next year are two examples.

If prices are viewed as "reflecting" other information, then prices can be used as a surrogate or proxy for that information. This perspective has led to research that examines the information content of prices with respect to future earnings. Beaver, Lambert, and Morse (1980) indicate that price-based forecasting models of earnings can predict future earnings "better" (with a lower mean error) than forecasting models based on a statistical extrapolation of past and current earnings. A widely used statistical model for forecasting earnings using current and past earnings data is called the random walk with a drift model. Under this model, next year's earnings are forecast to be equal to this year's earnings plus a drift term equal to the average change in earnings over some past period. Beaver, Lambert, and Morse (1980) use a price-based forecasting model that results in lower forecasting errors than the random walk with a drift model.

Beaver, Lambert, and Ryan (1987) extend this work by examining the relation between percentage changes in price and future percentage changes in earnings. Beaver, Lambert, and Ryan explain current percentage change in earnings as a linear function of current percentage change in prices and lagged percentage change in prices. The coefficients on both percentage change in price variables are positive and significant. The coefficient on last year's price change provides a basis for forecasting earnings based on price changes. Price changes lead earnings changes, and earnings reflects some economic events on a delayed basis relative to when prices reflect the effects of those events. At least a component of earnings is not timely relative to the information reflected in prices. This conclusion is further supported by the research of Collins, Kothari, Shanken, and Sloan (1994).

Price and earnings can be also be viewed as being simultaneously determined by a underlying set of information. In this setting, prices change for reasons unrelated to earnings, earnings change for reasons unrelated to prices, and both can be viewed as endogenously determined by a more primitive set of exogenous information variables. In this sense, neither is the predictor of the other in a literal sense. Beaver, McAnally, and Stinson (1997) adopt a simultaneous equations approach to estimating the price change–earnings change relation and find evidence consistent with simultaneity.

5-7 DELAYED RECOGNITION

A major feature of financial reporting under historical cost is delayed recognition. The reliance of generally accepted accounting principles (GAAP) on historical cost accounting induces substantial lags in the book values of assets and common equity relative to economic values and to market value. This feature of historical cost accounting is known as *delayed recognition*. Delayed recognition can induce substantial lags in the accounting numbers relative to security prices. As a result, the information content of prices with respect to accounting data may be greater than the one-year lead found in Beaver, Lambert, and Ryan.

Ryan (1995) constructs a model of delayed recognition that arises from a historical cost accounting for depreciable assets.[12] The economic value of the asset can

---

[12]Another example is investment securities in which the fair value of those securities changes subsequent to purchase. Under historical cost accounting, these unrealized gains and losses are deferred until the securities are sold. Statement of Financial Accounting Standards No. 115 has addressed this problem by requiring fair values for investment securities held for trading purposes and held available for sale.

change as the assessed expected value of the remaining cash flows changes. The economic value can be thought of as the present value of the expected future cash flows. Market values or fair values would respond to these changes in economic value quickly. However, the book value of depreciable assets equals the original cost less the accumulated depreciation, based on a depreciation expense schedule established at the outset of the asset's life. The difference between economic value and book value can be viewed as an unrealized gain or loss.

The historical cost system eventually reflects the unrealized gain or loss over the life of the depreciable asset. It does so implicitly via the depreciation expense. Specifically, suppose that a firm consists of a single depreciable asset. At acquisition, this asset has a market and book value of $1,000, a useful life of five years, and a zero salvage value. For simplicity, assume the asset depreciates both economically and for accounting purposes on a straight-line basis. That is, economic depreciation is *expected* to be $200 per year when the asset is acquired, whereas historical cost depreciation will be $200 per year regardless of subsequent events. Suppose that by end of the first year, the economic value of the asset is $960, because the present value of future expected cash flows for years 2 through 5 are now $960. The economic value of $960 exceeds the book value of $800, and an unrealized gain on the asset of $160 has occurred. In economic terms, the asset is expected to subsequently depreciate at $240 per year. The $40 difference of economic depreciation from historical cost depreciation ($240 − $200) is the portion of the unrealized gain that is implicitly recognized via understated depreciation in each subsequent year.[13] Under historical cost, the cumulative net income after depreciation expense is higher than it would be under economic depreciation by $160. In contrast, a fair value system would record the $160 gain at the end of year 1 and charge $240 a year depreciation expense in years 2 through 5. Extending this analysis to a multi-asset firm with acquisitions of depreciable assets over a number of years leads to basically the same conclusion. Historical cost induces substantial lags in the book value of assets and economic value of those assets, and the difference between the book value and market value of common equity is equal to the unrecognized gains and losses. The lag is equal to the useful life of the assets.

Ryan (1995) and Beaver and Ryan (1996) provide empirical evidence on the effects of delayed recognition. By assuming that the market value of common equity is equal to the economic value, an expression is derived relating book value and market value of equity. In particular,

$$BV_t = MV_t - \sum_{j=0}^{J} (\beta_j * \Delta MV_{t-j}) \quad \text{for } j = 0, J$$

[13]In this illustration, it is assumed to occur on a straight-line basis. However, regardless of the depreciation method assumed, the full $160 will be implicitly recognized over the remaining four years of the useful life of the asset. Of course, if the asset is sold before the end of its useful life, the net unrealized gain will be recognized at the time of sale.

or dividing both sides by MV_t

$$BV_t / MV_t = \alpha - \sum_{j=0}^{J} ((\beta_j * \Delta MV_{t-j}) / MV_t) \quad \text{for } j = 0, J$$

where BV_t is the book value of common equity in year t, $MV_t (\Delta MV_{t-j})$ is the (change in) market value of common equity in year t $(t - j)$, and J is the economic life of the depreciable assets. β_j is the proportion of the unrealized gain (or loss) that occurred j years ago, but still remains unrecognized as of year t. In a simple, idealized world, α equals one but empirically reflects the net effects of other factors on the differences between book value and market value, such as conservative accounting policy.

The expression leads to several empirical predictions. (1) The book-to-market ratio in year t is a function of lagged changes in market value of equity (in other words, the β_j is expected to be statistically significant). (2) The β coefficients are expected to be positive. (3) The β coefficients are expected to be between zero and one, because they reflect the *proportion* of unrecognized gains and losses. (4) The β coefficients are expected to decline as j increases. In other words, a greater proportion of an unrealized gain that occurred one year ago remains unrecognized relative to the remaining unrecognized gain that occurred two years ago. (5) The β coefficients are expected to be higher for depreciable assets with higher J. The longer the useful life, the more the unrecognized gain (or loss) after one year. (6) The β coefficients are expected to decay to zero later for assets with higher J.

The analysis predicts that the lagged behavior is due to the historical cost treatment of depreciable assets and is a function of the estimated useful lives of those assets. The coefficients are expected to vary with the relative importance of depreciable assets in the asset structure of a firm. The sample of firms is divided into subsamples based on the average estimated useful lives. The sample of firms with longer-lived assets are predicted to have estimated coefficients on the current and lagged market value changes that are larger and decay to zero more slowly than those firms with shorter-lived assets.

Two proxies for the average estimated useful life of assets are chosen. The first proxy is the ratio of net property, plant, and equipment to total assets (net PPE/Assets), which is the proportion of long-lived depreciable assets held by the firm. A firm with a greater proportion of depreciable assets is expected to have assets with a longer average useful life. The second proxy is the ratio of gross property, plant, and equipment to depreciation (gross PPE/Depreciation Expense), which is an estimate of the useful life of depreciable assets.

The ratio of the book value of equity to the market value of equity (in other words, BV/MV from the equation) is estimated as a function of the current and six lagged annual market value changes. The market value changes are expressed as a percentage of the current market value of common equity.[14] Figure 5-6 compares the coefficients (β) for the shortest-lived and longest-lived groups.[15]

Consistent with the first prediction, the changes in the market value of equity over the prior six years are significant factors in explaining differences in book-to-market ratios in a given year.[16] To understand the current book-to-market ratio, movements in the market value of common equity over the past six years must be considered. In other words, market values of common equity lead the book value of common equity for as much as six years. This is striking evidence of delayed recognition and the timeliness (or lack thereof) of book values based on historical cost accounting. Consistent with the second prediction, all of the coefficients are positive; and consistent with the third prediction, all of the coefficients are between zero and one. The coefficient has the natural interpretation that it is a percentage of the unrecognized gains or losses that occurred j years ago that remain unrecognized in the current year.

As stated in the fourth prediction, the magnitude of the coefficients declines as the lags increase. As predicted (fifth prediction), the coefficients on the current and lagged market value changes for the longer-lived subsample are higher. For example, 58% of the gain or loss is not reflected in book value by the end of the year in which it occurs for the longest-lived group, whereas only 32% remains unrecognized for the shortest-lived group. This pattern continues for the other years as well. For example, for unrealized gains and losses that occurred a year earlier, 45% remains unrecognized for the longest-lived group, whereas only 24% remains unrecognized for the shortest-lived group. For unrecognized gains that occurred six years earlier, 14% remains unrecognized for the longest-lived group, whereas only 6% remains unrecognized for the shortest-lived group. Consistent with the sixth and final prediction, the coefficients decay to zero sooner for the shortest-lived group. At the six year lag, the coefficient is not significantly different from zero for the shortest-lived group, whereas the coefficient still is significantly different from zero for the longest-lived group. An insignificant coefficient for the shortest-lived group implies that the gains and losses that occurred six years ago that remain unrecognized are not significantly different from zero. Although not reported in Figure 5-6, the coefficients for the longest-lived group for lags higher than six years are significant.

To understand the current book-to-market ratio, lagged changes in market values of up to at least six years must be incorporated into the analysis, and probably even longer for firms with longer-lived assets. These results document the delayed recognition and lack of timeliness of book values based on historical cost valuations.

---

[14]Only six lagged market value changes are included in the empirical model, even though many firms clearly have depreciable assets with longer useful lives, because including further lagged market value changes would diminish the time-series observations available for estimation.

[15]The longest-lived sample is defined as those firms with an above-average ratio of property, plant, and equipment to total assets and with an above-average ratios of property, plant, and equipment to depreciation. The shortest-lived sample is those firms with a below-average ratio of property, plant, and equipment to total assets.

[16]All of the coefficients reported in Figure 5-6 are statisitically different from zero at the 95% confidence level, with one exception—the coefficient in year 6 for the shortest-lived group.

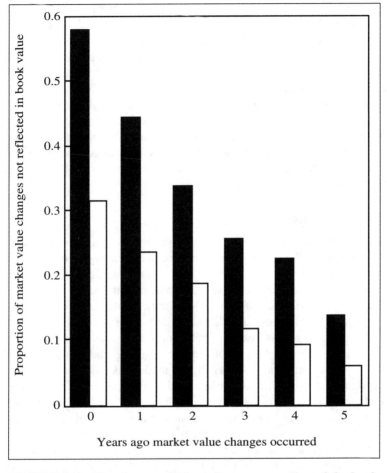

FIGURE 5-6 **The slope coefficients from a regression of the book-to-market ratio on current (year 0) and lagged (years 1 through 5) changes in market value. ■ denotes coefficients for sample of firms with longest-lived assets. ☐ denotes coefficients for firms with shortest-lived assets.**
Source: Beaver and Ryan (1993), Figure B, p. 54.

5-8 CONSERVATISM

Conservatism (biased recognition) is considered to be a major feature of financial reporting. Conservatism is a property commonly attributed to financial statements under GAAP. Prominent examples of conservatism under GAAP are lower of cost or market for inventories, the recording of contingent losses but not contingent gains (FAS No. 5), and the expensing of advertising and many types of research and development (R & D) expenditures in the year of expenditure. Staubus (1985) surveyed financial reporting standards and concludes that conservatism is a major component of approximately one-third of the standards. Conservatism also arises from voluntary practices, such as choice of LIFO inventory valuation or the use of deprecation methods more accelerated than economic depreciation.

Conservatism can also arise to the extent that firms systematically invest in positive net present value (NPV) projects. The excess present value is eventually reflected in the cash flow and earnings stream of the firm, but historical cost accounting does not permit that excess expected NPV to be recognized at the time of acquisition. A major issue is how conservative accounting policies affect the relation between earnings, book value, and market value.

Definition of Conservative Behavior

In simplest terms, conservative behavior involves choosing lower (rather than higher) revenues, higher (than lower) expenses, and recognizing unrealized losses but not unrealized gains. However, there is also a timing dimension to the choice not reflected in this definition. The sum of income over the life of the firm (or over the life cycle of some series of transactions) must be the same regardless of accounting choice.[17] What constitutes "conservative" earnings behavior in one period may imply "nonconservative" earnings behavior in some later period. For example, fully expensing an item in the year of acquisition implies that no expenses will be recorded in subsequent periods. This will lead to lower net income in the period of the expenditure but higher net income in the subsequent periods. An alternative definition of conservative accounting method adopts a balance sheet perspective. Under this view, a more conservative accounting method produced a lower book value of equity than a less conservative method.

From this valuation perspective, an accounting method can be labeled conservative or not depending on the relation of the reported amounts to some notion of economic value. Consider the example of fully expensing an expenditure in the year of acquisition. Full expensing will lead to conservative accounting if the asset has any residual value at the end of the year of acquisition. A similar, but less extreme, example is when accounting depreciation exceeds economic depreciation. To pursue the analysis of Chapter 3, sum-of-the-years-digits depreciation could be conservative for some assets but not for others, depending on the pattern of the net cash flows (and hence present value) over the life of the asset. For the asset example displayed in Table 3-3, sum-of-the-years-digits depreciation could be conservative because economic depreciation for the asset is straight-line depreciation.

This brief discussion only begins to explore the various dimensions of conservatism. Not surprisingly, as with many of the primitive notions in financial accounting, there are ambiguities associated with the use of the term *conservatism*.

---

[17]Implicit in this statement is identity, the "clean surplus" condition discussed in Chapter 4.

Empirical Evidence of Conservatism

As discussed in section 5-3, Beaver and Dukes find that price-earnings ratios systematically vary with depreciation method. Hence, the evidence is consistent with market participants at least partially adjusting for differences in more conservative versus less conservative depreciation methods. However, depreciation differences are only one dimension of conservative reporting.

Although certain aspects of conservative accounting are apparent, such as use of LIFO, use of accelerated depreciation, expensing of R & D expenditures, many other aspects are not, such as excess present value projects and conservative estimates of uncollectible accounts receivable. For example, determining whether a firm follows a policy of a conservative estimate of net accounts receivable is not a straightforward exercise (McNichols and Wilson 1988). However, one empirical manifestation of conservative behavior is persistence of book value below market value over a number of years, in a manner that cannot be explained by delayed recognition.

If conservative accounting policies are empirically important, the average book-to-market (BTM) ratio is predicted to be less than one, because book value will persistently be below market value of equity. Beaver and Ryan (1993) find a median BTM ratio of .73 for 1974 to 1993. Similarly, Penman (1996) finds a median BTM ratio of .85 for 1968 to 1985. Delayed recognition could explain a BTM ratio different from one for some firms in some years, but the average effect of delayed recognition across a number of firms and years is zero. Rather than attempt to look at explicit measures of conservatism, Beaver and Ryan infer conservative behavior from the observed BTM ratio and measure conservatism as the BTM ratio different from one that persists and cannot be explained by delayed recognition (in other words, by lagged changes in market value).

Beaver and Ryan decompose the BTM ratio into two components, a component due to delayed recognition and a component due to conservatism. Based on this decomposition, they forecast future earnings, as measured by return on equity (ROE). As predicted, firms in which the BTM ratio is dominated by delayed recognition show a difference in ROE, and the difference decays over time as the gains and losses are eventually recognized in earnings and book value. In contrast, those firms whose BTM ratio is dominated by conservatism (or biased recognition) have an initial difference in ROE, but these do not decay over time because differences induced by conservative accounting produce permanent differences in book values and earnings, as reflected in Table 3-7 of Chapter 3.

5-9 BOOK VALUE ALSO EXPLAINS SECURITY PRICES

Although much of the security price research has focused on the relation between prices and earnings, several empirical studies have adopted a balance sheet approach to relating accounting data to equity valuation. Under this approach, the market value of equity (MVE) equals the sum of the market values of assets (MVA) less the sum of the market value of liabilities (MVL). By virtue of the accounting identity, the book value of common equity (BVE) equals the book value of assets (BVA) less the book value of liabilities (BVL). The difference between market value and book value of equity (called the cumulative unrecognized gain or loss) is equal to the sum of the unrecognized gains (or losses) on each of the assets and liabilities.

In a simple setting of perfect and complete markets, market value of equity is a linear function of the market values of the individual assets and liabilities. If there were no measurement error in book values, market value of equity would be a linear function of the book values, where the implied intercept (α) is zero, the implied coefficient on each asset and liability component (β) is one, and there is nothing left to be explained (in other words, the residual term, $u = 0$).[18] However, in general the market value of individual assets is not equal to its book value, and the difference is called measurement error. In the presence of measurement error, the intercept term can be nonzero, the slopes can be different from one, and the residual term is nonzero.[19] Empirically, regressions explain the market value of equity as a linear function of the book value of assets and liabilities with an intercept and residual term included.

Empirical Evidence

The evidence indicates that both assets and liabilities are significantly priced by the market. For example, Barth, Beaver, and Landsman (1993) find that assets have a significant positive coefficient, whereas liabilities have a significant negative coef-

---

[18]More formally, for a firm with J assets and K liabilities:

$$MVE = \sum_{j=1}^{J} MVA_j - \sum_{k=1}^{K} MVL_k \text{ (the valuation relation)}$$

$$BVE = \sum_{j=1}^{J} BVA - \sum_{k=1}^{K} BVL \text{ (the book value identity)}$$

$$MVE - BVE = (\sum_{j=1}^{J} MVA - \sum_{j=1}^{J} BVA) - (\sum_{k=1}^{K} MVL - \sum_{k=1}^{K} BVL) \text{ (the difference)}$$

$$BVA_j = d_j + g_j MVA_j + e_j \text{ (measurement error in assets)}$$

$$BVL_k = d_k + g_k MVL_k + e_k \text{ (measurement error in liabilities)}$$

$$MVE = a + \sum_{j=1}^{J} b_j BVA_j - \sum_{k=1}^{K} b_k BVL_k + u \text{ (empirical estimation equation)}$$

[19]The magnitude of the intercept and slope coefficients will depend on the structure of the error term. In particular, they will depend on how error terms of various asset and liabilities items are correlated with one another. An extreme example of measurement error is an omitted asset or liability, where the book value is zero.

ficient. However, the coefficients are not equal to one and vary among asset and liability accounts. For example, the nonperforming assets portion of a bank's loan portfolio is assigned a significantly lower coefficient than the rest of the loan portfolio (Beaver, Eger, Ryan, and Wolfson 1989).[20] This would be expected because of measurement error in the net book value of loans induced by GAAP, which does not permit the recording of some aspects of the economic impairment of the loan, such as lost future interest income from the loan.

Evidence indicates that unrecorded assets and liabilities are also priced. Research by Landsman (1986), Barth (1991), and Barth, Beaver, and Landsman (1992, 1993) finds that an unrecognized portion of pension assets and liabilities (unrecorded but disclosed in the footnotes) is priced by the market in ways that imply that the market regards the pension assets as assets of the company and pension obligations as liabilities.

The balance sheet approach has also been applied to the fair value of financial instruments, which is disclosed in the footnotes in annual reports. Barth, Beaver, and Landsman (1996a) find that a significant portion of the cumulative unrecognized gains on common equity can be explained by the unrecognized gains (the difference between the disclosed fair value and the recognized book value) on loans, investment securities, and long-term debt, although the same does not hold for deposits and off-balance sheet items. In addition, several proxies for unrecorded intangible assets, such as core deposits, are also significant in addition to the unrecorded fair value gains and losses.

In many respects, the balance sheet approach is at the other end of the continuum from an earnings approach to valuation. The balance sheet approach is plausible to apply to some industries (for example, banks, which consist largely of financial claims) or for some issues (for example, pensions, which are essentially financial assets and liabilities). However, in general, income would be expected to be a significant valuation variable. Barth, Beaver, and Landsman (1993, 1996a) include net income as an additional variable. In both cases, while net income is significant, the balance sheet variables remain significant.

Book Value and Earnings—Empirical Evidence

In these studies the empirical estimation equation incorporates both book value and earnings variables. In its simplest form, there are only two explanatory variables: one balance sheet variable (the book value of equity) and one income variable (net

---

[20]Essentially, nonperforming assets consist of (1) loans that are at least 90 days delinquent; (2) loans that have been restructured because of financial difficulty; (3) loans, although current, whose future principal payments are in serious doubt (the so-called performing, nonperforming loans); and (4) other real estate owned (properties obtained in foreclosure). Nonperforming assets are more comprehensive than nonperforming loans, which includes only categories 1 through 3. However, the two variables are highly correlated, and specification tests on selected analyses indicate no differences in findings.

income). The Feltham–Ohlson model discussed in Chapter 4 provides one motivation for this approach. If the coefficient on a particular financial statement variable is significant and of the predicted sign, market prices act as if that variable is being priced conditional on the other variables in the equation and that item is defined as *value relevant*. The interpretation of value relevance is subject to the same caveats discussed earlier regarding correlated omitted variables.

Both book value and earnings are significant value-relevant factors. For example, Barth, Beaver, and Landsman (1993) report that book value of assets, book value of liabilities, and net income are all significant factors, explaining approximately 75 to 80% of the variation in market value of equity. Barth, Beaver, and Landsman (1996b) find that the relative importance of the book value and earnings varies by industry and by degree of financial difficulty. For industries in which intangible assets are relatively more important, such as pharmaceuticals, the income statement is relatively more important. For industries in which the intangible assets are relatively smaller, such as financial institutions, the balance sheet is relatively more important. In intermediate industries, such as durable manufacturers, both are about equally important. Barth, Beaver, and Landsman (1996b) also find that the relative importance of book value increases and net income decreases with the degree of financial difficulty experienced by the firm. Collins, Maydew, and Weiss (1996) find that over time the coefficient on earnings has declined and the balance sheet coefficient has increased. Their evidence indicates that much, but not all, of the decline is due to the presence of transitory, one-time charges against earnings (such as extraordinary items, special charges, restructuring changes) and the increased frequency of firms reporting losses, which is associated with a lower coefficient. Francis and Schipper (1996) use a similar approach to address the issue of whether financial statements have lost their relevance.

Easton and Harris (1991) explore this relation in first difference form and find that both the change in book value (as measured by earnings) and the change in earnings are significant variables in explaining changes in security prices. However, the implied coefficients are lower than in the levels studies. Kothari and Zimmerman (1995) confirm this in a broader setting that compares levels and first differences. Landsman and Magliolo (1988) and Kothari and Zimmerman suggest that the lower coefficients may reflect a poorer specification in the first differences, although neither specification dominates in general.

5-10 FOOTNOTE DISCLOSURES EXPLAIN SECURITY PRICES

Footnote information is often not prominently displayed and is complex and difficult to interpret, such as pension disclosures. Research indicates that in many cases information that is disclosed in the footnotes to the annual report is priced, although that information is not recognized in the body of the financial statements themselves. The examples discussed earlier in the chapter include disclosures about pension assets and obligations, fair value of investment securities, fair value of financial instruments, nonperforming loans, interest-rate sensitivity schedule for investment securities, and information related to the intangible value of core deposits. Moreover, evidence by Barth and McNichols (1994) regarding environmental liabilities indicates that the market looks beyond the financial statements to assess the assets and obligations of the firm. The implications of these findings for the issue of recognition versus disclosure are discussed in Chapter 6.

5-11 DISCRETIONARY COMPONENTS ARE PRICED DIFFERENTLY BY THE MARKET THAN NONDISCRETIONARY COMPONENTS

As discussed in Chapter 4, discretionary behavior with respect to accounting numbers is a major financial reporting issue. Opportunities for discretion arise because of the difficulty in estimating and latitude allowed in providing accounting numbers. For example, Statement of Financial Accounting Standards No. 5 (FAS No. 5) on loss contingencies calls for the estimation of losses from receivables or loans when they are *probable* and *reasonably estimable*. The standard and its interpretations provide only general guidelines as to how the measurement will take place, and mandated disclosures constitute a floor or minimum standard. Management has the discretion to voluntarily disclose more than the minimum required. Accounting research has examined four major areas of accounting discretion: voluntary disclosure, earnings forecasts (which are a particular type of voluntary disclosure), choices in accounting method, and accruals. Discretionary behavior with respect to accruals received considerable research attention.

Discretionary behavior is important because of the nature of, motivations for, and effects of discretionary behavior. Discretionary behavior can affect the effectiveness of the financial reporting system. Traditional forms of discretionary behavior have often assumed that someone was being "fooled." Alternatively, discretionary behavior can be viewed as the natural manifestation of multiperiod contracting in an incomplete market in which management is expected to take discretionary actions. As described in Watts and Zimmerman (1986), this approach to discretionary behavior does not require that anyone be fooled.

One aspect of discretionary behavior is the effects on market value of common equity. The pricing of discretionary components of accounting numbers can affect both the incentives and economic consequences associated with discretionary behavior. The valuation evidence is of interest in its own right, because it not only can show whether security prices are affected by discretionary behavior, but also can serve as indirect evidence as to whether other parties are likely to be able to conduct a similar decomposition.

Empirical Research

Several studies have examined managerial discretion with respect to loan losses by banks. The allowance for a loan loss account is a plausible arena for the study of discretionary behavior.[21] The allowance for loan losses constitutes a high percentage of banks' common equity. The account is perceived to be subject to discretionary behavior due to the manner in which allowance for loan losses is defined under GAAP and the uncertainty surrounding the estimation of loan losses. The meaning of the terms *probable* and *reasonably estimable* under this standard are ill-defined and subject to great variation in interpretation and practice.

Moyer (1990) decomposes bank loan loss provisions and charge-offs into discretionary and nondiscretionary components based on a bank's proximity to the capital adequacy minimums and macroeconomic indicators of business failures. Scholes, Wilson, and Wolfson (1990) find that realized security gains and losses behave as if they are used to offset, rather than reinforce, the effects of loan loss provisions on earnings. Collins, Shackelford, and Wahlen (1995) examine several areas of discretionary behavior, including three accounting choice areas. They find evidence of discretionary behavior motivated by earnings management and capital adequacy management, but find that taxes play a minor role. Beatty, Chamberlain, and Magliolo (1995) examine five areas of discretionary behavior, including both accounting and financing choices. They find evidence of discretionary behavior in the provision and net charge-off accounts and offer a system of simultaneous equations in which each discretionary variable is endogenously determined as a function of one or more of the other endogenous variables.

Beaver, Eger, Ryan, and Wolfson (1989) find that nonperforming assets play a significant role in explaining cross-sectional differences in the ratio of the market value of common equity to the book value of common equity (the reciprocal of the BTM ratio) across banks. In attempting to isolate the incremental explanatory power of nonperforming assets, Beaver et al. (1989) included the allowance for loan losses as a "nuisance variable" to ensure that nonperforming assets had incremental explanatory power beyond that provided by simply adjusting the allowance for loan losses account by some scalar. The nonperforming assets variable was significant, and the coefficient on allowance for loan losses was significantly positive. Beaver and colleagues interpret this finding as suggesting that, conditional upon nonperforming assets, additional reserves for loan losses are treated favorably by the capital market despite adverse financial statement effects from lower earnings, net worth, and assets, among other accounts. Beaver and colleagues conjecture that discretionary reserving may be used by management to communicate favorable, private information about future earning power.

---

[21]In contexts other than loan loss accruals, studies of the effects of discretionary behavior include Collins and DeAngelo (1990), Healy (1985), Jones (1991), McNichols and Wilson (1988), and Subramanyam (1996).

Subsequent research examined this phenomenon in the context of an "events" study research design. Griffin and Wallach (1991) and Elliott, Hanna, and Shaw (1991) found evidence that unexpected additions to loan loss allowances by banks with large foreign loan portfolios were viewed favorably by the market at the time of the announcement of additions to the allowance account. Wahlen (1994) explores the conjecture that managers are signaling "good news" with unexpected increases in the loan loss provision account. In addition to finding a positive stock price reaction, Wahlen finds that the unexpected portion of the provision is positively related to changes in future prediscretionary earnings, which is consistent with the signaling perspective. Using quarterly returns, Liu, Ryan, and Wahlen (1997) further find that the finding largely applies only to financially weaker banks in the fourth quarter earnings.

The Beaver and Engel (1996) study finds that the market prices of banks behave as if the capital market conduct decomposes the allowance for loan losses into discretionary and nondiscretionary components and assigns significantly different "prices" to each component. The nondiscretionary component is negatively priced, and the discretionary component is less negatively priced.

5-12   EARNINGS VOLATILITY AND SYSTEMATIC RISK

The discussion thus far has focused on prices as a function of expected earnings, among other factors. Mean-variance portfolio theory suggests that price is also a function of perceived systematic risk (beta) of the security, among other factors.

Empirical evidence by Beaver, Kettler, and Scholes (1970) and Beaver and Manegold (1975), among others, has shown that measures of systematic earnings volatility (accounting earnings betas) show significantly positive correlation with a security's beta defined in terms of security returns. For example, the correlation at the portfolio level ranges from .7 to 8.[22] Beaver, Clarke, and Wright (1979) have shown that securities with the greatest percentage changes in earnings also have the highest betas. This is illustrated in Table 5-1 in which the extreme portfolios 1 and 6 have higher betas than the intermediate portfolios do.

5-13   CONCLUDING REMARKS

The chapter summarizes the results of some of the empirical research on the relation between earnings and security prices. Several conclusions are drawn from the empirical research. (1) A significant, positive correlation exists between price changes

---

[22]This is based on an average of the correlations for the net income to net worth accounting beta with the market beta, using total period data to compute the betas. See Table 7 of Beaver and Manegold (1975).

and earnings changes. (2) Although significant, it is not a simple one-to-one relationship. One reason is that prices behave as if earnings are perceived to possess a transitory component. (3) Security prices act as though investors adjust at least partially for many accounting method differences among firms, such as depreciation method differences. (4) Price changes appear to price both the cash flow and accrual components of earnings changes. (5) Prices anticipate earnings because of more timely sources of information. (6) Prices can be used to forecast earnings, a feature known as the *information content of prices*. (7) Prices behave as if market participants perceive there is a delayed recognition component to earnings and book value of common equity. (8) Prices behave as if market participants perceive there is a *conservative* component to earnings and book value. (9) Book value of equity, as well as earnings, appears to be important in explaining prices. (10) Footnote disclosures are also priced by the market. (11) Discretionary components of accounting numbers are priced by the market differently than the nondiscretionary components. (12) Measures of systematic risk in security prices are significantly positively correlated with measures of systematic volatility in accounting earnings.

A number of issues are open or unresolved. The issue of accruals is one such important issue, because accrual accounting is a key feature of the current reporting system. Moreover, virtually all of the studies have found a statistical dependency between earnings and prices, which is consistent with the hypothesis that earnings convey information. It is difficult to say whether the observed significant relationships are due to reliance by investors on earnings or whether earnings are correlated with the information that does affect security prices. Studies using daily or intraday data show a price reaction to earnings announcements and come closest to resolving this issue. Stock prices act as if accounting data convey important information or, at the very least, are correlated with important information.

BIBLIOGRAPHY

Archibald, T. "Stock Market Reaction to Depreciation Switch-Back." *Accounting Review* (January 1972), 22–30.

Ball, R., and P. Brown. "An Empirical Evaluation of Accounting Income Numbers." *Journal of Accounting Research* (Autumn 1968), 159–178.

Barth, M. "Relative Measurement Errors Among Alternative Pension Asset and Liability Measures." *Accounting Review* (July 1991), 433–463.

———, W. Beaver, and W. Landsman. "Market Valuation Implications of Net Periodic Pension Cost." *Journal of Accounting and Economics* (March 1992), 27–62.

———, W. Beaver, and W. Landsman. "A Structural Analysis of Pension Disclosures Under SFAS 87 and Their Relation to Share Prices." *Financial Analysts Journal* (January–February 1993), 18–26.

———, W. Beaver, and W. Landsman. "Value-Relevance of Fair Value Disclosures Under SFAS No. 107." *Accounting Review* (October 1996a), 513–537.

————, W. Beaver, and W. Landsman. "The Relative Importance of the Balance Sheet and Net Income: Tests of the Abandonment Option Hypothesis." Unpublished working paper, Stanford University, 1996b.

———— and M. McNichols. "Estimation and Market Valuation of Environmental Liabilities Relating to Superfund Sites." *Journal of Accounting Research* (Supplement 1994), 177–209.

Beatty, A., S. Chamberlain, and J. Magliolo. "Managing Financial Reports of Commercial Banks: The Influence of Taxes, Regulatory Capital, and Earnings." *Journal of Accounting Research* (Autumn 1995), 231–262.

Beaver, W. "The Information Content of Annual Earnings Announcements." *Empirical Research in Accounting: Selected Studies.* Supplement to the *Journal of Accounting Research* (1968), 67–92.

————, R. Clarke, and W. Wright. "The Association Between Unsystematic Security Returns and the Magnitude of the Earnings Forecast Error." *Journal of Accounting Research* (Autumn 1979), 316–340.

———— and R. Dukes. "Interperiod Tax Allocation and Delta Depreciation Methods: Some Empirical Results." *Accounting Review* (July 1973), 549–559.

————, C. Eger, S. Ryan, and M. Wolfson. "Financial Reporting and the Structure of Bank Share Prices." *Journal of Accounting Research* (Autumn 1989), 157–178.

———— and E. Engel. "Discretionary Behavior with Respect to Allowances for Loan Losses and the Behavior of Security Prices." *Journal of Accounting and Economics* (September 1996), 177–206.

————, P. Kettler, and M. Scholes. "The Association Between Market-Determined and Accounting-Determined Risk Measures." *Accounting Review* (October 1970), 654–682.

————, R. Lambert, and D. Morse. "The Information Content of Security Prices." *Journal of Accounting and Economics* (March 1980), 3–28.

————, R. Lambert, and S. Ryan. "The Information Content of Security Prices: A Second Look." *Journal of Accounting and Economics* (July 1987), 139–157.

———— and J. Manegold. "The Association Between Market-Determined and Accounting-Determined Measures of Systematic Risk." *Journal of Financial and Quantitative Analysis* (June 1975), 231–284.

————, M. McAnally, and C. Stinson. "The Information Content of Earnings and Prices: A Simultaneous Equations Approach." *Journal of Accounting and Economics* (forthcoming 1997).

———— and D. Morse. "What Determines Price-Earnings Ratios?" *Financial Analysts Journal* (July–August 1978), 65–76.

———— and S. Ryan. "Biased Recognition (Conservatism) and Delayed Recognition in Accounting and Their Effects on the Ability of the Book-to-Market Ratio to Predict Book Return on Equity." Unpublished working paper, New York University, 1996.

————. "Accounting Fundamentals of the Book-to-Market Ratio." *Financial Analysts Journal* (November–December 1993), 9–13.

Benston, G. "Published Corporate Accounting Data and Stock Prices." *Empirical Research in Accounting: Selected Studies.* Supplement to the *Journal of Accounting Research* (1966), 1–14.

————. "There's No Real News in Earnings Reports." *Fortune* (April 1976), 73–75.

Bernard, V. "Capital Markets Research in Accounting During the 1980s: A Critical Review." In *The State of Accounting Research As We Enter the 1990s*, edited by T. Frecka. Champaign–Urbana, Illinois, University of Illinois, 1989.

———— and T. Stober. "The Nature and Amount of Information Reflected in Cash Flows." *Accounting Review* (October 1989), 624–652.

Collins, D., and L. DeAngelo. "Accounting Information and Corporate Governance: Market and Analyst Reactions to Earnings of Firms Engaged in Proxy Contests." *Journal of Accounting and Economics* (October 1990), 213–247.

——— and S. P. Kothari. "An Analysis of Intertemporal and Cross-Sectional Determinants of Earnings Response Coefficients." *Journal of Accounting and Economics* (July 1989), 143–182.

———, S. P. Kothari, J. Shanken, and R. Sloan. "Lack of Timeliness Versus Noise as Explanations for Low Contemporaneous Return-Earnings Association." *Journal of Accounting and Economics* (November 1994), 289–324.

———, E. Maydew, and I. Weiss. "Changes in the Value-Relevance of Earnings and Book Values Over the Past Forty Years." Unpublished working paper, University of Iowa, 1996.

Collins, J., D. Shackelford, and J. Wahlen. "Bank Differences in the Coordination of Regulatory Capital, Earnings, and Taxes." *Journal of Accounting Research* (Autumn 1995), 263–291.

Dukes, R. "An Investigation of the Effects of Expensing Research and Development Costs on Security Prices." *Proceedings of the Conference on Topical Research in Accounting*. Edited by M. Schiff and C. Sorter. New York University, 1976.

Easton, P., and T. Harris. "Earnings as an Explanatory Variable for Returns." *Journal of Accounting Research* (Spring 1991), 19–36.

——— and M. Zmijewski. "Cross-Sectional Variation in the Stock Market Response to Accounting Earnings Measurements." *Journal of Accounting and Economics* (July 1989), 117–142.

Elliott, J., J. Hanna, and W. Shaw. "The Evaluation by the Financial Markets of Changes in Bank Loan Loss Reserve Levels." *Accounting Review* (October 1991), 847–861.

Foster, G. *Financial Statement Analysis*. Englewood Cliffs, N.J.: Prentice-Hall, 1978.

———. *Financial Statement Analysis*. 2nd ed. Englewood Cliffs, N.J.: Prentice-Hall, 1986.

Francis, J., and K. Schipper. "Have Financial Statements Lost Their Relevance?" Unpublished working paper, University of Chicago, 1996.

Griffin, P., and S. Wallach. "Latin American Lending by Major U.S. Banks: The Effects of Disclosures About Nonaccrual Loans and Loan Loss Provisions." *Accounting Review* (October 1991), 830–846.

Hayn, C. "The Information Content of Losses." *Journal of Accounting and Economics* (September 1995), 125–153.

Healy, P. "The Effect of Bonus Schemes on Accounting Decisions." *Journal of Accounting and Economics* (April 1985), 85–107.

Holthausen, R., and R. Verrecchia. "The Effect of Informedness and Consensus on the Price and Volume Behavior." *Accounting Review* (January 1990), 191–208.

Hong, H., R. Kaplan, and C. Mandelker. "Pooling vs. Purchase: The Effects of Accounting for Mergers on Stock Prices." *Accounting Review* (January 1978), 31–47.

Jones, J. "Earnings Management During Import Relief Investigations." *Journal of Accounting Research* (Autumn 1991), 193–228.

Kormendi, R., and R. Lipe. "Earnings Innovations, Earnings Persistence, and Stock Returns." *Journal of Business* (July 1987), 323–345.

Kothari, S. P., and J. Zimmerman, "Price and Return Models." *Journal of Accounting and Economics* (September 1995), 155–192.

Kritzman, M. ". . . About Event Studies." *Financial Analysts Journal* (November–December 1994), 17–20.

Landsman, W. "An Empirical Investigation of Pension Fund Property Rights." *Accounting Review* (October 1986), 662–691.

───── and J. Magliolo. "Cross-Sectional Capital Market Research Model Specification." *Accounting Review* (October 1988), 662–691.

Lev, B. "On the Usefulness of Earnings and Earnings Research: Lessons and Directions From Two Decades of Accounting Research." *Journal of Accounting Research* (Supplement 1989), 153–192.

───── and T. Sougainnis. "The Capitalization, Amortization, and Value-Relevance of R&D." *Journal of Accounting and Economics* (February 1996), 107–138.

Liu, C., S. Ryan, and J. Wahlen. "Differential Valuation Implications of Loan Loss Provisions Across Banks and Fiscal Quarters." *Accounting Review* (January 1997), 133–146.

McNichols, M., and P. Wilson. "Evidence of Earnings Management from the Provision for Bad Debts." *Journal of Accounting Research* (Supplement 1988), 1–31.

Morse, D. "Price and Trading Volume Reaction Surrounding Earnings Announcements: A Closer Examination." *Journal of Accounting Research* (Autumn 1981), 374–384.

Moyer, S. "Capital Adequacy Ratio Regulations and Accounting Choices in Commercial Banks." *Journal of Accounting and Economics* (July 1990), 123–154.

Patell, J., and M. Wolfson. "The Intraday Speed of Adjustment of Stock Prices to Earnings and Dividend Announcements." *Journal of Accounting and Economics* (June 1984), 223–252.

Penman, S. "The Articulation of Price-Earnings Ratios and Market-to-Book Ratios and the Evaluation of Growth." *Journal of Accounting Research* (Autumn 1996), 235–260.

Ryan, S. "A Model of Accrual Measurement with Implications for the Evolution of the Book-to-Market Ratio." *Journal of Accounting Research* (Spring 1995), 95–112.

Scholes, M., P. Wilson, and M. Wolfson. "Tax Planning, Regulatory Capital Planning and Financial Reporting Strategy for Commercial Banks." *Review of Financial Studies* (1990), 625–650.

Sloan, R. "Do Stock Prices Fully Reflect Information in Accruals and Cash Flows About Future Earnings?" *Accounting Review* (July 1996), 289–315.

Staubus, G. "An Induced Theory of Accounting Measurement." *Accounting Review* (January 1985), 53–75.

Subramanyam, K. R. "The Pricing of Discretionary Accruals." *Journal of Accounting and Economics* (September 1996), 249–281.

Wahlen, J. "The Nature of Information in Commercial Bank Loan Loss Disclosures." *Accounting Review* (July 1994), 455–478.

Watts, R., and J. Zimmerman. *Positive Accounting Theory.* Englewood Cliffs, N.J.: Prentice-Hall, 1986.

─────. "Positive Accounting Theory: A Ten-Year Perspective." *Accounting Review* (January 1990), 131–156.

Wilson, G. P. "The Relative Information Content of Accrual and Cash Flows: Combined Evidence at the Earnings Announcement and Annual Release Date." *Studies on Alternative Measures of Accounting Income.* Supplement to the *Journal of Accounting Research* (1986), 165–200.

————. "The Incremental Information Content of the Accrual and Funds Components of Earnings After Controlling for Earnings." *Accounting Review* (April 1987), 293–322.

6

Market Efficiency

Market efficiency is a central feature of the capital markets and deals with the relation between security prices and information. In an efficient market, prices "fully reflect" information. More precisely, a securities market is defined to be efficient with respect to a particular information system if and only if the security prices act as if everyone observes the signals from that information system. Market efficiency deals with how the capital markets process information in general and financial reporting information specifically.

Market efficiency is important to financial reporting for several reasons. It influences whether public disclosure is expected to have significant effects on security prices. It also affects whether disclosure of an item in the footnotes versus recognition of the item in the body of the financial statements is expected to make a difference in security prices. It influences how important financial reporting data are relative to the total mix of information.

In an inefficient capital market, financial statement data are not necessarily reflected in prices, and hence an individual investor is not necessarily a "price taker" with respect to that information. An inefficient capital market affords opportunities for investors to earn abnormal returns from investment strategies keyed on financial reporting data that are not fully reflected in prices.

Each of the major constituencies has a vital interest in the prices of a firm's securities and the effect of information on prices. The interest in security prices arises because of the economic consequences associated with security prices. For example, changes in prices of a security alter the market value of the investor's wealth. The price of the security also affects the terms on which the firm obtains additional financing. This in turn can affect management's perceived cost of capital and alter the nature of the projects undertaken. At an economy-wide level, capital formation and resource allocation can be affected. Although prices may be of immediate interest, the ultimate concern is with the attendant consequences. The economic consequences of market efficiency are essentially the same as the consequences of financial reporting discussed in Chapter 2.

The purpose of this chapter is not to take a position in favor of or against market efficiency with respect to a particular information system. Nor is it to provide a detailed, in-depth technical evaluation of the research. The summary of the research will be brief and nontechnical. Instead, this chapter focuses on the origins, definitions, various forms, evidence, research design theories, and implications of market efficiency and its importance to the financial reporting constituencies.

6-1 ORIGIN OF THE MARKET EFFICIENCY CONCEPT

The issue of market efficiency with respect to financial statement information originated in the practice of security analysis, which is defined as the process of finding mispriced securities. In this context, market inefficiency was expressed as a departure of a security's price from its "intrinsic value." Using financial statement data to find mispriced securities is exemplified by Graham and Dodd (1934), who formalized the art of security analysis as it is practiced by the professional investment community. Much of the professional investment industry offers services to clients based on the contention that they can successfully find mispriced securities.

The concept of the *intrinsic value* of a security is an intriguing aspect of security analysis. A security, such as a common stock, possesses value because it is perceived to possess attributes desired by individuals. Common stocks are thought to possess value because they represent claims to future, uncertain cash flows in the form of future dividends. In elementary discussions of the demand for a commodity, prices are viewed as reflecting individuals' wealth, tastes, and beliefs. These factors are typically viewed as being personal or subjective and different across individuals. Indeed, for most commodities, the influence of endowments, preferences, and beliefs on prices and the subjective nature of the "value" of a commodity are readily acknowledged. Yet security analysis has introduced the notion of the intrinsic value of a security. The use of the term connotes an objective concept, independent of subjective influences.[1]

6-2 DEFINITION OF MARKET EFFICIENCY

Subsequent notions of market efficiency did not explicitly rely on concepts of intrinsic value. For example, Fama (1970) states that a securities market is efficient if security prices "fully reflect" the information available. As Fama points out, the terms *fully reflect* and *information available* are ambiguous.

---

[1]For example, Graham and Dodd (1934, p. 17) defined intrinsic value as "In general terms, it is understood to be that value which is justified by the facts."

Market Efficiency and Universal Access to Information

Market efficiency is defined in terms of universal access to the information system of interest. Specifically,

> The market is efficient with respect to some specified information system, if and only if security prices act as if everyone observes the information system.[2]

If prices have this property, they are said to fully reflect that information. This definition can be illustrated by an event that is the subject of several empirical studies of market efficiency. The event is a firm's announcement that it switched from an accelerated method of depreciation to straight-line depreciation in reporting to shareholders in the annual report. However, both before and after the change the firms used an accelerated depreciation method for tax purposes.

In this example, market efficiency means that prices act as if every investor knows that the firms changed depreciation methods, knows what those methods are and what impact they have on reported earnings, knows that there was no change in depreciation method for tax purposes, and knows the potential implications for managements' motivation to make such a change. Obviously, such universal knowledge does not literally exist. However, the definition of market efficiency states only that prices act as if such a condition holds. In other words, the prices that prevail with limited knowledge of such information among investors are the same as prices that would prevail if everyone literally knew such information. This may explain in part why many find the concept of market efficiency difficult to accept.

Much empirical research in market efficiency focuses on a major implication of market efficiency known as the "fair game" property.[3] If the market is efficient with respect to some information, the investor is playing a fair game with respect to that information. Under the fair game property of market efficiency, the abnormal expected returns from trading strategies based on that information are zero. The inability to earn abnormal returns is a particularly important implication of market efficiency to the professional investment community.[4]

The fair game approach requires that abnormal returns must be defined relative to some benchmark of normal expected returns. In many early empirical studies, the returns on a market portfolio were used as the benchmark against which to compare the return performance of portfolios arising from a trading strategy based

---

[2]A more formal statement of this definition is: The market is efficient with respect to some information system if and only if the prices of the securities are the same as they would be in an otherwise identical economy (with the same configuration of preferences and endowments and information systems) except that every individual has access to the information system as well. See Beaver (1981) for a further discussion of this definition.

[3]An analogy is a "fair coin" in which the probability of a head is .50. If the coin is "fair," the probability remains .50, regardless of the frequency and sequence of heads and tails of past tosses.

[4]*Return* is defined as the cash dividend plus the change in price over the defined period divided by the price at the beginning of the period. Return can be viewed as a percentage change in price adjusted for dividend. Hence, the terms *return* and *price change* will be used interchangeably throughout.

on information. However, some felt that such a benchmark might be inappropriate if the strategy tended to result in portfolios whose "risk" was different from that of the market portfolio. Portfolio theory and the capital asset pricing model permitted the specification of a risk-adjusted return benchmark and was perceived to be a contribution to empirically testing market efficiency. However, tests of market efficiency are a joint test of market efficiency and the assumptions made about how to measure the appropriate benchmark, which means the issue is a particularly difficult one to test empirically.

6-3   FORMS OF MARKET EFFICIENCY

A discussion of market efficiency must specify the information systems for which the market efficiency condition is being defined. This is critical because the market may be efficient with respect to some information systems but not others. In general, statements such as "the market is efficient" or "the market is not efficient" are ambiguous and incomplete.

Fama (1970) delineated three major forms of market efficiency: weak, semistrong, and strong:

1. The market is efficient in the weak form if prices fully reflect information regarding the past sequence of prices. This form of market efficiency has obvious implications for technical analysis, and it includes the random walk theory of stock prices.

2. The market is efficient in the semistrong form if prices fully reflect all publicly available information, including financial statement data. Trading strategies based on published financial statement data will not lead to abnormal returns.

3. The market is efficient in the strong form if prices fully reflect all information, including inside information. Hence, even having access to privately held information will not lead to strategies promising abnormal expected returns.

In a 20-year retrospective, Fama (1991) suggested that empirical tests for market efficiency be classified as tests for return predictability, event studies, and tests for private information. These classifications are best thought of as coarse partitioning of all information systems into three broad categories in which the boundaries between them are not precisely defined. However, the distinction is useful for classifying empirical research on market efficiency.

For many purposes, the information systems of interest may need to be more finely partitioned. For example, market efficiency with respect to the prices of firms that switched accounting methods is a finer partition of semistrong form efficiency.

The relationship among the three types of market efficiency must be distinguished. The information systems described in weak form efficiency are a proper subset of the information systems described in semistrong form efficiency, which in turn are a proper subset of the information systems described in strong form efficiency. As a result, strong form efficiency implies semistrong form efficiency implies weak form efficiency. However, the implication does not work in the reverse order.

6-4 EVIDENCE REGARDING MARKET EFFICIENCY

This chapter does not contain an in-depth discussion of the evidence regarding market efficiency for several reasons. (1) Some of this research is summarized in Chapter 5. (2) Excellent, detailed reviews of this research are available in Dyckman and Morse (1986) and Fama (1991). (3) The nature of the evidence and the strength of the findings either supporting or rejecting market efficiency are continually changing and are the subject of current controversy and debate. However, the concept, implications, and theory of market efficiency are likely to be of continuing interest and concern. This chapter focuses on these aspects of market efficiency. This section briefly summarizes a sample of the major studies that provided evidence on market efficiency.

Empirical research characterized as efficient market research has been the subject of considerable attention in recent years. Critics of financial accounting standards implied that securities are mispriced because of accounting practices. The empirical research (for example, on changes in accounting method) arose in response to these contentions and were offered as tests of these contentions. The research represents an important methodological contribution to financial accounting research because it subjects the allegations to empirical testing. It constitutes a more systematic and more rigorous use of evidence than had occurred previously and is one of the major areas of research that contributed to the introduction of empirical testing in accounting research. As such, the research is a considerable revolution in financial accounting research. Following Fama's (1991) classification, three classes of empirical tests of market efficiency are discussed: tests for return predictability, event studies, and tests for private information.

Tests for Return Predictability

The earliest forms of these tests are tests of weak form efficiency. Is the past sequence of returns helpful in predicting future abnormal returns? If current prices fully reflect the past sequence of prices and price changes, the answer is no. One form of the tests consists of examining the serial correlation of security return. Under some simplifying assumptions, in an efficient market the serial correlation of successive price changes (or returns) is expected to be zero. This is also known as the random walk theory of stock prices. If this is the case, then investors are playing a "fair game" with respect to the past sequence of price changes.

Prices respond only to the unexpected portion of any new information and do so in an unbiased fashion. Because price changes reflect the reaction to the unexpected portion of an announcement, they will be uncorrelated with past price changes. News, by definition, is unanticipated and cannot be predicted by past price changes. In contrast, consider a market in which prices are "slow" to react to information. This is a form of underreaction to information and would lead to positive correlation in price changes (price increases tend to be followed by price increases). By contrast, consider a market in which prices "overreact" to information. Good news is associated with an excessive price increase and with a later reversal by the market. In this setting, price changes would exhibit negative serial correlation. Price increases tend to be followed by price declines, and price declines tend to be followed by price increases.

Now consider a market in which prices respond quickly and in an unbiased fashion to news. The expected serial correlation of successive price changes is zero. Price increases are no more likely to follow price increases than they are to follow price declines. Just as a fair coin has no memory, neither do price changes. The expected value of future change in price conditional on past price changes is the same regardless of the past sequence of price changes. This is also known as the random walk theory of stock price changes. The empirical tests of serial correlation have been collected since 1900 and are summarized in Cootner (1964). More recent tests are summarized in Fama (1970, 1991). The evidence suggests that the behavior of successive stock price changes is well approximated by zero serial correlation, except over extremely short time intervals such as within a given trading day.

An illustration is provided in a study by Beaver and Landsman (1981). Starting in a given month (month 0), all securities on the New York Stock Exchange (NYSE) are placed into one of two portfolios based on their abnormal return behavior over the past 20 months. The "winner" portfolio consists of those stocks whose price changes outperform the changes in the market index during the previous 20 months. The "loser" portfolio consists of those stocks that underperformed the market over the same 20 months.[5] Figure 6-1 shows the behavior of the two portfolios during those 20 months (month −20 to month 0).

The winner portfolio outperformed the market as measured by the cumulative residual price change by over 30% during the time period, whereas the loser portfolio underperformed by over 30%. The result is not surprising, because "wisdom by hindsight" was used to select the two portfolios. The magnitude of the difference in the cumulative average residual (CAR) performance (+30% versus −30%) is a function of how many months of "wisdom by hindsight" is exercised. The difference would be smaller if a 5-month rule had been used or larger if a 30-month rule had been used. It is a reflection of how much information can affect prices within a given period.

As far as market efficiency is concerned, the issue is the expected behavior of the cumulative residual price change in the months after month 0, the month the

---

[5]More precisely, the variable is the *unsystematic return*, which is the u term defined in Chapter 2 footnote 9. The price change is adjusted for dividends (hence, returns) and for each firm's systematic risk (beta) as well as market-wide conditions (hence, residual return). The unsystematic return is then cumulated over the 20 months and labeled the cumulative residual price change. This is the same variable as discussed in footnote 5 of Chapter 5.

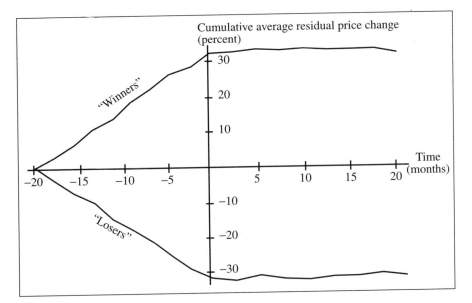

FIGURE 6-1 **Cumulative residual price change for "winner" and "loser" portfolios; vertical axis = cumulative average residual price change (CAR), horizontal axis = time in months relative to portfolio selection (month 0 is month of portfolio selection).**
Source: Beaver and Landsman (1981), Figure 1, p. 238.

portfolios are formed. In other words, is there abnormal price change behavior from the point of selection onward? In months 1 through 20, "wisdom by hindsight" is no longer operating. If stock prices are slow to react to information, the "winners" should continue to be "winners," and the cumulative residual price change should continue to rise. Similarly, the losers portfolio should continue to decline. If stock prices overreact systematically, then the winners should turn into losers and the cumulative residual price change should decline, whereas the loser portfolio should turn into winners.[6] If the stock prices behave as a "fair game" with respect to past price changes, the *cumulative* residual price changes should remain flat, because the average residual price change being *added* to the cumulated sum is zero.[7]

---

[6] The sum of the two portfolios constitutes the entire market, which cannot outperform itself. Hence, at any point in time the sum of the two cumulative residual price changes must be zero by construction. Hence, if one portfolio's cumulative residual price changes increase, the other's cumulative residual price change must decline.

[7] By analogy to the fair coin, suppose you start with $100 and toss a fair coin where $3 is won if a head is tossed and $3 is lost if tail appears. Even with a fair coin, the tosses will not be evenly split after 20 tosses. If 15 heads and 5 tails occur after 20 tosses, the wealth has now grown to $130. If the coin is fair, the expected wealth of continuing to play the game is $130. This is analogous to the winner portfolio. Similarly, suppose on the first 20 tosses, 5 heads and 15 tails had occurred. At the end of the twentieth toss, the wealth is $70, which is analogous to the loser portfolio. What is the expected wealth of continuing to play the game? If the coin is fair, the expected wealth is $70. If you were to graph this behavior, it would look essentially the same as Figure 6-1.

Figure 6-1 reports the behavior of the portfolios for the 20 months after the selection. The cumulative residual price change is flat for both portfolios, which is consistent with the market neither systematically overreacting nor underreacting to information but on average reacting in an unbiased manner. The major exception to the fair game behavior is for extremely short time intervals, such as transaction-to-transaction price changes. This is generally considered to be due to market "microstructure" reasons, such as nonsynchronous trading and bid-ask phenomenon. The microstructure literature is reviewed by Patell and Wolfson (1984) and Fama (1991). Nonsynchronous trading tends to induce the appearance of correlation in price changes over short intervals. The bid-ask phenomenon induces the appearance of negative serial correlation in observed price changes (reversals) over extremely short intervals. In both cases, the appearance of serial correlation is induced by a form of measurement error in the observed prices, not because of market inefficiency, and in any event, persists over only short time intervals.

Prediction of Returns—Other Conditioning Variables

Past price changes is only one variable on which to condition the prediction of future returns. Some of the variables that have some ability to predict future returns are systematic risk, firm size (as measured by the market value of common stock outstanding), and the book-to-market (BTM) ratio (Fama and French 1992). The capital asset pricing model (CAPM) suggests that systematic risk (beta) is the sole determinant of differential expected returns at any point in time. Both size and BTM appear to have predictive power even after controlling for differences in systematic risk. In particular, the average returns for small firms is higher than for large firms, and the average return for firms with high BTM ratios is higher than firms with lower ratios.

The tests are testing a joint hypothesis of market efficiency and a model of market equilibrium that reflect the factors that affect expected returns. As a result, the interpretation of these empirical results has been the subject of considerable controversy. Is the predictive ability of size or BTM evidence of market inefficiency, or does it merely reflect the fact that the CAPM is not a correct model asset pricing equilibrium? This is difficult to resolve, and the evidence is open to either interpretation.

The BTM evidence is particularly interesting because the accounting book value of equity is a component of this ratio.[8] The market inefficiency interpretation is that a high ratio implies that market value is small relative to book value and is an indication that the market value is currently underpriced. Eventually, the underpricing will correct itself and hence future returns are expected to be higher during this interval (Lakonishok, Shleifer, and Vishny, 1994).

---

[8]Other studies that document a relationship between current accounting measure and future returns are Ou and Penman (1989), and Lev and Thiagarajan (1993).

Event Studies

Event studies examine the residual price change of a sample of firms for a window of time on either side of an identifiable "event," such as announcements of earnings, stock splits and dividends, cash dividends, earnings forecasts, or changes in accounting methods. The influence of economy-wide and, if necessary, additional factors such as industry-wide information on stock prices is extracted to obtain a residual return. The expected value of the residual price changes, not conditioning on the event, is zero. Events studies have examined several aspects of market efficiency with respect to accounting data.

Speed of Adjustment to Earnings Announcements

The evidence indicates that weekly residual price changes respond quickly to announcements of annual and quarterly earnings (see Figure 5-2), and Morse (1981) also finds a rapid speed of reaction on daily data (see Figure 5-4). In both graphs, the dotted line indicates the magnitude of the average price change during nonearnings announcement period. As discussed in Chapter 5, the large spike on day (week) 0 reflects the fact that price changes are more likely to occur during earnings announcements. The average residual price change returns to normal very quickly.

Patell and Wolfson (1984) inspect transaction-to-transaction price changes based on intraday data. Their study finds similar results, which are reported in Figure 6-2. Here, price changes are measured on an *hourly* basis. The major reaction occurs during the hour the earnings announcement is reported on the newswire. There is a small, but statistically significant, reaction for as much as four hours afterward. Beyond four hours, price change has returned to normal. Often the earnings announcement is closely followed by other information, such as other news releases by management, teleconference calls between management and analysts, and reports by analysts. Thus, the subsequent significant, albeit small, reaction could be due to the tendency of other announcements to cluster around or follow the earnings announcements. Even four hours is a relatively short time interval and is much shorter than the interval over which abnormal returns are observed in the prediction of returns studies discussed earlier.[9]

The Patell and Wolfson (1984) study of intraday data suggests an extremely rapid reaction to earnings announcements, where rapid is defined in terms of hours after the announcement. Security prices may react significantly yet only partially to the information when it is released. Even if this were the case, there is no reason to see why the slowness to respond is particular to earnings information. Because of the attention given to earnings by the investment community, it is an unlikely candidate to be subject to slowness to respond.

---

[9]In fact, addressing this issue becomes increasingly difficult as the window is shortened because of market microstructure issues, such as the bid-ask phenomenon. In fact, Patell and Wolfson use a measure of price reversal as one of the indicators of speed of response.

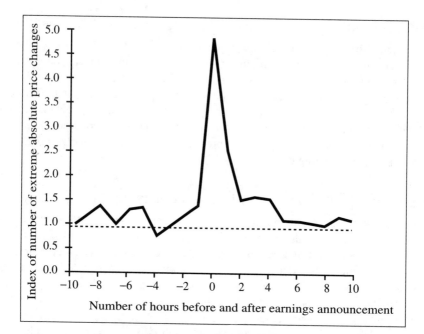

FIGURE 6-2 **An index of the number of extreme price changes (ignoring sign) in the hours surrounding the earnings announcements. The actual number is divided by the expected number of extreme price changes based on a nonreport period. If the actual number is equal to the expected number, the index is 1.0.**
Source: Patell and Wolfson (1984).

Prices Lead Earnings—The Information Content of Prices

Studies find that security prices anticipate earnings prior to the earnings announcement. For example, Figure 5-1 from the Ball and Brown (1968) study indicates that for the firms with good earnings news the cumulative residual price changes are positive well before the announcement month, which means prices are anticipating the earnings news for several months prior to the annual announcement. Part of this anticipation is simply due to the release of quarterly earnings announcements. However, this anticipatory effect also occurs because of the availability of other information that permits investors to revise expectations about earnings.

Furthermore, this anticipation could be because prices are responding to more timely nonearnings information. For example, the research on the information content of prices and on delayed recognition discussed in Chapter 5 indicates that price changes lead earnings changes and lead the book value of equity for as much as six years. Thus far, the picture is one of a market that responds quickly and in an anticipatory manner to earnings. It may not say much for the timeliness of earnings, but it is a remarkable testimony to the efficiency of the market with respect to earnings announcements.

Evidence on Pricing of Disclosures

As discussed in Chapter 5, the research documents a number of instances in which data that is disclosed in the footnotes to the annual report is priced. The examples included disclosures about pension assets and obligations, fair value of investment securities, fair value of financial instruments, nonperforming loans, and interest-rate sensitivity schedules of banks. Many of these disclosures, such as the pension disclosures, are complex and difficult to interpret. In this sense, one would think they would be a natural candidate for being ignored by a naive, inefficient market. Yet this information appears to be priced by the market. Similar statements could be made regarding the other disclosures. This evidence is consistent with a market in which prices reflect a fairly high degree of sophistication in the interpretation of financial reporting information and in which footnote information is incorporated into the total mix of information affecting price.

Evidence on Changes in Accounting Method and Differences in Accounting Method

As discussed earlier, diversity in accounting methods under GAAP and the ability to change accounting methods are two of the major features of the financial reporting system. As a result, the research on market efficiency has focused on the switch in depreciation methods from accelerated to straight-line depreciation for reporting purposes (Archibald 1972; Ball 1972). These studies assume that if the market were efficient with respect to this information, the changes in prices, ceteris paribus, would be zero.[10] These studies found that there were no abnormal residual price changes associated with a firm changing accounting method even when the effect of the change was to make earnings higher than it otherwise would have been if no change had taken place.

Alternatively, prices act as if investors look beyond accounting numbers and take into account the fact that earnings are being generated by a different accounting method. Further evidence supporting this contention is provided in the analysis of price-earnings ratios of firms using different depreciation methods. As discussed

---

[10]Tests of market efficiency have assumed that the information effect would be zero in a market that fully reflected the information. A contextual argument (in other words, no direct impact on cash flows) was typically offered to justify such an assumption. Although the empirical evidence is viewed as supportive of market efficiency, an argument could have been advanced that the change in method itself conveyed information, consistent with the signaling literature discussed in Chapter 2.

in Chapter 5, Beaver and Dukes's (1973) study of accelerated versus straight-line depreciation indicates that the price-reported earnings ratios of these firms do significantly differ. However, when reported earnings adjusted to compute pro forma earnings based on a common method of computing depreciation, the price-earnings ratios are not significantly different. This finding is consistent with a market that adjusts for accounting method differences, in contrast to a market in which there is myopic reliance placed on reported earnings.

Postannouncement Drift in Earnings

However, the story is not clear-cut. A series of studies have documented abnormal returns for several months subsequent to the earnings announcements. The earlier studies in this series were criticized for having omitted potentially important factors that determine expected returns and having incorrectly misspecified the asset pricing model. However, later studies addressed these concerns and the postannouncement drift in residual return still remained.

Foster, Olsen, and Shevlin (1984) document a significant residual returns after the earnings announcement. In particular, the positive drift in the cumulative residual price change continues for the good earnings news portfolio, with a negative drift continuing for the bad earnings news portfolio. In defining residual returns, Foster, Olsen, and Shevlin use the returns on firms of comparable size as the benchmark. They find that the magnitude of the postannouncement drift is greater for smaller firms. Interpreted as evidence of market inefficiency, the evidence suggests that the market is slow to react to the full implications of an earnings announcement, although the research indicates that it clearly reacts significantly at the time of announcement. Moreover, it suggests that this inefficiency is greater for smaller firms. Presumably, there are systematic differences in the financial reporting environments of large and small firms, such as a smaller number of analysts follow smaller firms.

Subsequent research by Bernard and Thomas (1989, 1990) represents an econometric *tour de force* in attempting to control for other factors and for removing sources of misspecification. The postannouncement drift was observed in their study as well, and the effect was persistent. They also document the fact that the effect is larger for small firms than for large firms. Their research suggests that the market prices act as if they do not fully reflect the time-series behavior of earnings.

The interpretation of these results are the subject of much debate. In addition to the research design issues of model misspecification and risk mismeasurement, the findings are anomalous in at least two respects. The evidence appears to be in conflict with much of the other research discussed earlier, such as dramatic and swift response when intraday return data are inspected and the evidence that suggests prices lead earnings by several years. Can prices both lead and lag earnings?

The evidence is also anomalous because earnings are the least likely candidate for inefficiency. Earnings are widely analyzed by the investment community. No other single firm-specific variable receives more attention by the analysts and other capital market participants than earnings. The result is paradoxical.

Abarbanell and Bernard (1992) suggest that the reason for market naive processing of earnings information may be the financial analysts. The study concludes that analysts' earnings forecasts do not fully reflect the time-series behavior of earnings. There is serial dependence in the forecast errors when analysts' forecasts are used as the benchmark. A necessary condition for a forecast to fully reflect available earnings information is that the forecast errors (unexpected earnings) are serially uncorrelated. The study then examines the extent to which this may explain the postannouncement drift and concludes that it may explain part but not all of the drift.

With the view that analysts play an important role in the price formation process, Dechow, Sloan, and Sweeney (1996) address the new-issue puzzle by examining long-term earnings forecasts by analysts. The new-issue puzzle, which is summarized by Loughran and Ritter (1995), suggests that after an initial price rise shortly after stock in an initial public offering is publicly traded there is a negative abnormal return that persists for five years after the initial public offering (IPO). Dechow, Sloan, and Sweeney find that analysts' forecasts are optimistic for IPO firms relative to a sample of non-IPO firms. As the *ex post* earnings performance is revealed, the average forecast error is negative, and the stock price reacts negatively, leading to the relative underperformance of the IPO firms.

Contrary to conventional wisdom in which the analysts are thought to be part of the institutional framework that makes the market efficient, these studies suggest that analysts may in fact be a contributing factor. Of course, interpreting the future abnormal returns as evidence of market inefficiency is subject to the caveats already discussed.

Chapter 5 discussed the empirical evidence on the pricing of accruals. Although accruals are priced by the market, research by Sloan (1996) suggests that the market may be mispricing the accrual component of earnings. In particular, Sloan provides evidence consistent with the contention that the market treats both the accrual and cash flow components of earnings as having the same degree of persistence. However, the time-series behavior indicates that the accrual component actually has less persistence than the cash flow component. Sloan then forms a trading strategy based on the accrual component and demonstrates that the future residual returns are negative (positive) for those firms with a relatively high (low) amount of accruals. Again, why the market participants would systematically ignore a difference that apparent from an analysis of past time series is a mystery.

Summary of Evidence

The results taken as a whole are indeed a paradox. Foster (1986, p. 399) observes

Notwithstanding this evidence, the efficient market model continues to play an important role in the literature. One reason is that competing models are not well articulated. A second reason is that non-market inefficiency explanations for the anomalous evidence exist.

Similarly, Fama (1991) concludes

> In short, some event studies suggest that stock prices do not respond quickly to some specific information. Given the event-study boom of the last 20 years, however, some anomalies, spurious and real, are inevitable. Moreover it is important to emphasize the main point. Event studies are the cleanest evidence we have on efficiency (at least unencumbered by the joint-hypothesis problem). With few exceptions, the evidence is supportive. (p.1602)

Returns to Private Information

Ignoring information costs, there are potential returns to private information. The events studies on earnings announcements clearly show that, if an investor were to trade on advance earnings information, abnormal returns are possible. However, because there are costs to information, there is no economic reason to believe that the market would be efficient in the strong form (with respect to all information, including privately held information). The costs of obtaining and trading on privately held information can be sufficiently high to preclude abnormal returns, after costs. The costs include not only search and analysis costs, but also transactions costs of trading and legal liability associated with trading on privately held information. Bernard and Thomas (1990) claim that the postannouncement drift is within the range of reasonable estimates of transactions costs.

Moreover, if some of these strategies from apparently readily available data lead to such large abnormal returns, one might expect this to be reflected in the investment performance of portfolios managed by professionals (for example, mutual funds, pension funds, and endowment funds). However, the evidence of superior performance by managed portfolios is quite weak, with many studies finding the abnormal performance to be negative once fund expenses, including management fees and trading costs, are included. This literature is reviewed by Fama (1991), who concludes that if these are the superior, informed individuals, they are trading beyond the point where the marginal benefits to investors equal marginal cost.

6-5   RESEARCH DESIGN ISSUES

As with empirical research in many other areas, efficient market research is the subject of controversy and the evidence is subject to diverse interpretation. One reason for diverse interpretations is that some features in the research design reduce the power of the tests. This section focuses on six research design issues: (1) the relationship between the definition of market efficiency and the tests of market efficiency, (2) the power of the test and the choice of the null hypothesis, (3) interstudy comparability and the variety of topics and methods choices available to the researcher, (4) self-selection bias, (5) the markets studied, and (6) joint hypothesis testing and model misspecification.

For the first issue, the empirical studies do not directly test market efficiency. The security prices that would prevail if there were universal knowledge of the information are not observed, because not every investor is literally aware of the change in accounting methods and its potential implications. Instead, the empirical studies attempt to infer that the security prices behave *as if such a condition held.* The research on change in depreciation methods provides an example.

The empirical evidence is interpreted as showing no price effects associated with the change in method and is further interpreted as evidence consistent with an efficient market. Prior to these studies, advocates of market inefficiency argued that a change in depreciation methods would induce a price change because of a myopic reliance on the earnings number (in other words, market inefficiency with respect to this information). Hence, the evidence, which indicates no average residual price change, is interpreted as consistent with market efficiency.

For the second issue, market efficiency is typically formulated in terms of the null hypothesis of no price change. Market efficiency is then not rejected, unless it can be rejected at "publishable" levels of significance. In this context, the power of the test (the ability to reject the null when it is false) is critical. Failure to control for other factors influencing price changes (even when they are uncorrelated with the event of interest) can reduce the power of the test. An alternative approach would be to adopt "market inefficiency" as the null. The purpose of the analysis would be to see whether extant research methods produce results that are capable of rejecting the null of inefficiency. This, of course, requires a specification of what "inefficiency" means in terms of prices. In many cases this is unclear. However, in the change in depreciation methods example, positing a constant price-earnings multiple provides an estimate of the expected price change and constitutes one possible specification of the inefficiency. The alternative was rejected by the evidence.

The third issue of research design concerns interstudy comparability in general and specification of the security return metric in particular. Since Ball and Brown's (1968) study the literature has extended this early work by expanding the set of signals examined, by expanding the technology for measuring the informational variable (for example, choice of earnings forecasting model), and by expanding the technology for deriving a security return metric. As a result, we have experienced a contemporaneous expansion of both the topics studied and the methods used to study them. In many cases, a study will alter both topic and method simultaneously, making comparison with previous studies difficult. When a difference in results is observed, it is difficult to identify the source of the difference, because more than one dial on the research machine has been turned. Because of the tendency to turn more than one dial at a time in each additional study, it is difficult to infer the reason for the different results.

A fourth research design issue is self-selection bias. Evidence suggests that many of the firms studied differ from other firms in a systematic fashion. Their residual price change behavior in the month before the change is very much like the "loser" portfolio in Figure 6-1. Firms that switch depreciation methods do so for a reason and differ in systematic ways in addition to price behavior, such as earnings performance. Similarly, firms that use the pooling versus purchase treatment for business combinations differ from each other. In particular, the residual price change behavior of firms that use the purchase treatment is similar to the "winner" portfolio in Figure 6-1. If firms differ in a systematic way in the months prior to the event of interest, there is a confounding effect, which can increase ambiguity in the interpretation of the results.

A fifth research design issue is the securities markets studied. For the most part, samples have been drawn from firms listed on the exchanges. Most frequently, the New York Stock Exchange has been the population from which the samples are drawn. Although listed securities represent the bulk of the market value of common stocks traded, it is difficult to determine the extent to which the evidence of listed securities can be generalized to the over-the-counter (OTC) market. For example, those who believe that analysts are the "force" that makes the market efficient often argue that the OTC market may be inefficient with respect to many items of information. Evidence indicates that such companies receive less analyst following. Is it then appropriate to infer less market efficiency for such securities? Research by Shores (1990) indicates that earnings announcements are relatively more important for such firms, but that the OTC stock prices behave similar to listed securities as far as the speed of reaction to earnings announcements are concerned.

There may be alternative mechanisms. For example, for OTC securities, the broker-dealers who "make" the market in that particular stock may fulfill this role. They stand ready to buy and sell shares at announced bid and ask prices. Such individuals would appear to have natural incentives to ensure that no one "knows" more than they do. As a result, the bid and ask prices may reflect the information in the possession of the broker-dealer, and such an information system may be extensive. Moreover, as will be shown, theories of market efficiency need not rely on the existence of "experts" such as analysts or broker-dealers.

The sixth research design issue is the joint hypothesis issue. A test of market efficiency is a joint test of efficiency, an equilibrium model of capital asset pricing, and the measurement of the relevant factors. For example, in the CAPM, systematic risk (beta) was assumed to be the only factor determining differential expected return. A finding of abnormal returns could occur because of market inefficiency, the incorrect choice of an asset pricing model, or measurement error in systematic risk. It can be difficult to disentangle the influence of each of these factors.

These research design issues that may lead to difficulty in interpreting market efficiency research are a common basis used by the research community in judging the power of the empirical evidence.[11] Such issues can explain why market efficiency is a controversial topic among the research community.

---

[11]While the discussion has focused on the research design issues of efficient market studies, many of these same issues arise in other areas of security price research, such as those discussed in Chapter 5.

6-6 THEORIES OF MARKET EFFICIENCY

Market efficiency involves a theory of the process by which information becomes reflected in prices. Unless individuals are characterized as throwing away something of value, information is not used because it is costly. The basic argument for market efficiency is one of competitive markets. Large numbers of buyers and sellers will compete with one another for the interpretation of financial reporting information. Competitive forces will cause prices to reflect unbiased assessments of the implications of the information for security prices. In this setting, investors would not process information in a biased or inefficient fashion, because it would be against their own economic self-interest do so. A related argument is even if individual investors might be prone to such inefficiencies prices will not, because inefficient prices would offer "arbitrage" opportunities (riskless abnormal returns) and competition among arbitrageurs would cause prices to fully reflect information and remove opportunities for arbitrage. In this setting, why would one expect prices not to "fully reflect" publicly available information? The answer, of course, lies in the possibility that such data are not universally available at zero cost to all individuals.

Knowledge of the change in methods may not be universal. Moreover, there may not be universal (costless) access to other information on the implications of the change. In other words, obtaining the training (for example, knowledge of depreciation methods, understanding that a firm can have a different set of books for tax and for annual report purposes) may be costly and hence such knowledge is not universal. However, interpretation of the change goes beyond this and involves the assessment of management's motivations for changing depreciation methods (for example, reflecting management's expectations about future earnings or plans for additional asset acquisitions). Such analysis (information) is provided by the financial and accounting community, but perhaps not costlessly. Hence, market prices might not reflect this potentially costly information. This constitutes a simplified explanation of why a nonzero probability of market inefficiency with respect to "publicly available" information might be assessed. However, despite the cost of the information, security prices might act as if the information were costlessly available to all investors. This provides one interpretation of the empirical research on semistrong form efficiency. In particular, from this perspective the empirical studies of change in accounting methods are viewed as testing market efficiency with respect to more information than merely the knowledge that a change took place (in other words, "sophistication" of the use of the data is also an issue).

Grossman (1976) and Grossman and Stiglitz (1980) provide analyses of conditions under which market efficiency would or would not be obtained. In these models, individuals "extract" information from prices. In the Grossman and Stiglitz model, individuals choose to become informed or uninformed, and at equilibrium each individual is indifferent, because either action (after deducting information costs) offers the same expected utility. For there to be incentives to purchase information, prices cannot "fully reflect" the information obtained. Hence, the market must be inefficient with respect to that information. In the Grossman model every individual is equally uninformed in that each receives a garbled signal, but prices act as an aggregation of everyone's information, such that the price "reflects" information that is superior to that held by each and every individual. However, individuals extract this superior information from prices and the price "fully reflects" that superior information. This model also has issues of private incentives for information production, because each individual is assumed to costlessly observe price (and extract information from it), which eliminates the incentive to privately seek information if it is costly (in other words, a free-rider phenomenon occurs).

In a related vein, Verrecchia (1979) has constructed a model in which price acts as an aggregator of beliefs (as distinct from an aggregator of information). As the number of individuals increases, prices behave as if everyone observed the ungarbled signal. The major difference is that there is no explicit learning from prices involved. Hence, while prices reflect the ungarbled signal, individual beliefs or portfolios may not reflect this information. Neither Grossman nor Verrecchia requires the existence of a subset of "initially" more informed individuals (for example, superior analysts). These analyses deal with private information production. One such collective choice would be centralized production of signal, thereby avoiding the costs of redundant production.

Bagehot (1971) and Treynor (1974) introduce a model of superior informed individuals (or at least perceive themselves to have superior information). As a result, they are the major "active" participants in the market, because the uninformed engage in buy-and-hold strategies that minimize trading. Although each informed individual is informed relative to the uninformed, no one individual observes a noiseless signal. When an active trader comes to the market, the person most likely to be on the other side of the transaction is another active trader. In this setting, they trade because they cannot perfectly extract the noise from their own private signal. The price reflects some average of the two private signals and hence reflects their information, but returns to each trader are normal, because no one active trader has consistently superior information to any other active trader. Treynor characterized this model of market efficiency with a quotation from the Pogo comic strip, "We have met the enemy, and he is us."

Illustration of a Theory

The crux of a theory of market efficiency that does not rely on the existence of a set of "experts" is that the level of knowledge reflected in prices is greater than merely the "average" level of knowledge among investors in the market. Some simple analogies illustrate this point. Consider each individual containing a "small" amount of knowledge and a considerable amount of idiosyncratic behavior. This can be modeled as each individual receiving a garbled signal from an information system that provides an ungarbled signal disguised by a "noise" component. The garbling is so large that any inspection of that individual's behavior provides little indication that such an individual is contributing to the efficiency of the market with respect to the ungarbled information system. Moreover, assume that this is true for every individual who comprises the market. However, the idiosyncratic behavior, by definition, is essentially uncorrelated among individuals. As a result, security price, which can be viewed as a "consensus" across investors, is effectively able to diversify away the large idiosyncratic component, such that only the knowledge (the ungarbled signal) persists in terms of explaining the security price. By analogy, the individual investor beliefs can be viewed akin to individual securities and the security price can be viewed as an aggregate akin to a portfolio.

The small amount of knowledge is the systematic component across investors. Although it is dwarfed by the idiosyncratic behavior at the individual investor level, it is the only portion that persists at the security price level. This does not require the existence of any "experts." Moreover, the quality of the knowledge reflected in prices is considerably higher than the average quality of knowledge across the individuals who comprise the market. Analogously, in portfolio theory the variance of return of any portfolio is strictly less than the average variance of the securities' returns that comprise the portfolio, if securities' returns are uncorrelated with one another.[12]

Forecasting Football Games

The fact that a consensus can reflect "greater than average" knowledge or insight is illustrated in a seemingly unrelated context—the prediction of outcomes of football games. Each week during the football season, the sports staff of the *Boston Globe* predicts the outcomes of the NFL professional football games for the coming Sunday or Monday. They are to pick which team will do better than predicted by the Las Vegas "line." The Las Vegas line is determined by the market for legalized gambling and represents a market consensus of which team is favored and the "spread," the expected difference in the scores. Members of the sports staff can be viewed as experts potentially possessing superior insight or superior information. However, the market has at least two factors operating in its favor. It represents a consensus and has the power of diversification relative to the forecasts of any individual. Also in the market, money, as well as pride, is at stake.

Individual sports staff members forecast which team will do better relative to the spread. The cumulative results for the last week of the NFL season are summarized in Table 6-1 for 1987 through 1996. If individual staff members have no superior insight to the market, by purely guessing they can expect 50% accuracy. Overall, the individual forecasters were right 50.2% of the time and wrong 49.8% (5,064 versus 5,023), which is not significantly different from 50%. The best forecaster

---

[12]In fact, much stronger statements can be made. The variance of return for the portfolio will be strictly less than the average variance, as long as the returns are less than perfectly correlated (there will be some diversification effect). Moreover, the variance of the return of the portfolio can be strictly less than the variance of even one of the securities that comprise it. For example, assuming uncorrelated returns and equal variances across security returns, the variance of the portfolio return will be strictly less than the variance of every one of the security returns for any portfolio with two or more securities.

TABLE 6-1 Forecasting Football Games[a]

	YEAR										
FORCASTER	1996	1995	1994	1993	1992	1991	1990	1989	1988	1987	TOTAL
Will McDonough											
Beat the line	115	110	91	112	114	97	96	115	101	69	1020
Lost to the line	110	111	113	93	93	104	111	91	105	82	1013
Michael Madden											
Beat the line	128	114	100	112	109	99	101	95	107	84	1049
Lost to the line	97	107	104	93	98	102	106	111	99	67	984
Ron Borges											
Beat the line	120	108	110	107	109	103	106	93	102	73	1031
Lost to the line	105	113	94	98	98	98	101	113	104	78	1002
John Carney											
Beat the line	116	104	97	102	103	107	107	97			833
Lost to the line	109	117	107	103	104	94	100	109			843
Nick Cafardo											
Beat the line	108										108
Lost to the line	117										117
Jim Greenridge											
Beat the line		94	103								197
Lost to the line		127	101								228
Frank Dell'Apa											
Beat the line				98	104	97	77				376
Lost to the line				107	103	104	52				366
Mark Blaudschun											
Beat the line								108	105	65	278
Lost to the line								98	101	86	285
Vince Doria											
Beat the line									104	68	172
Lost to the line									102	83	185
Overall											
Beat the line											5064
Lost to the line											5023

[a]*Taken from "Globe Staff's Pro Selections" of the* Boston Globe *for the final week of the regular NFL season for the years 1987 to 1996. Ties are omitted.*

had a accuracy of 51.6%. This "superior" performance could be due to either luck or to skill. However, even this difference is not significantly different from 50% at conventional levels of significance. Moreover, with nine forecasters, *ex post* some would be expected to do better by chance. Consistent with the luck interpretation, when the group as a whole is examined, four did better but five did worse. Consistency of superior forecasting ability across years is also an important factor. If individual years are examined, the best forecaster overall outperformed the line in only six years but fell short four years. Similar behavior was observed for the other forecasters.

The purpose of the example is not to demonstrate that no superior forecasters of football games exist. The illustration is certainly not introduced to show that no superior analysts exists. However, the example does illustrate that the consensus forecast imbedded in market prices can be very difficult to beat even by those who plausibly are viewed as experts with superior insight, knowledge, or skill.[13]

Interim Summary

The empirical research arose in response to claims in the financial and accounting community that market inefficiencies existed. As a result, the empirical findings have largely preceded a formal, conceptual development. A variety of theories of market efficiency have been explored, some of which compare informed with uninformed investors, some focus on competition among informed individuals, and still others focus on the consensus property of security prices that permit prices in principle to be better informed than most, if not all, the individuals that comprise the consensus. These theories help explain how privately held information may (or may not) become fully reflected in security prices, how costs are a potential barrier to market efficiency, and how market efficiency need not rely on universal sophisticated or even a subset of superior informed investors in order to function.

6-7   IMPLICATIONS OF MARKET EFFICIENCY

This section is devoted to a discussion of the implications of assuming that the market is efficient *with respect to publicly available information* (semistrong form efficiency). Discussing the implications is important but difficult. A difficulty arises because the potential implications of market efficiency cannot be discussed in isolation but rather in the context of other judgments of fact and value judgments. To the extent possible, the discussion will be explicit about the other judgments, perceptions, and assumptions being introduced. However, an element of subjectivity and personal opinion inevitably creeps into a discussion such as this. The statements that follow illustrate why many constituencies in the financial reporting environment have shown an interest in and perceive that they are affected by market efficiency. However, as will become apparent, many of the statements made have not been derived rigorously and rely on intuition. Moreover, empirical evidence is often lacking on critical links, which establish the importance of market efficiency to these various constituencies. With this disclaimer, the following implications are offered.

1. The efficient market implies that the substance rather than the form of disclosure may be the more important policy issue. A market that is efficient with respect to public information may not be efficient with respect to private information.

---

[13]Libby (1981) discusses several contexts where a consensus outperforms the average of those comprising the consensus. This is an extremely simple model of investor behavior mainly designed to illustrate the diversification effects that may be operating on price. Bagehot (1971) and Treynor (1974) question the lack of independence across investors.

Hence, bringing an item of information into the public domain (disclosure) is an issue of substance. However, once in the public domain, whether the format used to display the data is a substantive issue is unclear, at least in its impact on security prices. For example, although it may be important that an item appear somewhere in the annual report, it may not make any difference in terms of the price of the security whether the item is reported in the footnotes or in the body of the statement.[14] Similarly, it would make little difference whether the income statement effects of an item are explicitly reported if they could be inferred from balance sheet disclosure.[15]

2. To believe that merely because an item does not appear in the financial statements it is not reflected in prices may be naive. Security prices reflect a rich information system of which the financial statements may be only a part. Consider this implication in the context of fair value disclosures of financial instruments, pension assets and obligations, and nonperforming loans, all of which the evidence indicates are priced by the market. From an informational perspective, footnote disclosure may be substantively equivalent to recognition of the item in the financial statements.

Why might a disclosure versus recognition make a difference in security prices? There are several possible reasons even in an efficient market. The location of the item might affect management's behavior. For example, it has been contended that requiring fair value investment securities to be recognized will cause bank management to change its investment policy. In particular, it has been claimed that bank management will shift to shorter-term investment securities, whose market values are less volatile. The location of the item could also affect the value of the firm depending on how the contracts of the firm are written in terms of accounting numbers. Recontracting costs would be reflected in the security prices. Location of the item might affect how regulators view the item. For example, bank regulators may regulate a bank differently depending on whether the fair value of financial instruments are merely disclosed or recognized in the accounts. The form of financial statement presentation could affect the probability of changes in future tax legislation. The location of the item influences how much resources management and auditors place in estimating and auditing the item. However, the magnitude of these other effects is not clear.

3. The research, together with the informal evidence cited above, can affect the way in which we view the role of information intermediaries. Analysts constitute part of the process by which information becomes reflected in prices. Along some dimensions, the activities of the analysts are complementary to the financial reporting information. By their analysis of financial statements, complex information, such as pension footnote information, becomes reflected in prices. It does not re-

---

[14]In principle, the format could convey information regarding management's expectations. However, such an effect remains undocumented empirically. The discussion also assumes that there are no second-order effects that would alter the cash flows of the firm. For example, if the lending opportunities of a firm are influenced by the location of financial leases in the balance sheet, security prices could be altered by format choices. More generally, it assumes no effect that would alter the production or financing decisions of the firm.

[15]For example, the disclosure of the LIFO may be substantively equivalent to booking LIFO in the body of the statements from an informational perspective. Hence, a firm is able to use LIFO for tax, and the federal taxation constraint that LIFO must then also be used for reporting purposes may not be a substantive constraint. In other words, the disclosure permits investors to adjust the financial statements to a non-LIFO basis.

quire the ability of the "average prudent investor" to conduct such an analysis. However, along other dimensions, the analysts' activities are substitutes for financial reporting information. To the extent that analysts provide alternative sources of information to investors they are in competition with publicly available financial information.

However, if information is a perishable commodity and the analyst community is a competitive one, it may be difficult for any one analyst to demonstrate consistently superior performance. However, from a broader perspective, superior performance may not be the appropriate metric by which to measure the contribution of the analyst community. Every analyst may be playing approximately a zero-sum game against the rest of the community. But, this does not necessarily imply that the net effect of the activities is valueless. The process of competing analysts searching for information may in part result in security prices that reflect a richer information system. In this sense, the activities of the analyst community may in part be a public good. From this perspective, evaluation of performance in terms of ability to generate abnormal returns may be inappropriate.

The public good aspects of analysts' activities raises the issue of governmental regulation of their activities. The financial reporting regulations can alter the nature and level of such activities (for example, its powers over disclosure). Presumably, reduction of resources spent on private-sector information search and the prevention of wealth redistribution because of information asymmetries would be two of the concerns. In particular, the SEC can affect the analyst community not only by altering the nature of mandated disclosure but also by regulating the manner or process by which information flows from corporations to analysts.

4. In an efficient market, the vast majority of "average prudent investors" may not be actively and literally involved in trying to interpret the implications of financial reporting for the price of stock.[16] The average investor who has no expertise in financial or accounting matters may be deferring the analysis to those who have a comparative advantage (such as the information intermediaries). Hence, the demand for financial reporting information is an indirect one. The interest of the average prudent investor may be protected by ensuring that a given data item is disclosed to a number of analysts so that they compete with one another for the implications and interpretations of that item for the cash flows and price of security.

5. Regulators may wish to reconsider the nature of the concern for the naive investor. If the investor, no matter how naive, is in effect facing a fair game with respect to *publicly* available information, can the investor still be harmed? If so, how? If an investor holds a well-diversified portfolio, is a portion or all of the risk of nondisclosure diversifiable?

Harm can occur when firms are following policies of less than full disclosure, which gives some individuals the opportunity to trade on the private information. There may be other consequences as well. Portfolio positions held by investors may differ even though the prices are same. For example, "improperly" diversified portfolios is one of the consequences of "erroneously"

---

[16]The term *average prudent investor* refers to the investor who does not have professional skills in processing and interpreting the data. The indirect role of the average prudent investor is not a recent observation. Kripke (1973) discusses the myth of the informed layman, and Douglas (1933) notes the original intention of the Securities Acts was that the professional would act as an interpreter and disseminator of the SEC disclosures.

perceiving the market to be inefficient. Other consequences include the direct costs of reporting, disseminating, certifying, and processing the information; the costs of privately seeking the information if it is not publicly available; the costs paid to analysts and others to perform that function for the investor; and transactions costs such as brokerage fees.

Nonimplications

A number of unwarranted interpretations may be drawn from the assumption of market efficiency. In some cases, the interpretations cannot be drawn unless additional structure is assumed. In other cases, the interpretations do not fully appreciate the processes by which security prices arise and reflect information. Several specific illustrations are provided in an attempt to document these assertions.

1. Market efficiency does not connote social desirability. Market efficiency is concerned with the relationship between information and security prices. No value laden or normative connotations are implied. However, while the link cannot be explicitly made, many believe that greater market efficiency will indirectly lead to better resource allocation, lowering of risks of investing with a increased willingness to invest, greater capital formation, and a "fairer" system of more equitable dissemination of information.

2. Market efficiency does not imply clairvoyance. The future is uncertain, the prices reflect investors' expectations—expectations that may or may not be realized. Hindsight can often suggest that security prices reflected an expectation that differed greatly from the realization. However, this is not evidence of market inefficiency but rather of uncertainty. Even an efficient market does not have a crystal ball. A number of large "surprises," causing substantial revisions in security prices, is consistent with an efficient market. It is not valid to evaluate the efficiency of a set of security prices in the light of information that only became available after those prices were formed.

   A somewhat more subtle variation is to suggest that the market did have the information available but incorrectly interpreted subsets of the information. For example, certain signals were ignored, which with the benefit of hindsight we "know" should have received much greater attention. At any point in time a number of signals will be available and it is unlikely that each signal, considered individually, leads to the same prediction of the future. To examine the evidence retrospectively and determine what would have led to the best forecast is not valid and relies on hindsight just as much as the earlier scheme.

3. An efficient market does not imply that investors will necessarily perceive the market to be efficient. Perceived market inefficiencies may be widespread even though the security prices fully reflect published information for two reasons. First, any one investor may be aware of only a portion of the information that is reflected in prices. As a result, from this myopic perspective, securities may appear to be mispriced because prices reflect information not available to that individual. Second, interpreting price responses to information requires a model of the expectations underlying those prices. We may be tempted to interpret the market's response to prices in the light of a simplistic, naive expectations model. For example, annual earnings per share may be 30% above the previous year's figure; yet the prices might react adversely to the announcement if an increase of more than

30% had been expected. Information has arrived since the publication of last year's earnings, and this information may have led to a substantial revision in earnings expectations since the last year's earnings announcements. At a minimum, quarterly earnings and dividend announcements are capable of altering expectations. Forecasts by management and by analysts are also a source of expectations changes. More qualitative information on contract awards, acquisitions, litigation, and product development may also play an important role. In this respect, it is not surprising that the empirical evidence cited in Chapter 5 indicates that expectation models of earnings that use last year's earnings as their most recent input have limited ability to explain price movements in the one or two months prior to the announcement of the subsequent year's earnings.

In sum, understanding prices and price changes without knowledge of the information set reflected in prices and without knowledge of the expectations embedded in prices may be difficult. This inference process is particularly difficult because prices reflect a composite across investors, who differ with respect to information and expectations as well as other factors such as wealth and attitudes toward risk. It is not surprising to find particular cases in which the price reaction to information seems anomalous. However, one must be careful to avoid labeling our inability to explain such phenomenon as evidence of market inefficiency, market irrationality, or that all-absorbing residual, "market psychology."

The first three nonimplications of the efficient market deal with common misunderstandings about the meaning of an efficient market or the process by which information becomes reflected in prices. A second class of nonimplications deals with using the concept of market efficiency to evaluate adequacies or deficiencies in the current institutional structure. The concept of market efficiency by itself is not sufficiently rich to warrant inferences regarding institutional structure. Two illustrations are provided. For purposes of continuity, these will be numbered consecutively with respect to the previous nonimplications.

4. The efficient market does not imply that information intermediaries, such as analysts, are useless. The efficient market concept is silent on the value of their services. There is nothing in either the definition or the evidence concerning market efficiency that specifies the process or institutional mechanism by which information becomes reflected in prices. Analysts may play an important role in the process of generating and disseminating information to the investment community. However, although the efficient market evidence, in and of itself, does not indict analysts, it does not support them either.

5. The efficient market does not imply that no basis can be provided for governmental intervention in the disclosure process. To draw inferences regarding the role of governmental intervention in disclosure decisions, additional analysis of the nature of the institutional mechanism by which information becomes reflected in prices is required. Earlier it was suggested that the analyst community may play an important role in such a process. However, little is known in a formal way about the process. Corporations have incentives to provide information voluntarily to the analyst community, and the analyst community has incentives to search for information from corporations and other sources. Given this flow of information in the private sector, the additional information content of the mandated disclosures of the SEC may be minuscule. The basis for governmental intervention must stem from some aspect of the private-sector incentives that cause them to be imperfectly aligned with the social incentives. Chapter 7 discusses regulation in depth.

The choice among different financial reporting systems involves choosing among differing consequences, which affect individuals differently. Hence, some individuals may be better off under one method, and others may be better off under an alternative method. The issue is one of social choice, which involves making interpersonal welfare comparisons.

6-8 IMPORTANCE TO FINANCIAL REPORTING CONSTITUENCIES

This section attempts to summarize the importance of the implications from the perspective of the various constituencies in the financial reporting environment: investors, regulators, management, auditors, and information intermediaries. This discussion faces the same difficulties cited at the outset of the previous section. As a result, the same disclaimer that was tendered there applies here as well.

Investors

The relation between financial information and security prices can influence investors' demand for financial information. As previously discussed, in an efficient market much of the demand for financial information may be an indirect demand. Similarly, the consequences are indirect, albeit important, via the effect of financial information on security prices. For example, changes in security prices alter the wealth of the investor and in general alter the consumption-investment opportunities available to each investor. Security price changes can be viewed as inducing a redistribution of wealth among investors.

Investor behavior can also be affected by what information the investor possesses, by what information is reflected in prices, and by what information is held by others, including other investors and management. These factors can potentially influence investor behavior with respect to consumption, portfolio selection, and costs incurred, including information costs and transactions costs.

The perception that prices fully reflect a rich, comprehensive information system may reduce an individual's direct demand for financial information. In such cases, the individuals act as "price takers" and are willing to adopt, as their own, the consensus beliefs reflected in prices. In one sense, they can be "free riders" with respect to the information reflected in prices, and it may be optimal for them to pursue relatively simple, costless portfolio strategies.

Conversely, the perception that security prices do not fully reflect some information can lead to adopting portfolio strategies designed to reap abnormal expected returns by exploiting the informational inefficiency. (1) The perceived inefficiency can lead the investor to expend time and energy in searching for and interpreting such information, to pay others (such as information intermediaries) to provide such information, or to incur transactions costs pursuing active portfolio management. (2) It could also cause the investor to adopt less diversified portfolios by investing disproportionately in perceived "underpriced" securities.

The perception that some information is not fully reflected in prices may make the investor reluctant to trade in securities if it is felt that the information system is possessed by others, such as management or other investors. This approach to concern over information asymmetry could have several effects. (1) It could lead to an attempt to extract the information by observing the behavior of those perceived to have more information (for example, by observing the prices at which the more informed investors would be willing to trade).[17] (2) It could lead to a well-diversified, passive portfolio strategy designed to insulate the investor from trading with others who might have superior information. (3) It could cause the investor to retreat from such markets and invest in markets in which information asymmetry is of less concern. (4) It could also induce the investor to reduce the total amount of investment.

The potential effects of information asymmetries on investor behavior were discussed at greater length in Chapter 2. The list of potential effects is offered as illustrative and is not intended to be complete. Moreover, little is known about how important these effects are empirically, and it is not unreasonable to believe that the effects may vary across investors. The effects on investor behavior is of concern not only to investors themselves but also to the other constituencies. As a result, market efficiency is important to these other groups in part because of its potential effects on investor behavior.

Financial Reporting Regulators

The primary concern of the financial reporting regulators is investors (broadly defined to include creditors). The investor orientation is partially motivated by concern over the welfare of the investors and the "fairness" of the security markets in which they trade. Perceived adversities and inequities may happen to investors because of informational deficiencies (for example, failure to disclose). However, the regulators (SEC and FASB) also share a concern over the effects on resource allocation and capital formation. For example, fuller disclosure will tend to lead to a more efficient allocation of resources because investors will be in a more informed position to judge where their funds can be used most productively and profitably, given the risks involved. Some also argue that a more favorable climate for capital formation is provided by fuller disclosure because of the effect on the perceived "fairness" of the market. Investors are said to be more willing to invest funds in the new-issue market if there is greater disclosure and less risk of fraud or misrepresentation about the productive opportunities of the firm issuing the securities. Moreover, the subsequent "marketability" of the securities is said to be a function of the perceived "fairness" of the exchange markets. In other words, if the exchange market is efficient with respect to a rich, comprehensive information system, investors have less concern over information asymmetries at the time they eventually sell their shares and hence are more willing to invest in the new-issue market.

These arguments have not been developed rigorously and rely on intuition. Moreover, there has been little empirical evidence of the effect of disclosure on re-

---

[17]The literature on "learning from prices" cited in the section on theories of market efficiency is one example of extracting information from the behavior of other market participants.

source allocation or capital formation. A simple relationship between the level of disclosure and the rate of capital formation may not exist. For example, increased disclosure may not necessarily lead to increased capital formation. The disclosure (the particular signal reported) may lead investors to reduce their expectations regarding future returns or to increase their assessments of risk. As a result, capital formation may be lower than it would have been had the information not been provided and reflected in security prices.

The information that is fully reflected in security prices will partially determine the price effects of any given financial reporting regulation. For example, if prices fully reflect an information system, requiring disclosure of signals from that system will have no impact on prices, assuming the disclosure is expected to cause no change in the production and financing decisions of the firm (and, as a result, no change in beliefs regarding future cash flows). Of course, a price effect could occur if the disclosure is expected to alter the firm's future cash flows for the reasons stated earlier.

What are the implications of market efficiency for the SEC under the assumption that the market is not efficient in the strong form but is efficient in the semistrong form? The motivation for requiring disclosure would be essentially to bring private information into the public domain. In a market that is not efficient in the strong form, this is a potentially substantive issue, because privately held information is not reflected in prices. Once the data are placed in the public domain, semistrong form market efficiency provides the assurance that such data will be fully reflected in prices. In other words, requiring public disclosure is an effective remedy (at least in terms of security prices) for any perceived undesirable effects associated with the presence of nonpublicly available data.

In many respects, this pair of assumptions offers the most friendly or most favorable climate for disclosure regulation from the perspective of market efficiency. This does not deny that there are many other considerations as well, some of which are discussed in Chapters 2 and 7. Moreover, this pair of assumptions appears to be a reasonable description of reality based on an overall evaluation of the empirical research discussed earlier. From the above analysis, one might expect that the SEC has considerable incentive to adopt this pair of assumptions. In fact, by its policy of active disclosure regulation, the SEC can be viewed as acting as if it believes in semistrong form efficiency but not strong form efficiency. However, the stated policy position of the SEC makes no explicit reference to this concept.

Moreover, the *Report of the SEC Advisory Committee on Corporate Disclosure* (SEC 1977, p. XXXVIII) discusses market efficiency in essentially negative tones.

> The Committee believes that notwithstanding the interesting and clearly significant work done by economists and others in developing the efficient market hypothesis, the evidences that fundamental research is essentially useless are not yet, and may never be, sufficiently telling to justify the elimination of a disclosure system premised on the proposition that such research is useful and necessary.

The above statement contains two crucial premises: (1) Market efficiency implies that fundamental research is useless, and (2) the SEC disclosure system requires the assumption that such research is useful. Given these two premises, reticence by the SEC Advisory Committee, which supports the SEC, to accept the efficient market hypothesis is not surprising. However, neither premise is correct. Market efficiency in the semistrong form could in fact provide a "friendly" climate for mandated disclosure. However, given that the perception that such premises are valid and given that acceptance of market efficiency is equated with the demise of the SEC, market efficiency would probably not be accepted by supporters of the SEC.

Management

Management also has an interest in market efficiency and its effects on the investor. The maximization of shareholder wealth is a commonly cited criterion for managerial choice behavior. The stewardship view implies that management has a responsibility to act in the interest of the investor, and this is reinforced by the legal liability of management under legislation such as the Securities Acts of 1933 and 1934.

Management has a vital interest in the price of the firm's securities. Management compensation in the form of stock options and stock ownership is directly related to the performance of stock prices. Indirectly, other forms of compensation may also be affected by stock price performance. The maximization of shareholder wealth is often operationally taken to be equivalent to, or at least highly related to, the maximization of share price. The financing decisions of the firm are a prime responsibility of management. The stock price received on a new issue determines either how much proceeds are available for additional investment (assuming a fixed number of shares issued) or how much additional shares must be issued (assuming a fixed amount of desired net proceeds). In either case, the fortunes of the current shareholders are affected by the price of the new securities.

Financial reporting is considered to be a prime responsibility of management, and market efficiency is related to the effect on security prices of management choices among different financial reporting systems. Moreover, managements, competing among one another for investors' funds, have incentives to provide information to investors and information intermediaries, among others. Hence, management has incentive to voluntarily reveal private information (Healy and Palepu 1993), which can be influenced by costs, such as out-of-pocket costs, competitive disadvantage to unilateral disclosure of operations, and legal liability.

Market efficiency has potential implications for (1) certain management decisions, such as a change in accounting methods, (2) the legal liability imposed on management for nondisclosure, (3) the choice of the level of complexity of the financial reporting system, (4) the concern of investors over moral hazard (for example, fraud) by management, their willingness to invest funds, and hence the price that they are willing to pay for the firm's securities, (5) the concern of investors over marketability of the securities at some future time and hence the price they are willing to pay now, (6) the choice of format or form of disclosure (in other words, supplemental disclosure versus inclusion in the financial statements), and (7) the information content of accrual accounting and earnings determination, relative to other forms of financial disclosure.

Wyatt (1983) reports that management behaves as if it does not believe the efficient market hypothesis. Wyatt documents several transactions in which management appears to care about the accounting method and is willing to incur costs in order to structure a transaction to have a desired effect on reported results. Following are at least two explanations.

First, in many cases management does not believe security markets are efficient with respect to publicly available financial reporting data. Market efficiency does not necessarily require a majority of corporate management to believe in it. Corporate managements do not tend to be strong advocates of market efficiency. In many cases, the value of management expertise arises precisely because of some imperfection in the product or factors markets. Given that imperfections are the raison d'être of management, it is an easy leap for management to perceive capital markets to be inefficient as well.

Second, management may be motivated to structure a transaction in a particular way for reasons other than perceptions of market inefficiency. As discussed in Chapter 5, many of the firm's contracts, such as management compensation and bond covenants, are defined in terms of accounting numbers. These contracting effects can affect management behavior.

Auditors

A demand for auditing arises because of a potential asymmetry of information between management and investors. Auditing financial information potentially reduces that asymmetry and in this sense facilitates market efficiency. The auditor has a responsibility to investors as the independent certifier of the financial statements prepared by management. Hence, the auditor is concerned about the effects on investors.

More specifically, market efficiency has several potential implications for the auditor, including (1) the legal liability associated with nondisclosure, (2) the information content of the accrual accounting system, which is the heart of the accounting system being audited, (3) the resources of the auditor allocated to issues of form versus substance, (4) the advice given to management with respect to its financial reporting decisions, such as a change in accounting method, (5) the assessment of the potential effects of a change in reporting systems and whether it is a preferable one, and (6) the use of security prices as a means against which to evaluate the thoroughness of an audit.

Information Intermediaries

The information intermediary also can be affected by market efficiency. The information intermediary plays many information-related roles, including that of (1) a seeker of information not already fully reflected in prices, (2) a processor, interpreter, and analyzer of information for prediction (prospective analysis), and (3) an interpreter of events after-the-fact (retrospective analysis). Information intermediaries compete with one another in the gathering and interpretation of information. Moreover, information intermediaries compete with reported financial information in supplying information to the capital markets. As discussed earlier, information intermediaries can be an important part of the process by which information becomes reflected in prices. On the other hand, market efficiency may make it more difficult for individual intermediaries to reap returns from their analysis activities.

In the first role, these intermediaries have incentives to seek out and to disseminate information. In the second and third roles, the intermediaries are producers of information. Here more primitive information, such as financial statement data, is an input or factor of production. The conclusions of the analysis, interpretation, and processing are the output or product of the analysis and are a form of information.

Disclosure of an item can have different effects depending on the roles of the information intermediary. (1) To the extent that the information intermediary is a seeker of information not fully reflected in prices, publicly available information can constitute a competing source of information. In this sense, information intermediaries may oppose regulations for greater disclosure if they feel that such disclosures would intrude on their domain and effectively compete with the information they provide. (2) To the extent that the information intermediary is a producer of information, either of prospective or retrospective analysis, financial disclosure constitutes a factor of production. As a result, the information intermediary might favor a regulation to increase the disclosure of financial information because it is tantamount to providing more of a factor of production for the information intermediary.

Market efficiency can also influence the orientation of information search or analysis. (1) As a seeker of information, the information intermediary makes a decision on which sources of information to pursue. Market efficiency can influence the sources of information sought. For example, if the market is perceived to be efficient with respect to publicly available information, an information intermediary would concentrate on gathering information that is not publicly available. The information intermediary will seek out sources that are not fully reflected in prices. (2) As a producer of information, the information intermediary can have diverse objectives. For example, the analysis could be directed at detecting mispriced securities or it could be directed at assessing the risk of different securities. If the information intermediary felt that the market was efficient with respect to a rich, comprehensive information system, the information intermediary may choose to direct the analysis toward risk assessment rather than toward finding mispriced securities.

As indicated previously, the services of information intermediaries are commonly sold on the basis that they can select mispriced securities. Clearly, market efficiency can be viewed as a threat to such claims. Market efficiency of the semistrong form implies that mispriced securities do not exist with respect to publicly available data. An information intermediary who offers the services on the premise that mispriced securities can be selected based on publicly available information is unlikely to embrace semistrong form efficiency.[18] For example, the analyst community has typically expressed strong opposition to market efficiency.

6-9 CONCLUDING REMARKS

This chapter explores the definition, theory, evidence, implications, and acceptance of market efficiency. The market is efficient with respect to an information system if prices act as if everyone has access to that information system. In this sense, prices are said to "fully reflect" the information system. The origin of market efficiency with respect to financial information is security analysis. The empirical evidence arose in response to contentions in the financial and accounting communities that the market is inefficient with respect to certain financial statement information. The early evidence was interpreted to be consistent with the contention that security prices respond quickly and in a sophisticated manner to financial statement data. Although the bulk of the evidence is consistent with market efficiency with respect to publicly available information, some evidence is not so clear-cut. This research has been labeled anomalous evidence by some, open to a variety of interpretations, one of which is market inefficiency.

Research provides various theories of market efficiency. The theoretical and research design issues influence the acceptance of various forms of market efficiency by the research community. Conditional upon market efficiency of the semistrong form, several potential implications and nonimplications are presented, and their importance to various constituencies is discussed. The chapter also examines the acceptance by the financial reporting constituencies. It is suggested that the degree of acceptance may not rest primarily on the theoretical and research design issues previously discussed but rather whether the acceptance is viewed to be in the self-interest of that particular group. However, disclosure regulation is consistent with market efficiency with respect to publicly available data but market inefficiency with respect to nonpublicly available data. Whether recognition versus disclosure is a substantive issue is another matter, and one that is still largely unresolved. Several important implications of market efficiency cut across several constituencies. Moreover, there are constituency-specific implications of market efficiency.

BIBLIOGRAPHY

Abarbanell, J., and V. Bernard. "Tests of Analysts' Overreaction/Underreaction to Earnings Information as an Explanation for Anomalous Stock Price Behavior." *Journal of Finance* (July 1992), 1181–1207.

[18]Of course, the information intermediary claims an ability to select mispriced securities based on nonpublicly available information. However, such claims potentially expose the analyst to legal liability.

Archibald, T. "Stock Market Reaction to Depreciation Switch-Back." *Accounting Review* (January 1972), 22–30.

Bagehot, W. "The Only Game in Town." *Financial Analysts Journal* (March–April 1971), 12–22.

Ball, R. "Changes in Accounting Techniques and Stock Prices." *Empirical Research in Accounting: Selected Studies.* Supplement to the *Journal of Accounting Research* (1972), 1–38.

———— and P. Brown. "An Empirical Evaluation of Accounting Income Numbers." *Journal of Accounting Research* (Autumn 1968), 159–178.

Beaver, W. "The Information Content of Annual Earnings Announcements." *Empirical Research in Accounting: Selected Studies.* Supplement to the *Journal of Accounting Research* (1968), 67–92.

————. "Market Efficiency." *Accounting Review* (January 1981), 23–37.

———— and R. Dukes. "Interperiod Tax Allocation and Delta-Depreciation Methods: Some Empirical Results." *Accounting Review* (July 1973), 549–559.

———— and W. Landsman. "Note on the Behavior of Residual Security Returns for Winner and Loser Portfolios." *Journal of Accounting and Economics* (December 1981), 233–241.

Bernard, V., and J. Thomas. "Post-Earnings Announcement Drift: Delayed Price Response or Risk Premium?" *Journal of Accounting Research* (Supplement 1989), 1–48.

————. "Evidence That Stock Prices Do Not Fully Reflect the Implications of Current Earnings for Future Earnings." *Journal of Accounting and Economics* (December 1990), 305–340.

Cootner, P., ed. *The Random Character of Stock Market Prices.* Cambridge: MIT Press, 1964.

Dechow, P., R. Sloan, and A. Sweeney. "The Relation Between Affiliated Analysts' Long-Term Earnings Forecasts and the Overpricing of Equity Offerings." Unpublished working paper, Wharton, 1996.

Douglas, W. "Protecting the Investor." *Yale Review* (1933), 523–524.

Dyckman, T., and D. Morse. *Efficient Capital Markets and Accounting: A Critical Analysis.* 2d ed. Englewood Cliffs, N.J.: Prentice-Hall, 1986.

Fama, E. "Efficient Capital Markets: A Review of Theory and Empirical Work." *Journal of Finance* (May 1970), 383–417.

————. "Efficient Capital Markets: II." *Journal of Finance* (December 1991), 1575–1617.

———— and K. French. "The Cross-Section of Expected Stock Returns." *Journal of Finance* (July 1992), 427–465.

Foster, G. *Financial Statement Analysis.* 2d ed. Englewood Cliffs, N.J.: Prentice-Hall, 1986.

————, C. Olsen, and T. Shevlin. "Earnings Releases, Anomalies and the Behavior of Security Returns." *Accounting Review* (October 1984), 574–603.

Graham, B., and D. Dodd. *Security Analysis.* New York: McGraw-Hill, 1934.

Grossman, S. "On the Efficiency of Competitive Stock Markets Where Traders Have Diverse Information." *Journal of Finance* (May 1976), 573–585.

———— and J. Stiglitz. "On the Impossibility of Informationally Efficient Markets." *American Economic Review* (June 1980), 393–408.

Healy, P., and K. Palepu. "The Effect of Firms' Financial Disclosure Strategies on Stock Prices." *Accounting Horizons* (March 1993), 1–11.

Kripke, H. "The Myth of the Informed Layman." *Business Lawyer* (January 1973), 631–638.

Lakonishok, J., A. Shleifer, and R. Vishny. "Contrarian Investment, Extrapolation, and Risk." *Journal of Finance* (December 1994), 1541–1578.

Lev, B., and R. Thiagarajan. "Fundamental Information Analysis." *Journal of Accounting Research* (Autumn 1993), 109–215.

Libby, R. *Accounting and Human Information Processing Theory and Applications.* Englewood Cliffs, N.J.: Prentice-Hall, 1981.

Loughran, T., and J. Ritter. "The New Issues Puzzle." *Journal of Finance* (March 1995), 23–51.

Morse, D. "Price and Trading Volume Reaction Surrounding Earnings Announcements: A Closer Examination." *Journal of Accounting Research* (Autumn 1981), 374–384.

Patell, J., and M. Wolfson. "The Intraday Speed of Adjustment of Stock Prices to Earnings and Dividend Announcements." *Journal of Accounting and Economics* (June 1984), 223–252.

Securities and Exchange Commission. *Report of the SEC Advisory Committee on Corporate Disclosure.* Washington, D.C.: U.S. Government Printing Office, 1977.

Shores, D. "The Association Between Interim Information and Security Returns Surrounding Earnings Announcements." *Journal of Accounting Research* (Spring 1990), 164–181.

Sloan, R. "Do Stock Prices Reflect Information in Accruals and Cash Flows About Future Earnings?" *Accounting Review* (July 1996), 289–315.

Treynor, J. "Efficient Markets and Fundamental Analysis." *Financial Analysts Journal* (March–April 1974), 14.

Verrecchia, R. "On the Theory of Market Information Efficiency." *Journal of Accounting and Economics* (March 1979), 77–90.

Wyatt, A. "Efficient Market Theory: Its Impact on Accounting." *Journal of Accountancy* (February 1983), 56–65.

7

Regulation

Financial reporting takes place in a regulated environment. Given that regulation is an important part of the financial reporting environment, this chapter explores such issues as: Why regulate? How should regulation be conducted? Who should regulate (the SEC or the FASB)?[1] In doing so, the discussion will serve to synthesize the major concepts of the framework developed in the previous chapters.

7-1 MANDATED FINANCIAL REPORTING

The regulation of financial reporting receives its impetus from the Securities Acts of 1933 and 1934, which gave the SEC statutory power to ensure "full and fair disclosure" by corporations issuing securities on an interstate basis. The Acts specifically grant the SEC the power to determine the accounting standards for reports filed with the SEC. The SEC delegates authority to the FASB to determine generally accepted accounting principles with respect to statements filed with the SEC.[2] Often the illustrations refer only to the SEC. However, in general, the discussion of the rationale for regulation applies to the FASB as well as to the SEC.

[1]This chapter draws heavily on Chapter XX of the *SEC Advisory Committee Report on Corporate Disclosure* (SEC 1977). An excellent review of financial reporting regulation also appears in Chapter 7 of Watts and Zimmerman (1986).
[2]While the SEC has delegated such authority to the FASB, the SEC has often chosen to exercise "oversight" with respect to FASB decisions (see Horngren 1972, 1973; Armstrong 1977; among others).

Brief Review of the Financial Reporting Environment

The investment process involves giving up current consumption in exchange for securities, which are claims to future, uncertain cash flows. The investor must decide how to allocate wealth between current consumption and investment and how to allocate the funds set aside for investment among the various securities available. The investor has a potential demand for information that will aid in assessing the future cash flows associated with the securities and the firms that offer those securities. However, the investor is not acting in isolation but within a larger investment environment. This environment consists of several characteristics. (1) Investors, some perhaps with limited financial and accounting training, have the opportunity to avail themselves of the services of financial intermediaries, such as investment companies, to whom they can defer a portion of the investment process. (2) Investors, some perhaps with limited access to and ability to interpret financial information, have the opportunity to avail themselves of the services of information intermediaries, such as analysts, to whom they can defer a portion or all of the information gathering and processing function. (3) Investors have the opportunity to invest in a number of securities and to diversify out of some of the risks associated with a single security. (4) The information intermediaries compete with one another in the gathering and interpretation of financial information. (5) Managements, competing with one another for the investors' funds, have incentives to provide financial information to the investment community. (6) Investors and intermediaries have information available that is more comprehensive and perhaps more timely than the annual report to shareholders or the SEC filings. (7) Security price research suggests that security prices reflect a rich, comprehensive information system.

Under these conditions, why is it desirable to have a portion of the disclosure system contain a mandated set of disclosures?

Previous Rationale for Regulation

One approach consists of citing a litany of perceived abuses. Several questions can be raised in connection with such an approach. Were the actions in question in fact "abuses"? What one person might label "manipulation" another might label "arbitrage." In particular, what harm was inflicted as a result of such actions? Was inadequate financial reporting a contributing factor to the abuses? Will mandating financial reporting in some form deter or reduce such activities? What was the frequency of abuses relative to some measure of total activity? What are the costs associated with regulation attempting to deter such activity? These are potentially important questions because mandated disclosure tends to be imposed on broad classes of corporations, not merely on those that committed the perceived abuse.[3]

---

[3]After analyzing the perceived abuses at the time of the enactment of the Securities Act, Benston (1973, 1974) has concluded that they constitute an inadequate basis on which to justify the securities' legislation.

Any system, even a regulated one, will incur some frequency of "abuse." The central issue is whether there is some flaw in the private sector (for example, some market failure) that leads to the conclusion that governmental regulation is a more desirable solution.

7-2 WHY REGULATE? (POSSIBLE RATIONALE FOR REGULATION)

This section attempts to develop a framework for considering the issues regarding financial reporting regulation. In doing so, information is viewed as an economic commodity. The issue will be viewed as regulating the flow of information to the investment community. To examine this issue from an economic perspective, the nature of economic problems and the purpose of government with respect to those problems is discussed briefly.

Economic issues fall into two major categories: efficiency and equity. The first category is concerned with the most efficient means of achieving some specified result. Movement to a more efficient solution could in principle result in everyone in the economy being in a more preferred position (or at least as preferred a position) with no one being in a less preferred position (called a *Pareto-optimal solution*). The second category, equity, deals with the choice among efficient solutions in which each solution will leave some individuals better off but others worse off. Issues on how wealth should be distributed among individuals in the economy is one example of an issue of equity. The government becomes involved in both types of issues. However, the rationale for governmental intervention can vary considerably depending on the type of issue involved. Therefore, it is imperative to state the extent to which the rationale for disclosure regulation rests on efficiency or equity considerations.

In general, the government has a variety of means available to deal with these issues, including the enforcement of private contracts, the definition and enforcement of property rights, taxation, regulation, and direct ownership. The Securities Acts provide two primary means by which the flow of information to investors is affected. First is the general antifraud provisions; the second is the power to explicitly mandate financial reporting via the SEC filings and annual reports to shareholders.

The Securities Acts provide that it is unlawful to make a false or misleading statement or to omit a material fact in connection with the purchase or sale of a security. Laws against fraud are commonplace in the sale of a variety of commodities, and they reflect concern over the pervasive problem that the quality of the product or service being sold is uncertain. Moreover, often one party to the transaction may naturally be in a position of superior information regarding the quality. Under antifraud provisions, certain parties to the transaction face the prospect of civil or criminal penalties when and if the quality of the commodity is eventually discovered and their behavior is deemed "fraudulent."

Although the deterrence of fraud via legal liability is fairly commonplace, the presence of a regulatory mechanism that explicitly mandates what must be disclosed is a special (although not unique) feature of securities regulation. For example, neither federal nor state laws require filing a prospectus when an individual sells a home, even though the seller is in a potentially superior position with respect to information on the quality of the home.

The next sections deal with arguments that potentially provide a rationale for mandated financial reporting which by implication asserts that reliance solely on the antifraud provisions is inadequate.[4] The arguments fall into three major categories. (1) Financial reporting involve externalities and a form of market failure. (2) Left unregulated, market forces would lead to an asymmetrical or uneven possession of information among investors. (3) Corporate management has incentives to suppress unfavorable information.

7-3 FINANCIAL REPORTING EXTERNALITIES

An externality exists when the actions of one party have effects on other parties who are not charged (or compensated) via the price mechanism. This constitutes a form of *market failure*. Although in principle an elaborate price system could be conceived that would charge or compensate the third parties for these effects, such a system may be undesirable because it is too costly or simply not feasible.[5]

However, without some form of collective action, the party undertaking the action has no incentive to internalize the effects on third parties, and the actions taken may lead to an inefficiency. For example, in the classic public good analysis with positive external effects on third parties, there is an underproduction of the public good in the absence of a collective action that incorporates the third parties, who benefit from the public good but do not participate in the decision to produce or pay for it. For this reason, these third parties are often referred to as *free riders*. In this situation, the private incentives are less than the "social" incentives to produce the public good.

In the financial reporting context, two examples are frequently offered. Externalities could occur when information about the productive opportunities of one firm conveys information about the productive opportunities of other firms. Shareholders in the disclosing firm pay the costs of disclosure but shareholders in the other firms do not, even though they are affected by the disclosure. For example, disclosure by a firm about its success (or lack thereof) with respect to some product

---

[4]The rationale for the choice between regulation and antifraud provisions is discussed in Posner (1972), pp. 156–166.
[5]This is one of many possible ways of discussing externalities. It is used here because it serves to focus on the issue of "market forces" versus regulation, which is a focal point of the Report of the SEC Advisory Committee on Corporate Disclosure (SEC 1977) Introduction. Foster (1980) provides a more general discussion of the externality issue, which focuses on interdependencies without tying them to market "failures."

development may provide information to other firms about their chances of success in similar product developments. In fact, it might even obviate their having to expend resources on product developments. Thus the familiar objection to disclosure on grounds of competitive disadvantage can be viewed as one form of externality. This setting has a lack of incentive to fully disclose (even though there are benefits to other firms) because the disclosing firm is not being compensated.

The second example deals with positive external effects on prospective shareholders. Investors demand information to assess the risks and rewards (in other words, the array of potential future cash flows) associated with alternative portfolios of securities. In making consumption and investment decisions, the investor finds information about a security useful whether or not that particular security ultimately is one of the securities in the portfolio chosen by the investor. The process of selecting the "best" portfolio inherently involves a consideration of investment alternatives (alternative portfolios). Therefore, information on securities in these alternative portfolios may be valuable at the decision-making stage, even though subsequently some of those securities may not be included in the portfolio chosen. In this setting, prospective shareholders do not directly pay the costs, yet they share in the benefits of disclosure (they may be free riders).

Similarly, consider a securities market in which prices reflect a comprehensive information system. Investors without effort or incurring costs are able to act as "price takers" and can adopt simple, relatively costless portfolio strategies that reflect the information. In other words, they can act as if they are adopting, as their own, the consensus or composite beliefs reflected in price, which in turn reflect a comprehensive information system. In the context of Fama's "fair game" interpretation, investors are playing a "fair game" with respect to a comprehensive system of publicly available information. A variation of this argument is advanced in Chapter 6 with respect to information search. Investors may benefit from information when it is reflected in prices. However, because it is reflected in prices, the direct demand and incentives to pay for it may be zero.

Care must be exercised in advancing an externalities-based argument. Earlier chapters have highlighted the potentially diverse, complex, and indirect nature of the demand for financial reporting. However, diversity, complexity, or indirectness, in and of themselves, do not necessarily lead to any form of externality or to any form of market failure. The demand for many goods and services is indirect (such as raw materials), and yet no externality or market failure argument is involved. To induce an externality or market failure, something in the complexity or indirectness of the structure must produce effects or consequences that are not adequately reflected by or incorporated into the price mechanism.

Additional Considerations

A number of additional issues should be introduced in considering an externality or public good approach to regulation.

1. What is the materiality of the externality or public good aspect to financial reporting? Currently, little empirical evidence exists to assess the importance of potential externalities.

2. Issues of cost must be introduced. Once costs are considered, the term *market failure* is no longer clearly appropriate. The private sector may in fact be adopting a cost-effective response, relative to attempting to eliminate the effects of the externalities. These include the direct costs of disclosure, the indirect costs of disclosure, and the costs of regulation. (a) The direct costs of disclosure include the costs of the production, certification, dissemination, processing, and interpretation of disclosures. (b) The indirect costs include the adverse effects of disclosure on competitive advantage (creating a disincentive to innovate or invest in product development) and legal liability, which may induce an inefficient sharing risk by management and auditors, among others. (c) The costs of regulation include the cost involved in the development, compliance, enforcement, and litigation of disclosure regulations.

3. Some issues related to the information are demanded by the regulatory agency to develop and monitor the regulations. In disclosure regulations, the SEC attempts to determine the amount and nature of corporate disclosure that would take place and to avoid the inefficiencies induced by the externalities. When the prospective shareholders are free riders, this involves an attempt to determine their demand for information. In general, investor demand for information will be influenced by the wealth, risk preferences, and beliefs of investors. This implies a nontrivial demand for information by the regulatory agency. Economic analyses, which show the attainment of a more efficient solution via governmental regulation, typically assume perfect knowledge on the part of the regulatory body, which is obviously an unrealistic assumption. When obtaining the desired information is too costly or simply not feasible, implementation error by the regulatory agency due to imperfect information may occur.

   Individuals may not have incentives to honestly reveal their preferences for financial reporting. Individuals may understate or overstate the desirability of additional disclosure, depending on the extent to which they perceive that their expression of preferences will be used as a basis to assess their share of the costs. A clear illustration is provided when no attempt is made to include the free riders in sharing in the costs of disclosure. Suppose that some groups are invited to participate in the process that determines the quantity and nature of corporate disclosure but are not invited to share in bearing the costs of those additional disclosures (for example, financial analysts). In this situation, the result may be excessive disclosure instead of inadequate disclosure as suggested by the standard public good analysis. Issues of efficiency and equity are raised by such a process.

4. Some issues relate to the incentives of the regulatory agency itself. The economics of regulation offers two primary views of regulatory behavior.[6] The first is the *public interest* view, which states that regulatory behavior is directed toward furthering the public interest. This view implicitly assumes that the incentives of regulators are aligned so as to further the public interest and that the concept of public interest is well-defined. The second view is known as the *capture theory* and states that the prime beneficiaries of regulation are not the public (or investors, in the case of the Securities Acts) but rather those being regulated. This has led critics of the Securities Acts, such as Stigler, to argue that the primary beneficiaries

---

[6]The economics of regulation is reviewed in Posner (1974). Posner develops a comprehensive model of regulatory behavior, where the two primary views are special cases of his model.

of the Acts are various members in the professional investment community rather than investors at large.[7]

5. There is the issue of alternatives to governmental regulation, such as private-sector collective agreements. For example, many goods with externalities are dealt with in the private sector. Newspapers are an example. The issue of whether to deal with the problem collectively in the private or public sector revolves around the relative costs of the alternative approaches. It is argued that the government has a comparative advantage in dealing with certain types of collective agreements. In particular, when it is difficult to identify free riders or too costly to exclude them, it is intuitively felt that the comparative advantage favors governmental action.

7-4 UNEQUAL POSSESSION OF INFORMATION AMONG INVESTORS

A second major argument for a disclosure regulation is that, left unregulated, market forces would lead to an uneven possession of information among investors. Selective disclosure is one example. In other words, the result would be a continuum of informed investors ranging from well-informed to ill-informed. It is further argued that such asymmetry of access to information is inherently unfair and violates the meaning of "fair" disclosure under the Securities Acts. Hence, the basis of the argument is typically one of equity rather than efficiency. Simply stated, it is only fair that the less informed be protected from the more informed.

Recent economic analysis of the demand for privately held information suggests that considerable incentives exist to expend efforts searching for and obtaining nonpublicly available information for trading purposes.[8] However, the unfairness of such a process is not self-evident.

Presumably, the analysts pass along the benefits of the information search to their clients, either directly or indirectly. In this sense, the clients of analysts become more informed investors. However, they pay for the analysts' services either directly or indirectly. As long as the services are available to anyone willing to pay for them, there is no obvious way in which harm is occurring. At the margin, investors will purchase analysts' services to that point where investors are indifferent between being more informed or less informed, given the costs of becoming more informed. In other words, the expected benefits of being more informed (for example, in the form of expected superior returns due to better information) are equal to (or offset by) the costs incurred to obtain the additional information.[9] A common argument is that some investors cannot afford to purchase the services of analysts. However, the existence of financial intermediaries makes the force of this argument

---

[7]See Cohen and Stigler (1971, pp. 6–9).

[8]The term *information for trading purposes* refers to the demand for information for speculative purposes. In other words, information is demanded for the purpose of earning abnormal returns due to superior information at the expense of uninformed investors. The incentives to search for such information are analyzed in Hirshleifer (1971).

[9]The process is described in greater detail in Grossman and Stiglitz (1980) and Gonedes (1976).

unclear. Moreover, it ignores several alternatives open to relatively less informed investors. One such alternative is to partially insulate themselves from more informed traders via buy-and-hold strategies and index funds.[10] Also, the actions of the more informed may signal their information to the less informed and as a result prices may partially (in the limit, fully) reflect the information.[11]

The purchase of analysts' information can be viewed as the decision to purchase a higher-quality product (in this case, superior information). In general, quality differences exist with respect to any commodity, and usually it is not thought to be unfair when one consumer chooses to purchase a higher-quality product while another chooses a lower-quality item. The purchase of automobiles is one example, but illustrations could be provided for almost any commodity.

Although selective disclosure is commonly cast as an equity issue, there are grounds for considering it on the basis of efficiency. For example, Hirshleifer (1971) provides an example in which the social value is zero to the acquisition of private information in an exchange setting. If there are no costs to forming private-sector collective agreements, investors would agree among themselves not to privately seek information. Everyone who would gain in that society would no longer incur the costs of private search for information whose sole purpose is to redistribute wealth among investors via trading on superior information. In other words, the trading gains in the form of superior returns due to privately held information net out to zero across all investors. It is a zero-sum game in that every investor with superior returns is offset by other investors with inferior returns. However, to the extent that such search causes investors to incur real costs, it is not a zero-sum game, but these costs constitute deadweight losses to investors as a whole. Investors could be better off by collectively agreeing to avoid such costs.

However, reaching and enforcing such a collective agreement might be extremely costly or simply not feasible (for example, because of informational asymmetries). In the absence of effective enforcement, there would be an incentive to cheat on the agreement. Therefore, the SEC or the FASB may have a comparative advantage in effectively reducing private search for information. It could be accomplished by either or both of the two major means of regulation. (1) They could pre-empt private search for particular information by mandating the disclosure of that information in public filings or annual reports. (2) The SEC could impose sufficient legal liability on transmittal of information from management to analysts such that information flows would be deterred (or in the limit eliminated).

This poses a dilemma. Hirshleifer's argument suggests that there is a tendency for "excessive" information, as analysts and others privately search for information and disseminate it.[12] However, this is the converse of the public good argu-

---

[10]For a more complete discussion, see Marshall (1974) and Treynor (1979).

[11]For a more complete discussion of the ability of prices to reveal information, see Grossman (1976).

[12]Once the speculative positions have been taken based on the privately held information, there will be an incentive to disseminate or "push" the information. This will result in the prices reflecting the information, and the benefits of the superior information can be realized as soon as possible. The pushing of information is discussed in Hirshleifer (1971), Demski (1974), and Marshall (1974).

ment, which implies "inadequate" information. There are opposing forces operating. In one case, the private incentives are excessive; in the other case, the private incentives fall short. To the extent the latter exists, it might be desirable to permit a certain amount of private search to compensate for the otherwise inadequate incentives to publicly disclose.[13] However, permitting too much could lead to the inefficiencies described above.

7-5 MANAGEMENT INCENTIVES TO DISCLOSE

A third major argument for disclosure regulation is that management has incentives to suppress unfavorable information. Although investors may have a general awareness of this potential, they would not know specifically the nature of the suppressed information. As a result, investors will be unable to distinguish quality differences among common stocks to the same extent they would under fuller disclosure. Hence, security prices will not fully reflect quality differences among stocks, and there will be uncertainty about the quality of each stock. There may be a tendency for lower-quality stocks to be selling at a higher price than would prevail under fuller disclosure and conversely for the higher-quality stocks.[14] This can lead to a phenomenon known as *adverse selection* in which the managements (and investors) of poorer-quality stocks have greater incentives to offer additional shares for sale than the managements of higher-quality stocks.[15]

Firms can respond to this problem in a number of ways. (1) Higher-quality firms will attempt to signal their higher quality by undertaking actions that would be irrational unless they were in fact of higher quality. The effectiveness of this signaling behavior will be influenced by the extent to which the lower-quality firms can imitate the signaling behavior. Healy and Palepu (1993) discuss the incentives for management to use discretion to signal their private information. However, signaling may be a costly activity with no rewards beyond those of signaling. (2) Managements will offer to have their disclosure system monitored and certified by an independent party, which will lead to a demand for auditing services. (3) Managements may offer warranties to shareholders whereby they will incur penalties if it is eventually discovered that unfavorable information was suppressed.[16] In fact, managements' willingness to be audited and to offer warranties can be signals in themselves. Obviously, both auditing services and warranty contracts are not costless.

---

[13]Both Kripke (1976) and Lorie (1974) take the position that permitting some private search is socially desirable.

[14]A lower-quality stock is one whose price is overstated relative to the price that would prevail if greater disclosures were available to investors, and conversely for the higher-quality stock.

[15]Moreover, a *moral hazard* problem also can arise in which management changes the quality of the stock to take advantage of the information asymmetry. The moral hazard problem is discussed in Chapter 2. Obviously, adverse selection can also occur in the context of asymmetrically informed investors.

[16]This discussion heavily draws on a branch of economic theory known as signaling theory. A paper by Ross (1979) applies this literature to the disclosure regulation context. The bibliographic references to the signaling literature appear in the Ross paper.

One of the most important costs in the warranty is that management may end up bearing "excessive" risk.

After the fact, it may be difficult to disentangle a deterioration in the stock price that was due to correcting inadequate disclosure as opposed to other unfavorable events. As a result, management may become an insurer for events in addition to those induced by management's disclosure policy. This may lead to an inefficient sharing of risks, relative to that which would attain if there were no uncertainty about the quality of the stocks.[17]

The antifraud provisions can be viewed as requiring firms to provide disclosure warranties to investors. Presumably, the legal liability reduces the incentives of management to suppress unfavorable information. The argument for governmental intervention, as opposed to private-sector contracting, is that the SEC has a comparative advantage in achieving the same result. However, while this argument forms a basis for antifraud statutes, it is not clear why a mandated disclosure system is desirable. In other words, why is reliance on antifraud statutes deemed to be inadequate?

The antifraud provisions can be viewed as requiring firms to provide disclosure warranties to investors. Legal liability for financial reporting is substantial. Presumably, the legal liability reduces the incentives to suppress unfavorable information. Risk of litigation is a major factor in management's financial reporting decisions. Francis, Philbrick, and Schipper (1994) discuss litigation risk and its major determinants.

7-6   SUMMARY OF PREVIOUS DISCUSSION

The preceding discussion identifies some of the issues involved in defining the role of regulation of financial reporting. Three rationales are provided for the potential desirability of the regulation. All three arguments rest on the premise that a public agency, such as the SEC, has a comparative advantage in forming collective agreements of a certain form (for example, when the potential beneficiaries or affected parties are numerous and difficult to identify and hence when dealing with the same issue via market forces is more costly or simply not feasible. However, it is unclear empirically whether these arguments are valid. Hence, in the absence of evidence, the desirability of having a regulated environment is an open issue.

7-7   SUMMARY OF POTENTIAL
ECONOMIC CONSEQUENCES

The previous sections have dealt with various aspects of why a portion of information production and financial reporting should be regulated. This section takes the existence of regulatory bodies as a given, not because such bodies are necessarily

---

[17]Managers are unlikely to remain passive if such risk is imposed on them. For example, bearing this risk might alter the risk-reward trade-offs management makes in investment decisions. Management may tend to be more risk adverse because of the legal liability associated with higher-risk projects.

desirable but because they constitute an important part of the financial reporting environment. This section will deal with the issue of determining the content or desirability of specific proposals to regulate financial reporting.

Financial reporting regulations have several potential economic consequences, which have been discussed in Chapters 2 and 6. These potential consequences include (1) wealth distribution among investors and others; (2) the aggregate level of risk incurred and risk sharing among individuals; (3) the effects on the rate of capital formation; (4) allocation of resources among firms; (5) the use of resources devoted to the production, certification, dissemination, processing analysis, and interpretation of disclosures; (6) the use of resources in the development, compliance, enforcement, and litigation of disclosure regulations; and (7) the use of resources in the private-sector search for nonpublic information. These consequences may not have the same impact among or within the different constituencies. As a result, there may not be a consensus on the desirability of a particular proposed regulation. In terms of the framework in section 7-2, regulation of financial reporting may involve not only issues of economic efficiency but also issues of equity. The effects of a regulation, if enacted, may be analogous to redistribution of wealth among the constituencies. Hence, a trade-off is involved as to what importance to assign to the preferences of each group. The existence of an overall objective function, such as a social welfare function, is neither clear not is its nature well-defined.

In addition to this conceptual issue, there is the practical problem of determining the preferences of each group or the consequences. The earlier discussion indicated that individuals may not have the incentive to truthfully reveal their preferences and may distort them in unknown ways. Moreover, the reasons given for supporting or opposing a particular regulation may not honestly reveal the individuals' motives (Watts and Zimmerman 1979).

7-8 EMPIRICAL EVIDENCE ON THE EFFECTS OF FINANCIAL REGULATION

Many of the potential effects of reporting regulations would be difficult to assess, such as the effects on resource allocation. However, one class of evidence has examined the effects of regulation on security prices.

This class of empirical research examines security price behavior with respect to the disclosures *ex post.* As discussed in Chapter 5, the evidence indicates that many types of disclosures are significantly related to prices or price changes. Examples are pension disclosures (FAS No. 87) and banks' nonperforming loans and fair values of financial instruments (FAS No. 107). However, notable exceptions include the current cost and constant dollar disclosures (FAS No. 33).

Security price research can be informative in dealing with one aspect of disclosure regulation. With respect to the research into the price effects of disclosing the signals, the studies can provide evidence on whether prices behave as if such disclosure led to a systematic revision in beliefs. In other words, do prices behave as if investors perceive the signals as possessing information content? This is relevant to the extent that the rationale for disclosure is to provide information not already reflected in prices.

Of course, price effects deal only with one aspect of the effects of financial reporting regulation. They are a proxy or surrogate for economic consequences of ultimate concern: capital formation, resource allocation, wealth distribution, and costs, among others. For example, as indicated above, if the rationale for regulation is to add to the information system that is reflected in prices (in other words, to make the market efficient with respect to a richer information system), then price effects may be a reasonable expected consequence of the disclosure. However, failure to find price effects at the time of disclosure cannot necessarily be interpreted to imply that the regulation is valueless. For example, other effects of the regulation may have been intended or may be occurring. For example, one effect could be to provide the information via public disclosure by the corporation at a lower cost than would be incurred by the private sector's information network in seeking the same information and reflecting it in prices.

Similarly, when price effects are found, one must be careful in interpreting these effects. Although the presence of such effects may be consistent with the intent of the policy makers, it cannot be taken as *prima facie* evidence that the private-sector incentives to disclose are inadequate. It may be that the benefits were perceived to be not commensurate with the costs, such that disclosure was not worthwhile. The critical issue is to determine whether the failure to disclose was due to a misalignment of incentives in the private sector toward inadequate disclosure or due to a misalignment of regulators toward excessive disclosure.

Security price research cannot, in and of itself, answer this question. In sum, the absence of price effects is not necessarily an indictment of a regulation, and the presence of price effects is not sufficient to confirm the value of the regulation. However, security price research can provide evidence on one aspect of financial reporting regulation. As such, price effects can be a readily observable manifestation of the consequences of regulation and a reasonable implication that often naturally follows from rationale commonly offered for financial reporting regulations.

7-9 DUAL REGULATION

This section discusses some aspects of who should regulate financial reporting—the FASB or the SEC? More precisely, how should the respective jurisdictions be defined? Traditionally, the jurisdiction of the FASB is said to be *accounting standards* and the jurisdiction of the SEC is said to be *disclosure*. However, this distinction has not been successful in describing the jurisdictional boundaries. Many FASB standards contain disclosure provisions, as well as defining a new accounting standard. Similarly, the SEC has influenced accounting standards.

Horngren (1972, 1973) offers another interpretation of the relationship between the FASB and the SEC. Horngren suggests that the SEC be viewed as central management and that the FASB be viewed as decentralized management. The SEC manages "by exception" (in other words, by oversight). Several advantages to this dual regulatory structure are cited. (1) It permits the SEC to have access to the technical expertise of the accounting profession. (2) Such services are obtained by the SEC without having to pay for them. (3) The FASB serves as a "buffer" against criticism of a regulation that otherwise would be directed at the SEC if it were the sole regulatory body. (4) There may be greater acceptance of the regulations by management and the auditors.

The other side of the coin is, of course, what are the advantages of the dual management to the FASB? There are two possibilities. (1) It provides the "cosmetic" appearance that financial reporting standards are being set in the private sector, which may enhance the importance and status of the auditing profession with its clients and with other members of society. (2) It permits the FASB and the private sector, via the FASB, to have greater control or influence over the regulations. This raises the question of how much control the SEC and Congress are willing to give to the FASB.

The debate on financial reporting for stock options as compensation (FAS No. 123) was probably the most controversial standard in the FASB's history. Constituencies lobbied before the SEC not to support any standard that would require reporting the value of stock options as compensation. This lobbying process and the subsequent change in the structure of the board of trustees of the Financial Accounting Foundation, which is responsible for appointing FASB members, illustrates the tensions that are created by the dual regulatory structure.

Will the FASB and private-sector standard setting survive? At one time, the major power of the FASB was perceived to come from support of the public accounting profession itself, and its acceptance of FASB rulings was viewed as critical of the success of the FASB. However, under the view described above, the federal government (the SEC and Congress) is the prime factor in the future of the FASB. The success of the FASB will be influenced by the extent to which the FASB can promulgate regulations acceptable to the federal government, which in turn is responding to a variety of constituencies.

7-10   CONCLUDING REMARKS

This chapter explores the potential rationale for the regulation of financial reporting. The arguments rest on the assumption that the regulatory body offers some comparative advantage in forming collective agreements on the nature of such regulations. A number of other considerations are discussed that suggest that consequences of regulation in practice may fall short of "ideal" regulation. As a result, the efficacy of regulation is an open issue. Empirical research has assessed the effects of regulation on security prices, one of the consequences of regulation. Two effects are investigated: the anticipated effects of a regulation at the time it is announced and the effects of data at the time they are reported. Although the results vary with the context examined, this empirical research may be useful in providing evidence on one aspect of financial reporting regulations.

The selection among financial reporting systems is a social choice. As such, the choice deals with such questions as (1) What are the additional costs associated with the financial reporting regulation? (2) Are there alternative methods of dealing with the problem that might be more effective or less costly? Reliance on antifraud statues and private-sector collective agreements are two possibilities. In any event, no environment, even a regulated one, is likely to drive the level of "abuse" to zero. Even if it were feasible, it is not likely that such a result would be desirable because the costs of achieving that result could be prohibitive. Implementation error by the regulators, caused by a lack of evidence on investors' demand for information, must also be considered.

The desirability of financial reporting regulation is still an open question. However, the issues raised here provide a framework within which to structure future research. Notwithstanding the ambiguity with respect to the efficacy of regulation, it seems likely that extensive regulation of financial reporting will continue to be an important part of the environment.

Financial reporting regulation is a social choice because of the potentially diverse effects or consequences of regulation on the constituencies. These effects will typically entail considerations beyond those of accounting expertise. This social choice perspective naturally follows from viewing a financial reporting system as an information system in a multiperson setting. This perspective can lead to potentially dramatic changes in financial reporting, and these changes can be viewed as a form of accounting revolution.

This book has attempted to illustrate that a number of fundamental aspects of the environment are still open issues. One issue is the efficacy of accrual accounting, which is at the heart of financial accounting as it is presently structured. Another issue is the efficacy of financial reporting regulation, which is a major component of the financial reporting environment. In one sense, this uncertainty may seem frustrating; in another sense, it provides an opportunity for progress. These chapters have attempted to describe a conceptual framework within which to interpret the revolution and to possibly point to ways our knowledge of the environment may evolve.

Financial Reporting in the Twenty-First Century

The market for information responds on an minute-to-minute basis to a rich total mix of information that becomes available to the market through a variety of information sources. The rapid development of information technology could have a dramatic effect on the form and structure of financial reporting and generates a number of intriguing questions.

For example, what would financial reporting be like if the income statement and balance sheet format were abandoned in favor of a comprehensive database approach that consists of disclosures of the underlying primitive elements? Will users be in a better position to directly construct their own financial statements under a variety of different assumptions or construct none at all, if they so desire? Is the pattern of mandated quarterly disclosure of some items and annual disclosure of a fuller set of information compatible with a world of rapidly changing technology, including rapidly changing information technology? Several years ago Sandy Burton, as SEC Chief Accountant, advocated a system of continuous disclosure. Is that where the current private-sector information markets are evolving? What is the role and nature of regulation in this setting? Is the financial reporting environment changing so rapidly that regulation is too archaic and slow to be effective? Will regulation shift to the underlying set of primitive disclosures rather than a set of the financial statements? Can a world be imagined where regulation, at least as it is currently structured, has disappeared? Information technology has greatly reduced many types of information costs and provides an opportunity for another revolutionary change in financial reporting. Whether there is another revolution in financial reporting, however, is more likely to be due to political rather than technology factors. Interestingly, these same questions could have been raised several years ago (Beaver and Rappaport 1984).

BIBLIOGRAPHY

Armstrong, M. "The Politics of Establishing Accounting Standards." *Journal of Accountancy* (February 1977), 76–79.

Beaver, W. and A. Rappaport. "Financial Reporting Needs More Than the Computer." *Business Week* (August 13, 1984), 16.

Benston, G. "Required Disclosure and the Stock Market: An Evaluation of the Securities and Exchange Act of 1934." *American Economic Review* (March 1973), 132–155.

———. "Evaluation of the Securities Act of 1934." *Financial Executive* (May 1974), 28–36.

Cohen, M., and G. Stigler. *Can Regulatory Agencies Protect Consumers?* Rational Debate Seminars, American Enterprise Institute for Public Policy Research, 1971.

Demski, J. "The Choice Among Financial Reporting Alternatives." *Accounting Review* (April 1974), 221–232.

Foster, G. "Externalities and Financial Reporting." *Journal of Finance* (May 1980).

Francis, J., D. Philbrick, and K. Schipper. "Shareholder Litigation and Corporate Disclosures." *Journal of Accounting Research* (Autumn 1994), 137–164.

Gonedes, N. "The Capital Market, the Market for Information, and External Accounting." *Journal of Finance* (May 1976), 611–630.

Grossman, S. "On the Efficiency of Competitive Stock Markets Where Traders Have Diverse Information." *Journal of Finance* (May 1976), 573–585.

——— and J. Stiglitz. "On the Impossibility of Informationally Efficient Markets." *American Economic Review* (June 1980), 393–408.

Healy, P., and K. Palepu. "The Effects of Firms' Financial Disclosure Strategies on Stock Prices." *Accounting Horizons* (March 1993), 1–11.

Hirshleifer, J. "The Private and Social Value of Information and the Reward to Inventive Activity." *American Economic Review* (September 1971), 561–573.

Horngren, C. "Accounting Principles: Private or Public Sector?" *Journal of Accountancy* (May 1972), 37–41.

———. "The Marketing of Accounting Standards." *Journal of Accountancy* (October 1973), 61–66.

Kripke, H. "An Opportunity for Fundamental Thinking—The SEC's Advisory Committee on Corporate Disclosure." *New York Law Journal* (December 13, 1976), p. 1.

Lorie, J. "Public Policy for American Capital Markets." *Federal Securities Law Reporter* (1974), 79, 646.

Marshall, J. "Private Incentives and Public Information." *American Economic Review* (June 1974), 373–390.

Posner, R. *Economic Analysis of Law.* Boston: Little, Brown, 1972.

———. "Theories of Economic Regulation." *Bell Journal of Economics and Management Science* (Autumn 1974), 335–358.

Ross, S. "Disclosure Regulation in Financial Markets." *Issues in Financial Regulation.* New York: McGraw-Hill, 1979, 177–202.

Securities and Exchange Commission. *Report of the SEC Advisory Committee on Corporate Disclosure.* Washington, D.C.: U.S. Government Printing Office, November, 1977.

Stigler, J. "Comment." *Journal of Business* (1964), 414–422.

Treynor, J. "Trading Cost and Active Management." *Proceedings of Seminar on Investment Management: The Active/Passive Decisions.* Menlo Park, Calif.: FRS Associates, September 23–26, 1979.

Watts, R., and J. Zimmerman. "The Demand for and Supply of Accounting Theories: The Market for Excuses." *Accounting Review* (April 1979), 273–305.

———. *Positive Accounting Theory.* Englewood Cliffs, N.J.: Prentice-Hall, 1986.

Index

A

Abnormal earnings, sources of, 78–80, 136–37
Accelerated depreciation, 97–98
Accounting earnings, 50–51
  descriptive differences, 56–57
  forecasting future earnings, 70–71
  future earnings and future dividends, 70–71
  measurement error, 51–56
  past and future earnings relationship, 71–72
  permanent earnings, 71
  and price-earnings (P/E) ratio, 50–51
  relation to economic earnings, 66–67
  relationship to price of common stock, 69–72
  security prices as predictors of, 106–7
  shocks, 72
  under straight-line depreciation, 53
  transitory earnings, 71
  under uncertainty, 70–74
Accounting methods
  alternate. *See* Alternative accounting methods
  changes and market efficiency, 135–36
  choice of, 98–99
  different methods, example of effects, 97–98
  and security prices, 96–99
  See also Accrual accounting
Accounting revolution, 1–2
Accrual accounting
  alternatives, evaluation of, 3
  efficiency of, 5
  as forecast, 81–83
  in information setting, 5–6
  matching concept, 2–3
Accruals, for forecasting future cash flows, 80–83
Active trading, 9, 29
Adverse selection, 30–31, 167
Agency theory, 31
Alpha, 25
Alternative accounting methods
  descriptive differences, analysis of, 56–57
  evaluation of, 3
  and measurement error, 67
American Institute of Certified Public Accountants (AICPA), 1
Antifraud provisions, 167–68

Association for Investment Management and Research (AIMR), 1
Auditors
  market efficiency, implications for, 154
  role of, 12–13
Average prudent investor, 147n

B

Balance sheet approach, 115
Beliefs, and decision-making, 20
Beta, 25, 132
Biased recognition, and abnormal earnings, 79–80
Book-to-market ratio, 109–10
  components of, 113
  and market efficiency, 132
Book value
  and earnings, 115–16
  and security prices, 113–15
Book value of common equity (BVE), 114
Book value of liabilities (BVL), 114

C

Capital asset pricing model (CAPM), 132, 140
Capture theory, of regulation, 164–65
Cash flow oriented financial statements, 5
Cash flows
  and accrual method, 80
  definition, 99, 99n
  versus earnings, 49–50
  and earnings changes, 99–100
  and market values, 80–81
  over time, 39
  present value, 40
Certainty
  versus cash flows, 49–50
  economic earnings under, 40–48
  meaning of, 39
  permanent earnings under, 48–49, 50
Clean surplus relation (CSR), 77–78
Complete markets
  meaning of, 38–39
  and primitive claims, 67–68
  under uncertainty, 67–69
Compound claims, 67

Consequences, and decision-making, 19
Conservatism, 111–13
  and abnormal earnings, 79–80
  conservative behavior, elements of, 112
  empirical evidence of, 113
  examples of, 111–12
Constant dividend growth model, 50
  formula for, 46–47
Contracting hypothesis, 99
Contracting perspective, 32–33
Cost of capital, 61n

D

Decision-making, components of, 19–20
Delayed recognition, 66–67, 79, 107–11
  effects of, 108–10
  and historical cost system, 107–9
Depreciation
  accelerated depreciation, 97–98
  under accrual accounting, 83
  definition, 3
  economic depreciation, 43
  measurement error in, 53
  methods and P/E ratio, 97–98
  straight-line, 52–55
  straight-line depreciation, 97–98
  sum-of-the-years-digits (SYD), 79
Descriptive differences, analysis of, 56–57
Disclosures
  direct and indirect costs of, 164
  full and fair, 159
  management incentives to disclose, 167–68
  pricing by market, 135
  regulation of, 161–71
  selective disclosure, 166
  uses of, 11
Discounting, under uncertainty, 60–62
Discretionary behavior, 83–86
  and accounting numbers, 83–84, 117
  areas for use of, 118–19
  motivations for, 85–86
  views of, 84–85
Diversification, 9
  versus undiversification, 27

Dividends
  future dividends and future accounting
    earnings, 70–71
  future dividends and future earnings,
    70–71
  future dividends and prices, 69–70

E

Earnings
  abnormal, sources of, 78–80
  accounting earnings, 50–51
  and book value, 115–16
  versus cash flows, 49–50
  current earnings/current price
    relationship, 74–76
  earnings changes and price changes,
    90–92
  economic, 40–48
  ex ante earnings, 63–66
  ex post earnings, 63–66
  Feltham–Ohlson model of, 77–78
  forecasting future earnings from current
    earnings, 72–74
  future earnings, definition of, 71
  from informational approach, 69
  multiasset firm, 45–48
  permanent, 48–49, 50
  single-asset firm, 41–45
  timeliness of earnings, 100–104
  transitory components in, 93–96
Earnings announcements, 103–4
  anticipatory effect, 134–35
  market adjustment to, 133–34
  postannouncement abnormal returns,
    136–37
Earnings forecast error, measurement error
  in, 104–5
Earnings forecasting
  components of, 71
  of future accounting earnings, 71–72
Earnings rate, definition, 42–43*n*
Earnings response coefficient (ERC), 93*n*
Earnings volatility, and systematic risk,
  119
Economic depreciation, definition, 43
Economic earnings
  relation to accounting earnings, 66–67
  under uncertainty, 63–66

See also Economic income
Economic income
  definition, 3, 43
  and depreciation, 52
Economic income approach,
  meaning of, 3
Economic problems, categories of, 161
Equity, economic value under uncertainty,
  62–63
Events studies, 89, 119
  market efficiency, 133
Ex ante earnings, 63–66
Expected return, 24
Expected utility
  maximization of, 20, 23
  meaning of, 20
Expired cost, 3
Ex post earnings, 63–66, 68, 137
Externalities, and financial reporting,
  162–65

F

Fair game property, of market efficiency,
  127
Feltham–Ohlson model, 116
  of earnings, 77–78
Financial Accounting Standards Board
  (FASB)
  activities of, 1*n*, 11–12
  activities of, 159
  relationship to SEC, 171
Financial information
  costs of, 76
  economic consequences of, 13–14,
    34–35
  inferior system, effects of, 30–31
  information asymmetry, 28, 31, 32–33
  and moral hazard problem, 31–32
  and more/less informed investors,
    28–29
  in multiperson setting, 28–34
  in portfolio theory context, 26–28
  public information, 29–30
  roles of, 5, 25
  in simple setting, 21–24
  in single-person setting, 19–28
  social value of, 35–36
  total mix, 76

Financial information intermediaries, 10–11
  market efficiency, implications for, 154–56
  role of, 10–11
Financial reporting
  characteristics of, 15
  current trends in, 14–15
  and discretionary behavior, 83–84
  and externalities, 162–65
  future view for, 172–73
  informational view, 76–77
  measurement view, 76–77
  and portfolio theory, 24–26
Financial reporting environment, 6–13
  auditors, 12–13
  characteristics of, 7, 160
  information intermediaries in, 10–11
  investors, 8–9
  and management, 12
  and regulatory system, 11–12
Financial reporting revolution, 2
First difference studies, 89
Football games, prediction of outcome, 143–45
Footnote disclosures, on security prices, 116–17
Forecast error, $91n$
Forecasting
  accruals, role in, 80–83
  of earnings, components of, 71
  forecasting future earnings, 70–71
  of future accounting earnings, 71–72
  future earnings from current earnings, 72–73
  outcome of football games, 143–45
Free-rider phenomenon, 142, 150, 162
Full and fair disclosure, 159
Future dividends. *See* Dividends

G

Generally accepted accounting principles (GAAP), 33, 107

I

Imperfect markets, valuation in, 67–69
Incomplete markets, valuation in, 67–69
Index fund, $27n$

Informational approach, 69
  and accrual accounting, 5–6
  earnings from, 69
  and financial reporting, 76
  rise in use of, 4–5
Information content of earnings, and price changes/earnings changes, 90–92
Information. *See* Financial information
Information for trading purposes, $165n$
Internal rate of return, $43n$
Intrinsic value, of security, 126
Investors, 8–9
  activities of, 8–9
  market efficiency, implications for, 150–51
  nonprofessionals, strategies of, 8
  use of term, $7n$

L

LIFO method, $79n$

M

Management
  and financial reporting environment, 12
  incentives to disclose, 167–68
  market efficiency, implications for, 153–54
  stewardship function of, 2, 12
Market efficiency
  and auditors, 154
  and changes in accounting method, 135–36
  definition, 27, 126–28
  empirical tests for, 128, 129–38
  event studies, 133
  and financial reporting regulators, 151–53
  forms of, 128–29
  implications of, 145–48, 150–56
  importance to financial reporting, 125
  and investor behavior, 150–51
  and management, 153–54
  nonimplications of, 148–49
  origin of concept, 126
  postannouncement drift in earnings, 136–37
  prediction of returns, 132

prices lead earnings, 134–35
pricing of disclosures, 135
research design issues, 138–40
returns and private information, 138
speed of adjustment to earnings
announcements, 133
test for return predictability, 129–32
theories of, 141–45
and universal access to information,
127–28
Market failure, 162, 164
Market model, and security's return, 25
Market value
and cash flows, 80–81
of firm's equity, 77–78
Market value of equity (MVE), 113
Market values of assets (MVA), 113–14
Matching concept, 2–3
Measurement error, 114
accounting earnings, 51–56
and alternative accounting methods, 67
in earnings forecast error, 104–5
Measurement view, of financial reporting,
76–77
Moral hazard problem, 31–32, 167n

N

Net income, definition, 3
Net present value (NPV) investments, and
abnormal earnings, 79
Nonperforming assets, elements of, 115n

O

Objective function, elements of, 20
One-period return, 24
definition, 25n
Over-the-counter (OTC) market, 140

P

Pareto-optimal solution, 161
Passive trading, 9
Perfect markets
meaning of, 38
and uncertainty, 59–60, 63–66
Permanent earnings, 48–49, 50
accounting earnings, 71
computation of, 48–49
definition, 50

Portfolio theory, 9, 24–28
financial information, use of, 26–28
and financial reporting, 24–26
implications for financial reporting,
24–26
Preferences, and decision-making, 19–20
Present value, 4
cash flows, 40
under certainty, 60
under uncertainty, 60
Price
changes, and earnings changes, 90–93
price and future dividends, 69–70
Price–earnings (P/E) ratio, 50–51
and accounting earnings, 50–51
and depreciation method used, 97–98
formula, 50
under straight-line depreciation, 53, 54
and transitory components in earnings,
93–96
Price takers, 150, 163
Primitive claims, and complete markets,
67–68
Private information
and potential returns, 138
private information search, 10
Prospective analysis, 10
Public interest view, regulation, 164

R

Random walk case, 73, 130
Rate of return, and delayed recognition,
66–67
Regulation, 11–12
dual regulation, 170–71
economic consequences of, 168–69
empirical evidence on effects of,
169–70
externalities approach to, 162–65
Financial Accounting Standards Board
(FASB), 11–12
mandated financial reporting, 159–61
market efficiency, implications for,
151–53
rationale for, 160–62, 165–68
Securities and Exchange Commission
(SEC), 1n, 11–12
views of, 164–65

Report of the SEC Advisory Committee on Corporate Disclosure, 152–53
Residual change in price and earnings, 91*n*–92
Retrospective analysis, 10
Return, definition, 127*n*
Return on equity (ROE), 113
Reward, 24
Risk, 24

S

Securities Acts of 1933 and 1934, 11, 12, 159, 161
Securities and Exchange Commission (SEC)
  activities of, 1*n*, 11–12
  activities of, 159
  relationship to FASB, 170–71
Security prices
  and book value, 113–15
  and footnote disclosures, 116–17
  and prediction of accounting earnings, 106–7
Selective disclosure, 166
Shocks, 72
Single-person investment setting, 19–28
Social value, of financial information, 35–36
States, and decision-making, 19
Straight-line depreciation, 52–55, 97–98
  effects of, 53–54
  values under, 53–54

Sum-of-the-years-digits (SYD) depreciation, 79
Systematic risk, and earnings volatility, 119

T

Time adjusted rate of return, 43*n*
Timeliness of earnings, 100–104
Trading strategy, active versus passive, 9
Transitory earnings, accounting earnings, 71

U

Uncertainty
  characteristics of, 59–60
  decision-making under, 19
  discounting under, 60–62
  economic value of equity under, 62–63
  ex ante earnings, 63–66
  ex post earnings, 63–66
  and perfect and complete markets, 59–60, 63–66
Unsystematic risk, 25, 27
Utility function, 19

V

Valuation
  and earnings and dividends, 69–70
  in imperfect or incomplete markets, 67–69
Value-relevant factors, 116
Variance of return, 24